Caring for the Flock

Caring for the Flock

Pastoral Ministry in the Local Congregation

David L. Larsen

CROSSWAY BOOKS • WHEATON, ILLINOIS
A DIVISION OF GOOD NEWS PUBLISHERS

First printing, 1991

Printed in the United States of America

Bible quotations are taken from the *Revised Standard Version, New
International Version, Phillips* and *King James Version*

Library of Congress Cataloging-in-Publication Data
Larsen, David L.
    Caring for the Flock/ David L. Larsen.
        p.   cm.
    Includes bibliographical references and indexes.
    1. Pastoral Theology. 2. Church management. I. Title.
BV4011.L38 1991   253—dc20   91-2175
ISBN 0-89107-609-3

99		98		97		96		95		94		93		92		91
15	14	13	12	11	10	9	8	7	6	5	4	3	2	1

To Jean
partner and pilgrim with me
in pastoral ministry

Table of

Contents

III: RELATIONSHIPS

IV: RITES

V: RETHINKING

PREFACE

Coming down the stretch of the twentieth century and winding up this millennium, Christian leaders in both church and academy are looking at the balance sheets and the bottom-line. Where are we? Where are we going? Where should we be going? A gratifying willingness to analyze and strategize is in widespread evidence. The spiritual battle is heating up. The stakes are incredibly high for every community of believers. Time seems to be running out.

What is needed are men and women who will be like the "men of Issachar, who understand the times and know what Israel should do" (1 Chronicles 12:32). This book is a modest contribution to the current discussion and debate about Christian ministry in our time, most particularly the ministry of the pastor-teacher. Both pastors and laypersons must wrestle with the age-old issues in their contemporary and complex form. At every point our direction must be the conscious function of our ecclesiology, our doctrine of the church.

This study is intended also to serve as the basic text in a foundational course in pastoral theology or pastoral duties in seminaries and training schools. The discussions are not intended to be exhaustive, but suggestive. Such a course should include wide reading on specific issues from divergent perspectives as well as practical projects and field assignments. Reflective papers, particularly on personal philosophy of ministry, are critical for the crystallization of ideas.

The approach taken in this treatment is cautious and basically conservative. This is because primary values can easily be neglected and even lost in times like ours. According to the Greeks, *Chronos* (or Time) was the primordial deity who voraciously devoured his children. Yet our approach seeks to be honest with the data and open to the changes and adaptations bold strategies require.

Coming out of the trenches after thirty-two years in pastoral ministry, I have found my now ten years in the lively and theologically stimulating community known as Trinity Evangelical Divinity School an unspeakably bracing and stretching experience. I am in the deepest debt to all of my colleagues and students for what they are teaching me on the exciting but harrowing growing edge of ministry for Christ.

Ad Gloriam Dei.

INTRODUCTION

It was he who gave some to be apostles, some to be prophets, some to be evangelists, and some to be pastors and teachers, to prepare God's people for works of service, so that the Body of Christ may be built up until we all reach unity in the faith and in the knowledge of the Son of God and become mature, attaining to the whole measure of the fullness of Christ. (Ephesians 4:11-13)

This book is a study of the ministry of the pastor-teacher in the church. The application of the Granville-Sharpe Rule warrants our understanding these two coordinate nouns as describing a single function.[1] Apostles held an office, as may prophets and evangelists. The argument will be advanced here that similarly the pastor-teacher is both office and function.

Massive, sweeping changes in the cultural and societal environment of the church at the end of the twentieth century seem to call into question everything the church has believed about herself. Boisterous new and diverse models vie for attention. Incessant seminars often only further blur and confuse those who would chart the course for the local church. And in all of this the pastor-teacher becomes more and more what H. Richard Niebuhr described as "the perplexed profession."

Function always emanates from identity. Clearly the pastor-teacher is enveloped in a critical identity crisis in our time. Observe how our Lord's authentic sense of identity steadied and guided Him through a difficult passage:

Jesus knew that the Father had put all things under his power, and that he had come from God and was returning to God; so he got up from the meal, took off his outer clothing, and wrapped a towel around his waist. After that he poured water into a basin and began to wash his disciples' feet. (John 13:3-5a)

    The process of identity-formation is foundational in functioning. While normally achieved by the early twenties, delays are not unusual. Faulty formation will result in inordinate self-consciousness and brittleness as well as ineptitude in the forming of interpersonal relationships.[2] A Biblically and theologically sound identity for the pastor-teacher is of the utmost importance.

    Biff sadly observed of Willie Loman in Arthur Miller's *Death of a Salesman*, "He never knew who he was." One of Shakespeare's characters pleads, "Please tell me who I am." The late Anwar Sadat's moving autobiography is entitled *In Search of Identity*.[3] Don Quixote of La Mancha confidently asserted, "I know who I am."[4]

    The approach taken in this study conjoins identity and function. Only through a conscientious and constant reference to the Biblical understanding of the church and what it is in the plan and purpose of God can we find who the pastor-teacher is and what proper function in that office is to be.

I
Roots

CHAPTER 1

"The Church Which Is Christ's Body"

The Nature of the Church

It is dangerous to the health of the church for ministry to be practiced without good foundations in Scripture and tradition, reason and experience.[1]

Sometimes we feel with W. B. Yeats that "the center is falling apart." The very instability and uncertainty of our times, though creating great difficulties, are nonetheless conducive to what is beyond question the greatest time of gospel harvest in the history of the church. What is happening in sub-Sahara Africa, in Central and South America, and on the rim of the Pacific boggle the mind. The collapse of state socialism in Eastern Europe and most unexpected developments in the Soviet Union presage gospel opportunity on an unparalleled scale. Yet the affluent North American church seems currently more on the track of her declining Western European forebears than in sync with her fervent brothers and sisters in the Two-thirds World.

Seriously shaken by massive urbanization and a thoroughgoing secularism, the North American church is further beset by what *Time* magazine terms "evangelicalism's tattered image." The painful and debilitating effects of compromising acculturation have enveloped not only congregations but clergy.

Studies indicate that the pastor-teacher performs 192 different tasks. The frequently hapless pastor-teacher is much like a juggler trying to keep an ever-increasing number of objects airborne. And this in a time of a deepening and ever-more exaggerated individualism in our society where shared values are sharply eroding.[2] Thus the pastor-teacher's personal and professional pressures grow greater and greater. We are seeking to serve in community and to build community at a time when disruptive and disintegrative forces undermine and undercut authentic community on every side.

Ecclesiology—our doctrine of the church—has never been very vigorous among us, and yet has never been more important than today. The danger of a theologically rootless activism has never been greater. The malaise of the church and its ministry must be challenged by a return to our roots in divine revelation and sound doctrine.

GOD-FORMED ORGANISM

The Church of Jesus Christ is, as Aquinas so long ago pointed out, "that wonderful and sacred mystery." As the *ecclesia* of God, the church is the community of the redeemed. The church is both coming together and being together. The antecedent of "the Church which is Christ's body" (Ephesians 5:23) is the covenant community in the Old Testament. *Ecclesia* is used a hundred times in the Greek Old Testament for *qahal*, which simply means "gathering." The word *synagogue* says the same thing.[3]

The Lord Jesus spoke in Matthew's Gospel about building the New-Covenant community, and Acts portrays the constituting of this new, vital spiritual organism through the baptizing work of the Holy Spirit. Most commonly the word "church" describes a local congregation and in one instance a geographic clustering of congregations (Acts 9:31). Though spiritually it is the inclusive totality of believers in Christ, the church obtains her character and identity not from her members but from her Lord. We are talking about the Church of God or the Church of the Lord Jesus Christ.

Many New Testament images teach us concerning the nature and life of the church (for example, in horticultural, architectural, and marital illustrations). The church stands in symbiotic relationship to the Kingdom of God—the Kingdom being God's rule and regime, while the church is the community of persons who are subject and submissive to the Lordship of Christ (Colossians 1:13, 14).

The foremost metaphor for the life of the church is that which portrays her as the spiritual body of which Christ is the heavenly Head. The church is the new Messianic community, the eschatological community created when the powers of the age to come broke into this present evil age (Hebrews 6:5). There was nothing in the Graeco-Roman world comparable to this community (nor is there in our world today). The church is the direct result of the resurrection of Christ.

A body expresses the intent and ideas of the mind. The church—

the earthly Body of our living Head, Jesus Christ—expresses His plan and purpose. This headship implies union as well as Lordship (cf. Colossians 2:19); Christ and His church are inseparably linked. Christ is the fullness of His Father, and the church is the fullness of Christ (Ephesians 1:22, 23). An organism, the church is energized by life from a single source—her heavenly Head—through the Holy Spirit.

The church is one body, coupling the most extraordinary diversity with marvelous transcendent unity. Comprised of some forward and up-front members and some frail members who work faithfully in the background and attract little notice to themselves, the church is a supernatural wonder in Christ. In fact, the unity of the church parallels the unity of God (Ephesians 4:4-6).

GOD-ENDUED OPERATION

The objective and goal in all of this is "to prepare God's people for works of service, so that the Body of Christ may be built up" (Ephesians 4:12). This is for the glory and praise of God! Jesus Christ, our living Head, is the prototype of the ministry of the church. As T. W. Manson crisply stated it: "The ministry of Jesus is the standard and pattern of the church's task, but more than that, the church's task is the continuation of the ministry of Jesus."[4] Our ministry must be seen as His ministry.

Christ spoke of Himself as *diakonos* (minister) (see, for example, Mark 10:45). Christ lived His life in diaconal service. Any notion that the pastor-teacher is a religious entrepreneur dissolves in face of the fact that all believers are to be in ministry. We are involved in the ministry of the New Covenant (2 Corinthians 3:6), the ministry of the gospel (Colossians 1:23), the ministry of the Word (Acts 6:4), the ministry of the Holy Spirit (2 Corinthians 3:8), the ministry of righteousness (2 Corinthians 3:9), and the ministry of reconciliation (2 Corinthians 5:18).

Here is where our Christology shapes our ecclesiology. The church must never be arrogant or self-sufficient. All Christians are to be walking the way of the cross in self-giving, bearing the marks of the crucified Christ. What the new birth is for the individual, Pentecost is for the Christian community, vital incorporation into Christ's dying and living. We are to be incarnational Christians living as part of a kenotic or self-emptying community.[5] (In this regard, see Philippians 2:5-8.)

It is essential to bear in mind that, as Bromiley says, "Jesus Christ's is the supreme ministry within which all other ministries necessarily move."[6] His ministry is in a real sense unique and unrepeatable in the accomplishment of our redemption. It is a finished and completed work to which nothing can be added. Thus, when we speak of our extending Christ's ministry, we are describing something which is analogous to Christ's ministry but not identical with it.[7]

We are describing the vocation of *all* believers. This is the vision captured in the Protestant Reformation's trumpeting of the "priesthood of all believers." Extreme clericalism (an overemphasis on or overuse of the clergy) has stubbornly resisted the involvement of all believers in ministry. Yet think how Protestantism has been harmed by "one man ministry." (John Milton noted, "New Presbyter is but old Priest writ large.") One of the very heartening trends in recent years has been the resurgence of lay involvement in the church. To some degree this is a consequence of a new emphasis on spiritual gifts in the church, and to some extent this is a result of greater upward mobility in our ranks. The bottom line is an increasing sense that all of God's people are in ministry.

GOD-ESTABLISHED ORDER

Ministry in the wider sense in which we have described it derives from the unity of the Body of Christ in which "there is neither Jew nor Gentile, bond nor free, male nor female" (Galatians 3:28). Ministry in a narrower sense derives from diversity functioning within the Body. Modern egalitarian thinking may resist the implication of diversity, but God is a God of orderly variety of gift and ministry. The orders of creation are not negated by redemption. There are in point of fact men and women, there are the younger and the older, there are neophytes and the mature, there are differences in gifts. All these have their place and role within God's plan.

Leadership is such an order. God, for example, selected Joshua to succeed Moses. There were judges and kings and prophets. Jesus chose the twelve among whom there seemed to be an inner circle of three. Beyond them were the seventy. Within the larger covenant community in Israel there was the remnant. Certain bestowals were given to that remnant (Isaiah 8:16-20), and certain responsibilities were to be shared with the servant of the Lord (Isaiah 43:10, 12; 44:8). A. T. Hanson argues that the apostles were New-Covenant successors to the remnant.[8]

It seems abundantly clear that there have been offices and orders in the church from the very beginning. There has been a tendency in some circles to desacralize the ordained ministry or to abolish ordered ministry altogether. This is certainly a mistake. We see in Acts 1 that specific offices were immediately in mind as a successor was chosen to fill the place of Judas Iscariot. This required attention before the expansion of the church.[9] The teaching office of the ordained minister is more than a cultural accommodation. It is part of the divine order. On the other hand, an unhealthy separation between laity and clergy is a potential hazard in the exercise of leadership. We have much to fear from any elite, ecclesiastical and otherwise. Lay passivity is not to be blamed on the existence of leadership, but rather on the misuse of leadership.

While I would hold with Manson that the apostolate in a basic sense is nontransmissible, various functioning offices quite quickly and clearly came into existence as the early church developed. We see the ministry of word, of action, and of rule. The first involves proclamation and instruction, the second sacramental service and benevolence, the third guidance and direction in the assembly.[10] The fulfillment of these special ministries in the Body has involved a striking variety of forms. This is not regrettable but laudable and underscores the flex and freedom Scripture gives us within the bounds of revealed guidelines.

In the New Testament we find elders and overseers, deacons and deaconesses, stewards, prophets, evangelists, pastor-teachers, and an order of widows. The terms "elders" (*presbuteros*) and "overseers" (*episkopos*) are apparently used interchangeably. The first term reflects the dignity of the office (and shows continuity with the Old Testament background of "elders"), and the second term outlines the basic function of the office. We may well conclude that the precise title or appellation given to the office is not the critical matter. The one holding this office appears to have received regular remuneration. Careful study of the patterns in the Pastoral Epistles is very fruitful on these points.[11]

The plurality of elders would not seem strange to the early Jewish believers, for this is exactly what they had experienced in their Judaism. It would appear that within the eldership there was an inner core which had the responsibilities not only for oversight but for preaching and teaching (cf. 1 Timothy 5:17). The pastor-teacher as described by Paul in Ephesians 4:11 would thus appear to be a teaching elder.

There is clear Scriptural basis for monovocational ministry (full-time employment salaried by one congregation). The hierarchical, domineering mentality which has been such a curse and scourge through the centuries and which was so early in evidence in the early church expresses itself whether or not there is monovocational ministry. It is endemic in the human family and rears its ugly head in the most unstructured and informal associations. Left to ourselves, we all want to be in control or to do things our way.

While there is lack of uniform development in the functioning orders and offices of particularized ministry in the early centuries, we can see the emergence of permanent ministry in the Christian community. Even into the second century, as Lindsay notes, the *Didache* has "the control of all things evidently with the community in congregational meetings."[12] It is instructive that the epistles of Paul are addressed to the local congregations with the exception of Philippians, which is addressed to the church and its leaders.

GOD-DIRECTED ORDINATION

Flowing out of the nature of the church and its ministry are orders and offices for ministry. Beyond the essential ministry of the laity is the ordained ministry of the pastor-teacher. To deny the distinction between clergy and laity has long-term negative consequences. As F. D. Maurice insisted, "If we take away from the significance of the calling of the ministry, we inevitably depreciate the meaning of all other ministries in the church."

Ordination is the public recognition of God's call to ministry by prayer and the laying on of hands. Unfortunately, ordination has not received anywhere near adequate theological reflection in low-church evangelical circles. The background is the Old Testament consecration of priests, prophets, and kings. In line with this, we see in the New Testament the consecration of the apostles and others through the laying on of hands. (Note Acts 6:6; 13:3; 14:23; 1 Timothy 4:14; 5:22; 2 Timothy 1:6; 2 Corinthians 8:19.)

In his monumental study of classical pastoral care, Thomas Oden draws from the great wealth of material in the church up until 1700.[13] None should be "over-hasty in laying on of hands." Prior to ordination there should be a most careful and prayerful ordinal examination in regard to doctrine and fitness for ministry. The critical issue is the Christian community's affirmation of God's hand upon the ordinand. This is a significant facet of the pastor-teacher's sense of identity.

John Calvin spoke about the inner and the outer call. The inner call can come in various ways. Jowett movingly traces from Scripture how Moses was called by the burning bush, Gideon on the farm, Amos on the hillside, Isaiah at worship, Paul on the Damascus Road, Apollos apparently in the university, Timothy in his childhood home. The pastor-teacher needs to share along with these Bible personalities what Jowett calls in his great chapter in the Yale Lectures "the wondering sense of the greatness of his vocation."[14]

No issue finds Bible-believing Christians more divided than the question of ordaining women to the office of teaching elder. The Scriptural data itself describes "women deacons" (cf. 1 Timothy 3:11; Romans 16:1). It would appear that at Ephesus there was an officially recognized order of widows (cf. 1 Timothy 5:3-16).[15] Certainly women prophesied in the church (cf. 1 Corinthians 11:5). Many communions continue to wrestle with these questions.

The outer call is climaxed at the service of ordination, but is preceded optimally over the years by the gradual and growing perception in a local body of believers that here is a committed believer who demonstrates both aptitude and heart for ministry. What a momentous occasion it is when such recognition culminates in a public consecration for Christian ministry!

Beyond gifts and endowments, and beyond bowing in surrender to God's sovereign will, there must be a great love for the church of Jesus Christ. "Christ loved the church and gave himself for it" (Ephesians 5:25). Because the church is unspeakably precious to the Savior, it ought to be precious to us. The church belongs to Him. The pastor-teacher should not speak of "my church," for the church is Christ's. He is building it, adding those who are being saved. He is the foundation and the chief cornerstone. He is blessing His church and has guaranteed that "the gates of hell should not prevail against it" (Matthew 16:18).

With all its schisms and divisions, with all its weaknesses and obvious deficiencies, the church is that unique organism chosen by God to storm the very citadels of Satan and to prevail, to snatch the souls of men and women from the darkened bastions of death itself. What a high and holy privilege—to be part of the church and then to be able to serve Christ and His church.

No one has all of the spiritual gifts, but under the call of God we can dedicate the gifts we have to Christ for the expansion of His church. A godly woman once traced the experience of the congregation of which she was a member. Some time previously they had had a zealous evangelist as pastor-teacher. The emphasis was almost entirely on conversion, and many came to Christ during those days. The next pastor was a soft-spoken Bible teacher who built up the new converts in the knowledge of the Word of God and led them into the deeper things of the Spirit. When he moved on, the church called a man who turned out to be neither an evangelist nor much of a preacher. But he was an organizer and an administrator, and he rallied these studious Christians to go out in gospel teams through the whole state and down into the slums and skid-rows, giving their testimonies and leading others to Christ.

In hindsight, this assembly of believers perceived how the Head of the church supplied His people with variously gifted pastor-teachers for His glory and the growth of the people of God. What a thrilling adventure—to be part of what God is doing in and through "the church which is Christ's body" (Ephesians 5:23).

CHAPTER 2

"Christ's Ambassadors" and "Witnesses of the Resurrection"

The Mission of the Church

It is difficult to see a congregation—there are a few exceptions—frozen by their fears, afraid to reach out, afraid to think of numerical growth, afraid to share the gospel. These fears have caused a rather ingrown church. I pray I will be able to break a couple people out of that. (Letter from a young pastor in his first church)

The words *missile* and *mission* come from the same root, having to do with being sent. We moderns have become very conscious of missiles, but obviously the church by and large is not clear on its mission. While the mission of the church and the function of the pastor-teacher stem from the nature of the church, many congregations are in serious checkmate situations, with little reference to or reflection on Christ's marching orders for His New-Covenant community.

Some congregations have become unbearable activity traps, while others are suffocating in an oppressive malaise of passivity and purposelessness. The basic purpose of the church is perhaps outlined in the constitution or bylaws of the congregation, but it has become a meaningless motto. The widespread uncertainty of the church as to its role is seen in any typical community. On one corner is "The Church of What's Going on Now." Across the street is "The Church of the Immaculate Perception." Down the block for those with more New-Age tendencies is "The Mystic Church of Cosmic Vibrations." Within a short distance one can also find, for those to the left, "The First Church of Christ, Socialist." And perhaps the most popular of all is

"The Church of the Inner Spring," a refuge for many on a typical Sunday morning.

Common rejection of the pastoral role in favor of a therapeutic model bespeaks the current bewilderment. In the vacuum created by the absence of a sense of direction, the tendency is to piggyback on the latest fad, and our therapeutic society is well satisfied with a quiescent church which purrs "peace, peace" during any provocation.

THE MANDATE IS CLEAR

The Bible shares with us God's loving strategy through Christ to reach the sinful sons and daughters of Adam with His grace. Anticipated in the Old Testament, actualized in the Gospels, acclaimed in the Acts, and analyzed in the epistles, this glorious gospel is to be proclaimed to the whole world. "God so loved the world . . ." (John 3:16). "Go into all the world . . ." (Matthew 28:19). Sometimes preferring isolation, the church has failed to appreciate that in speaking of God's people as "salt" and "light" (Matthew 5:13, 14) our Lord used figures which describe *penetration*.

"The church exists by mission as fire exists by burning," Emil Brunner argued. Propagandism is inherent in every vital conviction. It is still true that "No heart is pure that is not passionate; no virtue is safe that is not enthusiastic." We sense this spiritual surge in the book of Acts, where the fresh air of Heaven is plainly blowing. To use J. B. Phillips' classic description, "These were the days before the church became fat and short of breath through prosperity or muscle-bound through over-organization."

The fact is, humankind is helplessly and hopelessly lost in sin, being alienated and estranged from a holy and just God. Apart from Christ men and women are ravaged by sinful selfishness and eternally condemned. Christ as the prophesied Messiah came "to save his people from their sins" (Matthew 1:21). "The Son of Man is come to seek and to save that which is lost" (Luke 19:10). The gospel is the death, burial and resurrection of the Lord Jesus Christ for guilty sinners (1 Corinthians 15:3, 4). This is our message.

The Great Commission of the risen Savior as found variously in all four Gospels and in the never to be forgotten words of Acts 1:8 is solidly anchored in the creation mandates of Genesis 1, the covenant promises to Abraham in Genesis 12:1-3, the words of worship in the Psalter, and the summons of the prophets in ancient Israel. The empowering Holy Spirit now owns and blesses the ministry of the church

(Acts 1, 2; 5:32) and directs her missionary work (Acts 8:29; 10:19, 20; 13:2; 16:6-8; etc.). Possessed by the Spirit, the early believers experienced a spiritual solidarity, a willingness to have goods in common, and a deep bond of *koinonia* (fellowship).

The broad ecumenical movement seems to have largely lost this common faith out of which the towering task of the church emerges unscathed. Pluralism has became the watchword. This is the age of discussion. Evangelism has been watered down to congeniality. A recent conference on mission and evangelism embracing seven hundred and fifty people from a hundred nations and scores of denominations, held in San Antonio, stated that while "it is important to speak about Christ to others, one must avoid offending people of other faiths with statements suggesting that salvation and the way to God are in him alone."[1] How can such a statement square with the claims of our divine Lord (John 14:6) or the emboldened witness of the early apostles (Acts 4:12)?

Factor analysis of this divinely-given Scriptural mandate would yield something like the following: The church is that fellowship of believers through which Christ works in the world for the glory of God, in:

1) *Evangelism*—the proclaiming and living out of that beautiful and good message of God's saving work in Christ. The early Christians told what they had seen and experienced in the power of the Holy Spirit.

2) *Edification*—the building up of the spiritual community. John Wesley was given some good advice which influenced him to found the Holy Club at Oxford: "Sir, you wish to serve God and go to heaven? Remember, you cannot serve Him alone. You must therefore find companions or make them; the Bible knows nothing of solitary religion." Those who were sent forth (as *apostoloi*) had already been called as disciples (*mathetoi*). The making of disciples is achieved through baptizing (initiation into the community) and teaching them everything Christ commanded (cf. Matthew 28:18-20).

3) *Expression*—the utilization of the gifts of the Spirit in harmony with the graces of the Spirit (Galatians 5:22, 23) in worship, benevolence, and service to the poor and needy both within and without the church. The local outcropping of Christ's great church then becomes "the community of awareness" and "the fellowship of the concerned."

In all of this is the recognition that the end will not come until the witness of the church is borne. An authentic eschatological perspective produces missionary obedience. Such working together with God is the peerless privilege and solemn obligation of the church.

THE MASTER HAS COME

The critical features of this mandate are embodied in the person of the Lord Jesus. Indeed He said, "As the Father has sent me, I am sending you" (John 20:21). Nowhere is this better seen than in the magnificent imagery of Christ as the Good Shepherd, "that great shepherd of the sheep" (Hebrews 13:20), the "chief shepherd" (1 Peter 5:4) who will appear again in a future day. The Bible is in a real sense a pastoral document. The shepherd-sheep relationship has rightly been called "the pivotal analogy of the Old Testament" (cf. Genesis 48:15; Psalm 23; 78:72; Ezekiel 34's unchanging manifesto). The word *pastor* is taken from the close contacts the shepherd has with his sheep.

Charles Jefferson's exquisite sentences do not overstate the matter: "When church leaders began to lose the vision of the good shepherd, they at the same time began to drift away from the New Testament ideal of ministerial service."[2] John 10 lays out some of the salient aspects of Christ's example:

1) The Good Shepherd knows His sheep. He calls them by name (v. 3). The shepherd individualizes and personalizes. Few sounds are sweeter to the human ear than the sound of one's own name.

2) The Good Shepherd leads His sheep and goes before them (v. 4). The true shepherd is available and accessible. He is not the butcher who drives the sheep. Nor is He the sheepdog snapping at their heels. He is their trusted and comforting companion on the journey.

3) The Good Shepherd is faithful (v. 12). In contrast to wolves (open enemies of the flock) and thieves (secret enemies) and hirelings (false friends) stands the faithful, hard-working shepherd. To be faithful is far more important than to be successful. In the sight of society there are the plum churches and there are the crumb churches. Shepherds may turn down a great advancement for the sake of the flock they love.

4) The Good Shepherd cares for the sheep (v. 13). One brother said, "I'd love the ministry if it weren't for people." But ministry is people! To minister is to love people. Jesus commanded: "Feed My sheep"— "Care for My lambs." He did not say, "Experiment with My rats" or "Train My dogs" or "Feed My giraffes." Every person is interesting and has a story to tell if we will just listen. This is one of the priceless privileges of pastoral ministry—to work with all ages and to share momentous high peaks of experience and passage. Jesus calls for searching affection and solicitous love which will leave the warm, cozy fireside and go out into the wilds to find the lost sheep. He did this!

5) The Good Shepherd lays down His life for the sheep (v. 11). Every good shepherd lays down his life for the sheep. All believers are supposed to do this (1 John 3:16). The self-giving of our Savior sets the example for Christ's people in a hate-filled and hostile world.

The shepherd figure is compelling because it emphasizes the ministerial as over against the magisterial for the pastor-teacher. The pastor-teacher himself needs a shepherd. We all do. We all need a Barnabas, a Timothy, a buddy like Epaphroditus. Jefferson again speaks to our questions about becoming good shepherds rather than hirelings: "But a shepherd he can become only slowly, and by patiently traveling the way of the cross."[3] He goes on:

> How then, can a young person with limited experience, undeveloped sympathies, an impatient temper, a love for self-expression, and passion for ideas become a true shepherd for his people? First of all let him study afresh the life of the ideal shepherd, and then let him day by day, both by prayer and self-sacrificing deeds, endeavor to build up in himself the mind of Christ.[4]

Few images capture more poignantly the mission of the church and its essential ministry than does the shepherding of the Lord Jesus Christ. We all need to imbibe deeply at this well and ponder how it translates into lifestyle in our highly competitive culture.[5]

OTHER MODELS SPEAK

Understandably the Apostle Peter shares a great concern for the shepherding of the flock of God (1 Peter 5:2-4). Likewise, all of Paul's epistles are intensely pastoral and are thus most germane in assisting us track how the mission of the church is appropriately reflected in the identity and function of the pastor-teacher. One senses an urgency attaching to the Apostle Paul's farewell remarks to the Ephesian leadership in Miletus (Acts 20:13-38), summarizing important values adhering to his pastoral history among them.

1) We see concern for the pastor's *character* (v. 19). Paul begins with the reminder, "You know how I lived the whole time I was with you, from the first day." Absolute personal integrity is top-priority for Paul here, as in the qualifications for leadership set forth in the Pastorals. Being must precede doing. "Take heed to yourself and to your teaching," he admonishes Timothy (1 Timothy 4:16). We're look-

ing here at "intrinsic credibility" in the Christian enterprise. Robert Murray MacCheyne used to say that what he owed his people more than anything else was "great likeness to Christ." Unfortunately this is being neglected in the conspiracy of trifles victimizing us today, but such a priority needs to be recovered. In the preserving of confidences, in the making and keeping of promises, in the use of true illustrations, we need to take pains to be right and to do right.

2) We see evidence of the pastor's *commitment* (v. 19). "I served the Lord with great humility and with tears, although I was severely tested." Here is the tough-mindedness/tenderheartedness which we sorely need in our time. There is humility here—not so much looking down on ourselves as looking up to God (cf. Philippians 3:4-10). We need to take the message to heart as much as do our hearers—with tears, sincerity and moral earnestness. Spurgeon's great chapter in his lectures aptly entitled "Earnestness—Its Marring and Maintenance" argues that the most important qualification for winning souls is earnestness.[6]

This commitment stands firm even in the face of severe testing. "I have the gift of criticism," announced a parishioner. We all sometimes are hurt by criticism. The challenge is to be constructive when we face the obstructive and the destructive. I think I have learned more from my critics than I have from those who have complimented me. As one of my predecessors said in a rather difficult spot: "We need more firemen and fewer brakemen around here."

3) We see the presence of the pastor's *courage* (vv. 20, 27). "I have not hesitated to preach anything that would be helpful to you but have taught you publicly from house to house. . . . I have not hesitated to proclaim to you the whole will of God." Paul was no pillar of Jello. Here is the boldness for which the apostles prayed. Both Jews and Gentiles received the message of "repentance toward God and faith in our Lord Jesus Christ." No watering down of the message was permissible. The pastor-teacher ought to choose with care the hill on which he stands and from which he refuses to be moved. It is prudent for the pastor to lose on some issues, but he should be immovable where it matters! Some of us perhaps need to be more confrontational and assertive, and others need toning down, but we all need to pray, "Increase my courage, Lord."

4) We see the signs of the pastor's *compassion* (vv. 22-24, 28-31). "Remember that for three years I never stopped warning each of you night and day with tears."

Paul's relationship with the New Testament churches is amazing. In his epistles he uses the names of ninety-nine different persons.

Notwithstanding his brilliance and his busyness as preacher, writer, statesman, and traveler, he was a real pastor! He shows us what it means "to keep watch over [the flock] as those who must give account" (Hebrews 13:17). He considered his own life worth nothing for the believers' sakes, and in this he reproduces through the Spirit the mind of Jesus. "I have you in my heart" was his testimony.

5) We see the basis of the pastor's *confidence* (v. 32). The pastor's love affair with the congregation makes his leaving like a bereavement. Yet no one is indispensable, and the real test as to whether we directed the flock closer to the Lord comes after our departure. "Now I commit you to God and to the word of his grace, which can build you up and give you an inheritance among those who are sanctified." The sovereignty of God, the sufficiency of grace, and the certainty of the goal provide the basis for our confidence in ministry.

Again we are impressed with how the mission of the church is implemented in the actual situation of ministry through dedicated and yielded human lives.

THE MESSAGE FOR THE LOCAL CHURCH

Every local church and its leadership need to have a carefully and clearly developed mission statement by which activity and organization are evaluated. Churches need to become goal-oriented. Nonadaptive forms need to be curtailed. Specific incremental objectives need to be formulated annually for each organization and functioning part of the fellowship. Some form of PERT (Program Evaluation and Review Technique) is required. The goals set should be specific, achievable and measurable.

A strong case can be made for using a program theme for the entire church each year. The planning needs to come from leadership as a whole, with generous grass-roots participation. What comes from the top down is not nearly as effective as what rises up with catalytic help from leadership. With constant attention to the Biblically mandated mission of the church, the local congregation should build year by year in a sequence of goals for growth. Growth is numerical, relational and spiritual.

Here is an example of what one congregation projected on the basis of serious self-study and the desire to go forward in the areas of chief challenge:

Year I: A YEAR OF EVANGELISM AT ELIM CHURCH
Year II: MISSIONS—OUR MANDATE

Year III: INTO THE WORD—INTO THE WORLD
(Nurture of the inner life—outreach)
Year IV: FARTHER AND DEEPER
Year V: IN LOVE AND LOYALTY TO CHRIST AND
HIS CHURCH (65th anniversary year).[7]

Each year's program theme encompasses preaching goals, involvement of each organization, overall programmatics for the congregation, and a spiritual state-of-the-church analysis as the context for goal-setting. The projections require ownership by the entire congregation. Each year's projection builds on the previous year and seeks to conserve the positive values already accrued, as well as targeting the unrealized and unfulfilled objectives.

Without clarity in our vision of what we ought to be doing and apart from honesty in our evaluation of how we are doing, it is very unlikely that a local congregation will make substantive progress in fulfilling God's will and purpose.

CHAPTER 3

"God's Household . . . The Pillar and Foundation of the Truth":

The Governance of the Church

The holy, catholic or universal church . . . this church I do honor and reverence in the Lord. But the rule of this church is the Word of God. The guide of this church is the Holy Ghost. The marks whereby this church is known in this dark world and in the midst of this crooked and froward generation are these: the sincere preaching of God's Word; the due administration of the sacraments; charity; and faithful observing of ecclesiastical discipline according to the Word of God. By God's grace, I will live and die the child of this church.[1]

What form is to content, structure is to function. Adversaries of structure in the church are the unconscious allies of anarchism and have always been with us ("In those days . . . everyone did as he saw fit," Judges 17:6). Structure is simply the principle and pattern of organized association. As such, no structure is itself a kind of structure, and a bad one at that. Structure is unavoidable; effective structure, like effective form, can greatly enhance function and content.

Our God is a God of order. It is His intention that in the church "everything should be done in a fitting and orderly way" (1 Corinthians 14:40). In the commonwealth of Israel, prophets, priests and kings functioned within divinely stipulated parameters. The Lord Jesus worked through the twelve and the seventy in the implementation of redemption's objectives. Church order emerged under the tutelage of the Holy Spirit as the church grew and faced new situations (cf. Acts 6). The apostles had a concern to establish government and structure for new churches as "they appointed elders for them in each church" (Acts

14:23; Titus 1:5). Paul in his Pastoral Epistles devotes no small space to matters of governance.

Overstress on the "invisible church" as God forms it, comprising the full number of the elect through the ages, may result in an under-emphasis on structure. This is the overidealization of the church. On the other hand, overstress on the "visible church" as we experience it may result in an overemphasis on structure. This can be the overmech-anization of the church. The systems approach to management, so widely used in modern business and industry, has much to teach us in the church, but it has limits due to the ultimately spiritual nature of the church.

THE TRADITIONAL CATEGORIES

Historically there have been three major church polities or structures of governance. Richard Hooker well argued long ago that there is that which is necessary in the church (the matters of saving faith) and there is that which is accessory in the church (ceremonies and matters of government).[2] Strands of each of the historic polities can be discerned in Scripture. A particular polity is largely historically and pragmatically derived, often greatly influenced by the personality and vision of a leader or leaders. Only thus can we understand the view of the long-time pastor of a mega-church who maintains: "A layman-led, deacon-led church will be a weak church anywhere on God's earth. The pastor is the ruler of the church. There is no other thing than that in the Bible." Though sincere, this is grotesque.

Beyond question there are structures of power and authority in the early church. In his very provocative study of *Paul and Power*, Bengt Holmberg argues impressively that "all authority is seen as ultimately flowing from the same source, viz. the Founder of the Church, and this is recognized as being the basis for the legitimacy of the exercise of authority in the church."[3] While originally the authority was more charismatic in nature due to varying degrees of proximity to "the sacred ratio," there is a gradual institutionalization, and the church lives with this dialectic in whatever its polity or structures of governance may be. Thus discussions and debates about governance need to bear in mind that power and authority in the church are not wholly Biblical and theological in nature, but are additionally complex historical and sociological phenomena.

1) *Episcopal.* This polity is essentially monarchial and illustrates straight-line management in its most direct form. While there is no evi-

dence of the uniform development of polity in the early centuries, the *Letters of Ignatius* (c. 110 A.D.) describe the three-fold ministry of bishops, priests and deacons. Cyprian's further exaltation of the bishop fits the hierarchical mentality of his time. Imperial governance in the church clearly images the great empires of antiquity and the Middle Ages, as well as the centuries of colonial expansion and manifest destiny.

Centralized leadership and authority are always the most efficient. It would be hard to argue that Paul and James and other apostles did not exercise strong and direct leadership. All of us have had moments when we sighed, "Oh for a godly bishop." But Lord Acton (himself a Roman Catholic) was right when he said that "power corrupts and absolute power corrupts absolutely." Without adequate checks and balances, such concentration of power in the hands of sinful beings is most perilous. It is fascinating how in more democratic times, the traditionally more monarchial communions have moved increasingly to more participative government (e.g., the Roman Catholic Church since Vatican II).

2) *Presybterial.* This polity is more contractual in nature and reflects the federalism of the seventeenth century. John Calvin's strong emphasis on covenant echoes in the Second Scots Confession of 1580 and the Irish Articles of 1615. The consequent Federal Theology provides "the necessary framework for a new theological and ecclesiastical system."[4]

Election of elders for rule in the local church and the development of a series of higher courts and adjudicatories beyond the local church have provided an admirable filter for problems. Similarity to western democratic and representative government is clear. Loyalties are substantially established. Influence of the clergy is strong, even though at the level of the synod and the general assembly ministers and ruling elders are equally divided. Historically this polity has found it difficult to halt and hinder the spread of heresy.

3) *Congregational.* This polity rests authority in the autonomous local church and its membership. Certainly there is leadership with consent in the New Testament (cf. Acts 6:1-6; 13:1-3; 15:1-34, especially 15:22). The involvement and responsibility of the members of the assembly is a cherished ideal in historic congregationalism and well reflects the individualism and participation which have been such a part of the New England town meeting and its progeny in American life. The right of franchise has been inviolable in theory if not always in practice.

Yet congregationalism has not always fostered loyalty within the community or filial ties with depth and significance in common endeavor. The larger and older congregations become, the less viable this pure kind of democracy seems to be. While limiting tenure has been one method of revitalizing congregational experience and meeting head-on the invulnerability of entrenched interests and the growing sense that decisions are already made and issues are cut and dry, many who argue vociferously for congregationalism in fact experience increasing apathy and more and more difficulty in achieving the already minimal quorum requirements for business meetings.

These are the three historic polities, but obviously we live in a time of great flux and ferment with regard to governance. Change is in the air. We can and must be open because Scripture does not give us a prescriptive exposition of any specific polity. At the same time, we must be ethically sensitive to the historic commitment of any local congregation or fellowship of congregations.

CONTEMPORARY CURRENTS

The fact is, the three historic polities are all converging and are increasingly becoming more similar. Democratization and the call for more participation now characterize the more authoritarian bodies. Curiously, many of the more historically democratic and participative bodies are seeing strong moves toward very rigid, self-perpetuating eldership modes, in sharp discontinuity with their historic commitment. What is happening?

All structures of authority are, of course, under question in our times. Anything traditional is suspect. Such a relentless review can of course be salutary. We need to summon all of our structures for scrutiny and examination before the bar of evaluation. There can be no progress without change. The church must be teachable. Infallibility belongs to no person, nor does does it belong to an institution. On the other hand, caution regarding change is prudent since we must recognize that there is continuity in the experience of God's people.

The notion that a drastic change in the structures of governance in a local church will bring about automatic change and improvement is naive. Such tinkering with the machinery guarantees no more than would the physical relocation of a church facility. Apart from spiritual vitalities, none of these externalia really address the essence of ministry. Shifting from a three-board/church council form to an eldership/commission form may increase participation in numerical and spiritual upswing, but in a down-cycle the concentration of decision-making in such a small circle reduces participation and deepens the sense of distance and remoteness from the congregational center.

No one has better described the dangers for the traditional Christian and the traditional church than Daniel Jenkins. The primary dangers are formalism, legalism (the ethical expression of formalism), and archaism.[5] The *status quo* is no option. The church has to be of divine origin to have survived as it has. Who has criticized the "old wineskins" more than the church herself? On balance, one would have to say the old wineskins have shown some incredible elasticity over the years. But winds of change and renewal are blowing over the church. What do they portend?

In some significant senses the differences within the historic polities now are more striking than the differences among the actual polities themselves. This has led Perry and Peterson to project three basic styles of local churches today: 1) the traditional church with quite customary and predictable moves in the direction of evangelism and nurture; 2) the super-aggressive mega-church, with a highly structured program and strong, visible leadership; 3) a renewal type with strong emphasis on the organic life of the church and innovative worship.[6]

Avery Dulles in his *Models of the Church* delineates five basic ecclesiastical options: 1) the church as institution (the very traditional church); 2) the church as mystical communion; 3) the church as sacrament (high church and liturgical renewal); 4) the church as herald (the pulpit and teaching center type); and 5) the church as servant (the sharing, caring community).[7]

In the fluidity of the present situation, the traditional tensions over governance have for the most part yielded to general confusion and uncertainty about worship styles, bewilderment over identity, increasing obsolescence of denominational distinctives and demarcations, restlessness among lay and clergy regarding the church, and an increasing tendency to follow fads.

Add to this the house church movement (especially strong in Britain), the charismatic renewal, "signs and wonders," power evangelism, power encounter and deliverance ministries, the shepherding movement, and the para-church.

The 1960s saw concentration on Christian education and management for the churches; in the 1970s the emphasis was on counseling; in the 1980s we saw the super-church models and major development expectations. With tremendous growth in many places abroad, we have seen renewal among some Christians and in some churches, but we have not seen renewal generally in the North American or European churches. Where are we going? What should the shape of structure and governance be for the situations we face in the nineties?

THE CRITERIA FOR OUR CHOICES

The role of the pastor-teacher in all of this is that of enabler, a facilitator, a catalyst and resource person who can be a change agent. The pastor-teacher needs to be a clarifier who faithfully focuses what Scripture says about the nature and ministry of the universal church in relation to the structures and governance of the local church. Each congregation has its own personality and character, as well as being heir to a tradition. The prayerful, sensitive undershepherd will foster and gently nurture toward growth without being insensitive to the flock.

The Scriptures supply basic principles and patterns. It is unfortunately possible to overstate what Scripture supplies us. Extravagant and overstated claims as to what is "the only pattern for church leadership given in the New Testament" must be resisted.[8] I believe W. D. Davies does not overstate the fact when he asserts, "The Church in the New Testament can assume many forms, and is not limited to any one particular form which is peculiarly the expression of its being."[9]

Peter Wagner makes a good case for strong pastoral leadership.[10]This is a needed corrective and balance to the flattening out of pastoral leadership found in Howard Snyder and Alexander Strauch (strange compatriots).[11] The permissiveness and laxity of our society are moving some to create highly authoritative pyramidal forms of government in which everyone is subject to someone else, except the primary leader who is ostensibly subject to Christ. But is he? Flexibility, not rigidity, recognizes that no one method solves all problems. Although no doubt well-intended, highly authoritarian and rigid approaches fail to recognize the diversity and variety in the workings of the sovereign Spirit of God through different personalities who can render effective leadership in the church. Old First Church downtown needs a particular structuring for ministry and staffing. The downtown pastor needs certain skills.[12] Since as Lyle Schaller urges, "The small church is different," the quest for pastoral leadership must take into consideration where the small church is and what the demographic picture is and what the ethos of the congregation is.[13]

Within our historic polities we need to craft and contemporize our structures and governance to be maximally responsive to our congregations and to increase participation. Much thought and care need to be given to more creative church meetings. Beyond question Findley Edge is on the mark when he prescribes freedom and variety, flexibility and adaptability as the criteria for structures in "the emerging church."[14] Much attention needs to be paid to the qualifications of those who serve (to be dealt with in the next chapter). I never cease to be amazed at how the Holy Spirit gives wisdom to the people of God as they wait before Him for guidance.

Clearly the greatest need of the church today goes far beyond structures and governance. We need the gracious, sweet, sweeping visit of the Spirit of God to energize all of our forms, to vitalize our mission, and to invigorate our worship. "Breathe on us, O breath of God!"

CONFLICT AND CHRISTIAN UNITY

The quest for structural and spiritual renewal in the church exposes us to the irritations and frustrations of the church's humanity. Ours is not the Docetic church with only the appearance of humanity. From the beginning scandals of division in the Body of Christ have caused the enemies of the gospel to blaspheme. Some in the church are on principle opposed to change. And spiritual mountaineers seem elitist to those who are stuck in the mud. The structures and governance of the local church need to take into account what will best proclaim the gospel and what will best maintain the unity of the church.

Church turmoil and splits seem to be on the increase, reflecting the general restlessness in our society and resulting in confusion in the church. Wayne Kiser has observed that congregational hypertension seems to be at epidemic levels. He quotes a denominational executive to the effect that "churches are splitting more today than in the past . . . and for more reasons . . . splits used to be primarily over doctrine, but now it's mostly personalities that clash."

Preventative maintenance dictates the formulation of a deliberate strategy for living with diversity in the local church, "rowing the boat together."[15] When conflict arises, a strategy needs to be built immediately by the spiritual leaders based on Matthew 18:15-17. If the problem does not respond, outside help needs to be sought. Persistent troublemakers should be disciplined. Perhaps a church consultant should be brought in for overall strategizing and long-range help.

Jesus prayed for the unity of His own—"that the world may believe" (John 17:21). We cannot urge people to be reconciled to God if we are not reconciled to each other. Of course there will be differences, and indeed there are divinely directed divisions. Could we deny that God has blessed the stand Martin Luther took on behalf of the purity of the gospel?

Visible unity is the great need of today's church. Disunity not only distracts the people of God from their task, but discredits the message which the church proclaims. Reaching "the unity of the faith" is an integral part of the maturity toward which we are to be moving (Ephesians 4:13).

In the household of God and its functioning, "Behold, how good and how pleasant it is to dwell together in unity!" (Psalm 133:1).

CHAPTER 4

"A Holy Nation . . . Chosen in Him to Be Holy"

The Integrity of the Church

I have walked in my integrity; and I have trusted in the Lord without wavering. Examine me, O Lord, and try me; test my mind and my heart. I shall walk in my integrity; redeem me and be gracious to me. My foot stands on a level place; in the congregations I shall bless the Lord. (Psalm 26:1, 2, 11, 12)

A bold claim, and, to our ears, sounds like boasting. Yet, in the psalmist, it is accompanied with a dread of sin, a sense of danger, and a prayer for deliverance. He knows that all goodness comes from God, and he clings to God in childlike trust. Two things will always be found together—love of God and recoil from sin.[1]

Integrity comes from a Latin root which means "untouched, whole, complete." God's people are called out of the world to become distinct and conspicuous by their godly character and holy living. MacCheyne used to say that "A holy church is an awful instrument in the hands of God," and in that regard shared his conviction that above all things he owed his congregation "a holy life" as their pastor.

The North American church has increasingly been conformed to and seduced by a culture which no longer thinks of immoral lifestyles, but rather alternative ones. The beacon-lights of western civilization have for the most part led the way in breaking our moorings in traditional law and morality.[2] As Ortega y Gasset has put it, "Twentieth century man is becoming a technologically competent barbarian." Tragically, and to our ceaseless chagrin and embarrassment, we Christians have not shown ourselves that much different.

Certainly from the beginning there have been Judas Iscariot and the Borgias and Elmer Gantry and Marjoe, all of whom have scarred the

Christian community with scandal and have blemished the testimony of the gospel. But there has come a change. As G. K. Chesterton opined, "Morality consists of drawing a line somewhere." Previously seven deadly sins were recognized even in western thinking. But now there are ostensibly no sins because there are no lines. Marital infidelity is on the rise, cheating is an accepted fact of life, and extramarital affairs are considered natural behavior. And sadly, the church has not taken significant exception to this paradigm shift in either word or example.

To put it another way, nothing in the church makes the world want to crucify it. One leading churchman excused his repeated unfaithfulness to his wife as simply manifesting the brokenness of the human situation. A woman fired her maid for stealing her priceless hotel towels. A publishing house discovered that a book entitled *Telling Right from Wrong* was largely plagiarized. Emerson's description of a speaker cuts even more closely today: "The louder he spoke of his honor, the faster we counted the spoons."

Beyond doubt we have catered to the meeting of needs and furthering self-fulfillment for the "me" generation. It is time for those of us in the church to rekindle our commission to build character. Reputation is what people think we are; character is what we are. "The English word character comes from a Greek word meaning 'an engraving tool and the mark it makes.' Our character is the 'mark' we make with our lives, the distinguishing qualities we display. In the highest sense, character is the mark of God upon a life, the noble qualities of godliness in a person."[3] This must be our aim and obsession if we are to be true to the high and holy calling which is ours in Christ Jesus.

QUALIFICATIONS

Reformed theology has always insisted that all truth is in line with goodness. This is everywhere taught in the Scripture (*inter alia*, Romans 8:2-4; 2 Corinthians 5:17; Ephesians 2:10; etc.). But a holy lifestyle must be embodied in the leadership of the church. Spiritual leadership is "a noble task" (1 Timothy 3:1), but we must recognize at the same time that "we who teach will be judged more strictly" (James 3:1). Christian leaders are called to a heavy responsibility, and Paul laid it on young Timothy to "set an example for the believers in speech, in life, in love, in faith and in purity" (1 Timothy 4:12).

If we are to stave off the mounting corruption in the church and the decline in the pulpit, we must revisit what the Pastoral Epistles teach about the qualifications of elders and deacons. We have endeavored to maintain here that pastor-teachers are part of a plurality of teaching and ruling elders. Whatever may be the nomenclature and polity in a local congregation, a more serious and spiritually purposeful approach needs to be taken to the nominating and election procedure for Christian workers at every level. In choosing those who would wait on tables and disperse funds to the neglected, the church chose people with high spiritual qualifications (Acts 6:3, 5). It would be better to leave positions unfilled than to thrust the unqualified prematurely into function.

Nominating committees and pulpit-search committees should ponder and pray over 1 Timothy 3:1-7 and Titus 1:5-9 on their knees if we are to avert total disaster through unqualified leaders. "Such as I have I give to you," Peter said to the lame man. We cannot give what we do not have. Leaders are to work as a unified team in ruling, feeding, protecting and caring for the flock of God. They are not self-appointed. They are to be respected (1 Thessalonians 5:12, 13), and they are not to be falsely accused (1 Timothy 5:19).

The preponderance of the qualifications have to do with inner traits and qualities of character. There is a strong emphasis on Christlike interpersonal relationships. Striking attention is given to the family life and marriage of the Christian leader. Competence for ministerial function is further stipulated and delineated. Wrestling with each of these qualifications with conscientious care using some good commentaries is a healthy discipline.[4]

Generally speaking the qualifications for leadership should characterize all believers, but they must exist at a high level and with consistency in those who would lead. Homer A. Kent has a good outline:[5]

I. The general qualification: "above reproach" (I Timothy 3:2). The leader "should present no obvious defect of character or conduct, in his past or present life which the malicious, whether within or without the church, can exploit to his discredit. In particular, his sexual life must be exemplary, and the highest standards can be expected of him."[6]

II. The moral qualification: "the husband of but one wife" (3:2). This is a very difficult and much debated qualification. The leader is to be a one-wife husband, a one-woman man. I believe this upholds the highest standard of faithfulness and loyalty within marriage but does not teach that divorce in pre-conversion days is the unforgivable sin.[7]

III. Mental qualifications: "sober (i.e. clear-headed, temperate), self-controlled, respectable (dignified, well-ordered), able to teach" (3:2).

IV. Personality qualifications: "Hospitable, not given to much wine (literally, 'not beside wine,' important in our time when pressurized modern life, modern methods of distillation and advertising conspire to make moderation in the use of ethyl alcohol very problematic. Abstinence is the best), not violent but gentle, not pugnacious (but magnanimous), not a lover of money" (3:3).

V. Domestic qualification: while the leader may be single and not married, if the leader is married there needs to be in evidence a godly concern for the establishment and maintenance of a truly Christian home (3:4).

VI. Christian experience: "not a recent convert, a good reputation with outsiders, sincere" (3:6-8).

What if Christian assemblies across the land were to take seriously what the Scriptures set forth about the qualifications of leadership? We cannot attain or recognize such leadership in our own strength (John 15:5), but we can do so through the abundant empowerment of our Lord Jesus Christ through the Holy Spirit (Philippians 4:13).

TEMPTATIONS

To the praise of God we are not ignorant of the devices and strategems of our adversary. The spiritual battle rages hot, for Satan knows his time is short and he is redoubling and retrebling his efforts to trip up the servants of Christ. No one is temptation-proof. "So, if you think you are standing firm, be careful that you don't fall!" (1 Corinthians 10:12). Thank God for His promises to the tempted (1 Corinthians 10:13) and for what He provides to make us "more than conquerors through him who loved us" (Romans 8:37).

There are certain temptations which are particularly common and prevalent for the pastor-teacher. Some of the most intense barrages are aimed at us toward the end of the pilgrimage of ministry. But throughout ministry, experience and observation indicate that some temptations are virtually endemic in ministry.

1) The *spiritual* temptation. No one is more dangerous than a backslidden preacher. We all experience undulation in our spiritual lives, but a down-drift and spiritual slippage take an unconscious and untold toll on our ministries and on those to whom we minister. If we

are not going forward in the blazing of new trails, we are falling back in our walk with Christ. There are, of course, dry times, and we are called to diligence "in season and out of season" (2 Timothy 4:2). We influence people more by what we are seven days a week than by what we say one day a week. Paul lived in dread of being spiritually "disqualified" (1 Corinthians 9:27)—that is, set aside from ministry. We need to live on short accounts with our Savior and to keep fresh spiritually.

2) The *intellectual* temptation. This is the temptation to become lazy and slovenly in our lifestyle. The pastor-teacher does not punch the clock. If we are not disciplined, we can fritter away our time and come to our preaching and pastoral opportunities unprepared. We need to get started promptly and use our time efficiently. It is real work to crack the Biblical text open in thorough exegesis and to project a message which has high interest and genuine relevance. There is no easy way for anyone to do this. The old-timers said we should study books in the morning and doorbells in the afternoon. The patterns of pastoral visitation may have changed, but the need for dedicated study and hard work has not changed. Lounge lizards who waste their days with endless prattle and chit-chat and playing with their computer toys (the latest minefield) will have much to answer for at the Judgment-seat of Christ.

3) The *vocational* temptation. Here we face the peril of professionalism. We get used to our role as a spiritual practitioner and soon perform it perfunctorily. The ministry becomes a habit, a routine, and a kind of spiritual boredom sets in. Our involvement becomes something of a yawn. The old Shepherd of Hermes described some in our time when he spoke of one serving Christ as: "empty himself, he gives empty answers." We can be chilled in our own spirits in this spiritual ice age. Is there warmth and enthusiasm in our praying, verve and nerve in our leadership, compassion and real feeling for those to whom we represent the Lord? Are we mechanical and automatic in our responses? Are we sensitive to the nuances of communication from the troubled and desperate? Has a kind of hardening of our hearts to human suffering and woe isolated us from our people?

4) The *material* temptation. North Americans enjoy the highest standard of living ever known in the history of our planet. Ministers as a whole are better paid and cared for than ever before. We find ourselves steeped in a very materialistic and narcissistic ethos. Are we taking care to escape "the love of money" and creature comforts (see 1 Timothy 6:10)? Will we succumb to a mercenary spirit? Peter warned spiritual

leaders in his day about being "greedy for money" (1 Peter 5:2). As servants of Christ we need to handle personal finances with impeccable care. We should not borrow too much. We need to be meticulous in our tax obligations. We should not pay a penny more than we owe the government, nor should we pay a penny less. We must be cautious lest we cater to the wealthy and special interests. There may be some gifts we cannot accept. Because of our essential humanness, perfectly innocent (and generous) offers may involve us in situations of obligation. We must not sell out because of the lure of a higher lifestyle. Too many who have fallen in our time have been victimized by this very temptation.

5) The *moral* temptation. The incidence and rampancy of moral defection among those in ministry goes across all denominational and ecclesiastical boundaries. About one in ten leaves ministry for a moral offense or problem. This is shocking and sickening. Even the thought of the lurid realities of our time should scare us. To paraphrase Luther, we can't keep the birds from flying over our heads, but we can keep them from building a nest in our hair. Casualty insurance by remaining close to Christ is essential if we are to avoid failure in this heartbreaking, family-wrecking, church-ruining, life-scarring, Christ dishonoring area.

a) Stay close to Christ. Times of exhaustion and letdown are times of great vulnerability. We can't afford to take our eyes off Christ.

b) Feed and fuel the flame of devotion to your spouse. Affectively starved people make easy psychological transference to caring, empathetic helpers.

c) Keep at arm's distance from the opposite sex in vulnerable situations. It is better to be thought a bit stiff and forbidding than to unwisely take risks.

d) Keep the thought-life pure. Lack of prudence in reading and visual materials in or out of the home can undercut the foundations of chastity and purity in any one of us. Lust begins in a mind where Christ is not allowed mastery over every thought. We live in a sexually suggestive and salacious age, and it is a battle for every one of us to keep a clean mind.

6) The *inescapable* temptation. This temptation which so plagues the ministry is the temptation to be discouraged. What William Willimon calls "the thus-and-so-ness" of the church leads to Spurgeon's "fainting fits" for the minister. Nothing seems to be happening; we keep dealing with the same impervious structures; the same neurotic people consume our time; all that changes is the calendar. Many a servant of Christ has withered and wasted in a prolonged

Elijah-like wilderness. This can be a time of ministry burnout and even leaving the ministry with a heavy load of guilt and shame. Here's where the pastor's pastor or some type of support group may be indispensable for the survival of the pastor and the pastor's family in ministry.

PREVENTIONS

Since prevention is obviously crucial for integrity in ministry both individually and corporately, it is imperative to trace and track some of the dynamisms which can inform and inspire spiritual overcoming. Several Biblical examples speak helpfully to this point.

The Life of Joseph

This Old Testament patriarch was truly a fruitful vine. In the face of great adversity and a very hostile environment, he maintained a godly life and testimony of extraordinary rigor. As a young man far from home, he faced the temptress. His response to enticement was: "He refused . . . he refused . . . and ran" (Genesis 39:8, 10, 12). He had no Ten Commandments, no Bible, no church fellowship. Six times we read, "The Lord was with him." He drew upon the resources of the Lord in order to hold his ground (cf. Genesis 49:22).

Joseph was truly a God-energized person. Though he had thirteen disappointing and discouraging years, his life was centered in the reality of the Lord's presence and provision. When he was asked to interpret Pharaoh's dream, he conceded, "I cannot do it" and relied on the Lord (Genesis 41:16). He persisted in exalting God (Genesis 41:25, 28, 32). In making himself known to his brothers in Egypt, he saw all of their mutually painful circumstances within a perspective of faith—"It was not you who sent me here but God" (Genesis 45:5, 7, 8, 9). Because Joseph knew God, he was mightily used by God to preserve his whole clan and to see to the feeding of the entire nation of Egypt. Notice the five titles for God used by Jacob with reference to Joseph's life and experience (49:23-25). There is a path to the peaks—and that path is intimate fellowship with God.

The Life of Daniel

Here is another Old Testament personality who long before the age of the fullness of the Holy Spirit demonstrated God's keeping power. Daniel at age fourteen or fifteen found himself in a foul and defiling foreign environment but determined he would not defile himself. Strong previous intention alone explains the firmness of his resolve (Daniel 1:8).

As Daniel and his friends faced extinction, their resort was to united prayer. Again we have a case of a very God-centered individual who lived and spoke in the conscious awareness of "the God of heaven" (Daniel 2:18). Daniel was an unbribed soul who was still going strong when past eighty. He wouldn't allow the power line of prayer to be cut. He proved Maclaren's contention that "There are no circumstances in which a person must have his garment defiled."

Our Divine Lord

Our great High Priest in facing all of the tempter's fury and force in the wilderness was "tempted in every point like as we are, yet without sin" (Hebrews 4:15). His three temptations are also ours: 1) temptation with regard to priority, 2) temptation with regard to methodology, and 3) temptation with regard to loyalty. And He will be our strength and stay—our living Savior!

Paul and the Early Church

A typical chapter which sets forth the prescription for community health is 2 Thessalonians 3. The inspired apostle's burden suggests what is always central in the preservation of the integrity of the church. We notice there: 1) the church is alive in intercession; 2) the church is active in proclamation; 3) the church is alert to discipline; 4) the church is aggressive in personalization. There is much language of kinship in Paul's epistles.

Surely though the dangers are many and formidable, our resources are superior in Christ. What dear Richard Baxter wrote long ago still obtains:

> If God would but reform the ministry, and set them on their duties zealously and faithfully, the people would certainly be reformed. All churches either rise or fall as the ministry doth rise or fall, not in riches or wealthy grandeur, but in knowledge, zeal and ability for their work.[8]

CHAPTER 5

"The Followers of This Way"

The Servanthood of the Church

Much self-deception still exists among leaders, particularly clergy, who perceive that leadership is handing down pronouncements, decisions and comments in a unilateral, authoritative manner. Leadership is a function of the people, as much as it is of the leaders. Strong, educated, resourceful people do not tolerate unilateral, authoritative leadership. Passive, dependent, under-educated persons tolerate so-called "strong leadership." Conditions no longer exist that made possible "the high doctrine of ministry" developed in feudal society. And that style will not solve the identity crisis for either clergy or laity. The model of clergy and lay leaders as reflective persons each with integrity in knowledge and function is more viable for our time. A role for clergy in teaching, assisting, equipping, organizing, supporting, and enabling leaders and members points to a higher doctrine of ministry, and one that is needed for both church and world.[1]

The thing that you are doing is not good. You will surely wear out, both yourself and these people who are with you, for the task is too heavy for you; you cannot do it alone. (Exodus 18:17, 18)

Leadership in essence is any behavior which helps the group meet its stated goals or fulfill its purpose. The leader is that person who initiates and enables this behavior to commence, continue, and find completion. Obviously leadership is needed in every aspect of human endeavor. In this basic respect the church is like the family, the government, the business, the union or the club. Leadership is necessary. We have discussed the structures of leadership in the church, but now we turn to how that leadership at any level functions.

Occasionally the officially designated leadership does not in fact lead. An unofficial power structure based on the long-standing role of a "tribal chief" exerts *de facto* leadership. It may take the new pastor a while to discern just where the power really is.

Evidence points to a mounting concern about leadership generally in our society. The complexity of problems facing modern government seems to exceed the capabilities of any one person, and there is a paucity of leadership as a result. A similar cry rises from education and from the church. Books and seminars multiply in the interest of addressing this need. Fifteen years ago R. M. Stogdill admitted after much research:

> Four decades of research on leadership have produced a bewildering mass of findings. Numerous surveys of special problems have been published, but they seldom include all the studies available on a topic. It is difficult to know what, if anything, has been convincingly demonstrated by replicated research. The endless accumulation of empirical data has not produced an integrated understanding of leadership.[2]

Where then does the church stand today in relationship to leadership?

LOOKING AT THE PATTERNS

The Lord Jesus Christ is our first-leader, our file-leader (Hebrews 12:2). But clearly there are under-leaders. The writer to the Hebrews admonishes: "Remember your leaders, who spoke the word of God to you. Consider the outcome of their way of life and imitate their faith" (Hebrews 13:7). "Obey your leaders and submit to their authority. They keep watch over you as men who must give an account. Obey them so that their work will be a joy and not a burden, for that would be of no advantage to you" (Hebrews 13:17).

Lack of leadership or a vacuum of leadership only invites disaster. Nature abhors a vacuum, and human systems do also, at all levels. Sometimes an *ad hoc* leadership will emerge by default, but this is asking for trouble. Sometimes a complete distortion or paralyzing disunity will eventuate when there is no responsible and proper exercise of leadership.

Secular theorists speak of task and maintenance functions in leadership. Task leadership facilitates moving toward goals, and maintenance leadership seeks to keep the social unit effective and viable. Some spiritual leaders have resigned themselves to a maintenance mode or have sensed that task leadership will not be received. This is a frustrating and defeating situation for many, and they yearn to get things going again.

Some leaders are tree-shakers, and some are jelly-makers. Varying congregational profiles call for appropriate but different styles of pastoral leadership. The leadership team in any setting needs the complementary gifts of diversely endowed leaders for healthy ministry. W. J. Phillips has helpfully pointed out that varying degrees of ownership and initiative will exist on committees and boards. He argues that the more passive congregation needs leadership with vision and inspiration. The church that is catching the vision needs engagers and interpreters. The congregation which has a clear sense of direction and purpose needs teachers and enablers. The church which is aflame and really on the move needs monitors and supporters. Phillips's counsel is wise:

> Few people can do all these forms of leadership well. Perhaps, rather than seeking some abstract, nebulous quality called "leadership," congregations and clergy should first examine their own context, to assess the leadership strengths that may already exist. Then it may be possible to determine with more precision just what kind of leadership is already needed.[3]

Tidball contrasts the more institutional with the more charismatic type of leadership. The more institutional type of leadership works more within structures and infrastructures. The emphasis is on continuity and order. The danger here is stodginess and being overly tradition-bound. On the other hand, the more charismatic type of leadership while trumpeting plural leadership may actually be in danger of new and tight authority structures. The peril of this style is fragmentation. Tidball points out that Paul argued against the separation of the charismatic gifts from institutional ministry. Both are needed, although doubtless any given leader will tend toward one or the other in emphasis and approach.[4]

Beyond doubt we are facing something of a crisis in leadership within the church. Observation and experience, as well as perusal of the superb evangelical publication *Leadership*, lead us to affirm that there is no one style of leadership which is wholly advantageous or strategic, but that within stylistic variation and diversity there is a unique and indispensable tone and texture in truly Christian leadership. It is to that consideration that we now turn.

LEARNING FROM OUR PARADIGM

As we have previously seen, Christian ministry is diaconal in nature. Ministry is "works of service" and is often menial and mundane.

Christian leadership is to be exerted not from status but through humble service, the lifestyle of the followers of Jesus Christ.

The world holds up hard-nosed and bruising assertiveness training. Wes Roberts's best-selling book *Leadership Secrets of Attila the Hun* is recommended by all of the moguls in this field. But our paradigm as believers must be the servant-leadership of Jesus Christ. The necessary background for us is the Suffering Servant of the Old Testament and the Servant songs in Isaiah (42:1-9; 49:1-13; 50:4-11; 52:13—53:12). We do not look to Rambo or Lee Iacocca for our pattern but to Jesus (Mark 10:45). If we are interested in long-range transformational leadership, rather than short-term transactional leadership, we must see that the effective leader is first a servant. The dominical model or the magisterial or managerial models may reflect the wisdom of this world, but this is not the wisdom which is from above.

"We are not gods," Paul shouted, and his example, as is ours, is the self-emptying of the Lord Jesus (Philippians 2:5-11). Servanthood is not transitional in ministry. Ours is not to be a kind of endless king of the mountain game of one-upsmanship. The Horatio Alger syndrome is much with us. But the Lord said to Baruch in the times of Jeremiah, "Should you then seek great things for yourself? Seek them not" (Jeremiah 45:5). Christian leaders are to be first and foremost lovers of God and people. Then we can be leaders.

This leadership begins with submission to the Lord. Howard Butt in a wise book on the nature of servant-leadership insists that submission is the key to power and that "the crown of Christian leadership is a crown of thorns." As Butt puts it so well:

> Christ's authority gave authority to Paul! Of his authority Paul had no doubt; he exercised it decisively and continuously ... this is no namby-pamby egalitarianism, no wishy washy leaderless group. Paul had a magnificent sense of command. Slave to Christ acting like a general! He showed us leadership up close; he was in charge and he knew it: his power to lead breathed strength.[5]

We need to candidate for ministry as servants. We need to commence ministry as servants (not with negative or critical remarks about our predecessor). We need to conduct ministry as servants. Christ Himself is our model for ministry, and He is by nature love. We see our Lord in John 13 dramatizing and enacting the character and nature of ministry. Jesus rises from the table (not intent on being the object of attention and ministration), lays aside His outer garments (the cultural equivalent of rolling up His sleeves), girds Himself about, pours water into the basin, and washes the disciples' dirty feet. These are the very terms of the Incarnation when our Lord took the form of a servant, the garb of the slave. The leader is to don the slave's apron.

Sometimes the ministry seems like life in the piranha bowl. We identify with the disciples when they pled, "Send them away." It seems like the urgent appeals always come at three o'clock in the morning. We so easily become robots. Hubris or pride are occupational hazards in ministry. Why aren't we more like Jesus who said, "I am meek and lowly in heart" (Matthew 11:29)? It is so easy to be grasping and self-seeking in ministry. We can be so possessive of our pulpit and our prerogatives that we fail to offer much-needed encouragement to young ministerial neophytes. Our Lord's willingness to do dirty work should make us ashamed of our ministerial conceits.

Clement Attlee's one telling criticism of Winston Churchill out of their experience in the British war cabinet was that Churchill was always asking the question, "How do you think I will look to history?" The servant-spirit is not so much looking down on ourselves and depreciating ourselves, but looking up to God. True and authentic worship will keep confidence from becoming arrogance. J. S. Bach would inscribe at the beginning of every composition, "J. J." (*Jesu juvet*—may Jesus help). Then he would conclude the composition with "S. D. G." (*soli Deo gloria*—to God alone be glory). That captures the spirit and tone of what is distinctively Christian in Christian leadership.

LIVING WITH PARADOX

Peter's exhortation to elders captures and articulates a kind of practical tension which everyone in ministry experiences. He wrote: "Be shepherds of God's flock that is under your care, serving as overseers—not because you must, but because you are willing, as God wants you to be; not greedy for money, but eager to serve; not lording it over those entrusted to you, but being examples to the flock" (1 Peter 5:2, 3). Two components exist within this equation. We see the exercise of oversight, and we see the example of servitude. These are authentic strands within ministry. Inspection of many passages clearly indicates that the leader is to lead, but this is to be in a spirit of deep subservience to Christ and His church. Ours is to be "the sacrificial expenditure of life" for the sake of Christ.

How do these two ingredients fit together? How shall we mix and blend aggressive, goal-oriented leadership (as in 1 Corinthians 16:15, 16; Acts 20:28; 1 Thessalonians 5:12, 13; 1 Timothy 3:4, 5; Hebrews 13:7,

17, 24) with the Venerable Bede's accurate and eminently Scriptural spirit—"We as clergy are simply the servants of the servants of God"? Abraham Kuyper put it well when he observed, "An office-bearer who wants something other than to obey his King is unfit to bear his office."

We see the tension of this paradoxical position in a memorable dialogue in an early issue of *Leadership* magazine when Larry Richards argues vigorously that because the church is an organism and not an organization, authoritarian and managerial models and attitudes are inappropriate. He prefers a more egalitarian and a much more unstructured renewal mode. Gene Getz comes back with a compelling argument for clear lines of leadership. There just have to be such structures when you get beyond seven or eight people. He feels Richards assumes levels of maturity which don't exist generally in the evangelical population and which must be predicated if such loose structure and leadership are to be employed.

The fact is, spiritually vital ministries are conducted within a considerable continuum of different styles. We can locate ministries which are very concentrated and heavy on the side of structure, and we can plot effective ministries which lean far more to decentralization and collegiality. Perhaps some entries could be made to illustrate the range and scope of diversity:

OVERSIGHT/CONCENTRATION:
From Jerry to Larry
JACK HYLES, JERRY FALWELL ,W. A. CRISWELL
Very Strong Pastor Leader
BILL GOTHARD
Chain of Command, Umbrella of Authority
JAY ADAMS
Confrontational Counseling
MUMFORD/ORTIZ
Shepherding Pattern in the Local Church
ENGSTROM/DAYTON/SCHULLER/PERT
Strong Leadership Role
PETER WAGNER
Church Growth School
ELTON TRUEBLOOD
Pastor as Coach
RAY STEDMAN
Body Life

BRUCE LARSON/KEITH MILLER
Small Groups
FINDLEY EDGE
Church as Miniature Theological Seminary
LARRY RICHARDS
Egalitarian, Unstructured, Collegiality

SERVANTHOOD/COLLEGIALITY

All of these ministries attempt to blend or mix the two essential strands of leadership consideration as set forth in the New Testament. Where on the spectrum will a given individual in ministry come out? Some basic axioms must be advanced to assist us with this important issue.

1) The leader must find his or her own basic style (out of the variety of combinations legitimately possible on the spectrum), and this style will be the function of temperament, experience, and the local situation (its size and age). We are shaped by various factors to be a certain basic type of leader.

2) The leader needs to develop considerable and consistent flexibility within the framework of the Biblical "givens." For instance, Paul in writing to the Galatians asserts his authority with rigor and force (cf. Galatians 1). The situation called for firmness. On the other hand, in writing to the Thessalonians he writes "like a father" and "like a mother" (1 Thessalonians 2:8ff.).

3) The leader has the responsibility of developing leaders. This is to be done in one-on-one discipling, in terms of existing leadership units in the church (such as the diaconate, Sunday school staff, etc.), and through the formation of small groups, support groups, 2:7 groups, etc., and then in the church as a whole. Jesus beautifully balanced His training of the twelve with ministry to the larger groups of needy humanity. We must beware of an elitism which will only deal with cutting-edge people.

4) The leader must lead. Paul's holy audacity is never more striking than when he says, "Be a follower of me as I am a follower of Christ" (1 Corinthians 11:1). Field Marshall Bernard Montgomery of Alamein (and a dear Christian believer in the resurrection) gave this splendid definition of leadership: "Leadership is the capacity and will to rally men and women to a common purpose, and the character which inspires confidence."

The Christian leader will ever seek to hold in proper and balanced tension the need for oversight and direction and the call to genuine servanthood.

LABORING THROUGH THE PROCESS

Undeniably in the area of leadership there is no substitute for competence. The "Peter Principle" operates: we all tend to rise to the level of our own incompetence. One district superintendent wrote:

> The trouble with most of the clergy that I supervise is that they either are lazy or don't like people. Nobody watches a minister on a daily basis. A lot of our people are just plain lazy . . . then there are the ones who don't like people at all. They say they do, but not really. They avoid people. They don't get to know people. They don't make calls on people.[6]

Sometimes problems in an inept or ineffective leader are the result of demoralization and acute anxiety and insecurity. We are in a general time of employee turmoil. There is much cultural unemployment (i.e., the employee doesn't fit the company's style). There is a general lessening of employee loyalty with a greater meanness and leanness seemingly in the very atmosphere of our time. Even *Time* magazine commends the committed Christian manufacturer Max DePree's advice: "Try a little kindness."[7]

Alert and responsive leadership must dig deeply into the nature and mission of the church and must be open to learning from good models (although not slavishly aping any of them). Frank Tillapaugh's *The Church Unleashed* is a positive example of the kind of thing we all need to consider. Taking key board members to seminars and conferences for a fresh breath of new possibilities can revolutionize and wake up everyone.

Leadership needs to plug into basic spiritual renewal if it is to demonstrate vitality and vision. Our lagging efforts in leadership may sometimes be the function of drying up spiritually. Perhaps the elders need a study retreat centering around J. Oswald Sander's *Spiritual Leadership*. Perhaps it's Eugene Peterson's *Working the Angles: The Shape of Pastoral Integrity* that we need. Here is an admirable exposition of prayer, the reading of the Scriptures, and spiritual direction. The pastor's struggle between Sundays is addressed with immense practicality in Eugene Peterson's *The Contemplative Pastor*.[8]

All leadership needs periodic renewal and firing up if we are to be and become truly "followers of this way."

II
Roles

"Preach the Word"

The Pastor as Communicator
of the Truth

Nor was the pulpit itself without a trace of the same sea taste
that had achieved the ladder and the picture. Its panelled front
was in the likeness of a ship's bluff bows, and the Holy Bible
rested on a projecting piece of scroll work, fashioned after a
ship's fiddle-headed beak.

What could be more full of meaning . . . for the pulpit is
ever this earth's foremost part; all the rest comes in its rear; the
pulpit leads the world. From thence it is that the storm of
God's quick wrath is first descried, and the bow must bear the
earliest brunt. From thence it is that the God of breezes fair or
foul is first invoked for favourable winds. Yes, the world's ship
is on its passage out, and not a voyage complete; and the pulpit is its prow. (Herman Melville, *Moby Dick*)

The primacy of the written Word of God is clear and compelling
in reference to the church and everything Christian. Jesus Christ is the
foundation of the church, and "she is His new creation through water
and the word." The Holy Spirit ever "in, with and under the Word"
uses that Word as the instrumental agency in effecting conviction for
sin and new birth, growth in godliness, and incorporation into the Body
of Christ (1 Corinthians 12:13).

The pastor-teacher has no higher responsibility than the faithful
and dutiful preaching and teaching of the Word of God. The feeding of
the flock of God must be at the head of his agenda. "The hungry sheep
look up and are not fed" was John Milton's complaint in his day and
tragically is the legitimate lament of many in our own time. They ask
for bread but are given a stone.

Preaching and teaching are seen virtually interchangeably in the
New Testament. C. H. Dodd in his classic study has unquestionably

overstated the distinction. Beyond question good preaching will contain much teaching, and effective teaching will have some preaching. Teaching is above all occupied with a subject in a generally homogeneous setting. Preaching is additionally concerned with application, generally in the more heterogeneous setting of the congregation as a whole in the context of corporate worship. Our focus here will be primarily on the communication of truth through preaching.

THE SUBSTANCE OF OUR COMMUNICATION

"Take thou authority to preach the Word of God," the ordinand is enjoined in *The Book of Common Prayer*. God has spoken (Hebrews 1:1, 2) and entrusted the gospel to us. God's truth has been embodied and personified in the living Word, Jesus Christ (John 1:14). Here is the ultimate contextualization. Then, "not in words taught us by human wisdom but in words taught by the Spirit, expressing spiritual truths in spiritual words" (1 Corinthians 2:13) God's truth is conveyed. Though words are culturally conditioned, they bear meaning. In fact, all communication is predicated on the ability of language to carry meaning.

Truth is propositional correspondence with reality. Our message is translatable. The very notion of meaning is under serious assault in western civilization today. The "new hermeneutic," while helpfully reminding us that we bring presuppositions and baggage to the task of interpretation, frequently boils down to the idea that a text is what the reader makes of it. Like a Rorshach ink-blot test or a Thematic Apperception Test, the text tells us about ourselves with no objective referent. The structuralism of de Saussure moves the locus of attention away from the author or the reader to the relations of words to the text (semiotics). The ultimate absurdity is deconstructionism, which denies meaning altogether and views even grammatical construct as fascistic.

We must argue that language is the fundamental institution of society and is capable of carrying and communicating meaning. The Word of God written is God's special revelation to humankind. The Bible is not only inspiring, it is inspired. It is not man reaching up to God, a kind of religious anthology, but in fact God reaching down to man. God addresses us reliably and trustworthily in the words and sentences of Scripture.

Herein lies the necessity and urgency of preaching. As Amos expressed it, "The Lord God has spoken; Who can but prophesy?" (Amos 3:8). Preaching, then, is not an improvisation. Preaching is to be the proclamation and exposition of a God-given message. What F. W.

Robertson termed "the intense excitement of preaching" derives from this unimaginably high privilege of sharing God's message with our people. While Scripture has perspicuity (an essential clarity in its message), there are difficult things in Scripture as well, and a preacher-teacher has been appointed in the strategy of divine providence to aid hearers in understanding and applying the Word of God. The Reformers did not have a Scripture reading in addition to the text for the sermon (the "naked Scripture"). The Scripture read was to be expounded. So Paul urges Timothy, "Devote yourself to the public reading of Scripture, to preaching and to teaching" (1 Timothy 4:13).

Private Bible reading is not enough. Immediately in the Acts the very vocabulary of preaching alerts us to the nature and necessity of proclamation. Four main words are used to describe what was at the heart of apostolic ministry: to announce or publish (*katangello*, six times); to herald (*kerusso*, eight times); to announce the good news (*euangello*, ten times); to speak (*laleo*, several times). It is not our role to merely share trendy opinions, or to try to be stand-up comedians. Our responsibility is to open up the Scriptures. Thus the expository sermon in which the text of Scripture actually shapes the sermon gives us the best opportunity for sharing God's Word with believers and nonbelievers, to be like the preacher of whom F. D. Maurice said, "He seemed to be the channel for what he said, not its source."

THE SETTINGS FOR OUR COMMUNICATION

While many gifts are entailed in pastoral ministry, significant priority is given to the gift of public proclamation. In most instances the search committee is still called "The Pulpit Committee." The first question ordinarily asked is, "Can this candidate preach?"

The stated services of divine worship remain the primary preaching opportunities. Multiple morning services present their own challenge physically and psychologically. Only when a congregation is pressing capacity for some time does going to a second service guarantee the 10 to 12 percent increment frequently described. Good stewardship of our resources, however, cannot justify construction of large edifices needed only for Sunday mornings.

Preaching in a series (*lectio continua*) rather than randomly preaching appealing texts (*lectio selecta*) has much to commend it. The evening service, while in some difficulty, provides its own special opportunities (see Chapter 22 for a full discussion of the developing situation). Some congregations are going to a Saturday night service to accommodate a special constituency.

Likewise the midweek prayer service is taking its lumps. This service should be primarily devoted to prayer. Robert Murray MacCheyne had thirty-nine prayer meetings weekly in Dundee (five of which were children's prayer meetings). However, a brief Bible lesson primes the pump of intercessory prayer, though it should not preempt the time for prayer. It is so much easier to talk about prayer than to pray. Yet "the ministry of the Word" (Acts 6:2) is so closely allied to the practice of prayer that we cannot artificially segregate them.

Bible classes and small-group Bible studies have proliferated in recent years. Part of the pastor's responsibility is to train leaders who are competent to teach in these settings.

One great advantage of expository preaching is that it models how the Bible is to be studied and taught. It not only exhibits the fruit of study, but leads the listener into and through the passage at hand.

The whole Christian education enterprise is of prime concern to the pastor-teacher. Even where there may be capable staff or lay leadership, the pastor-teacher needs to demonstrate confidence in and concern for this vital arm of the church. It may not be possible or desirable to have the pastor regularly teach in the Sunday school (especially if there are multiple services). Participation in an advanced adult elective or an occasional appearance in a children's department or high school or college class makes a valuable statement respecting the undeniable priority of the educational task.

In many traditions there is the custom of a confirmation class or Bible instruction class for eighth- and/or ninth-graders. In my own tradition I would teach the eighth-graders Old and New Testament with memory work and catechism and then the ninth-graders church history and doctrine with catechism. This afforded me an invaluable opportunity to become acquainted with our youth, to interview them, and to press the claims of Christ upon those who had not yet made decisions for Christ.

Beyond the local church there come innumerable opportunities for the pastor to share the Word in nursing homes and penal institutions, in street meetings and rescue missions, in park services and service clubs, in school baccalaureates (still common in small-town America). There are always gifted and articulate believers in a local assembly who should be encouraged to use their gifts in many or all of these settings. It is a serious blunder to imply that only the pastor can or should speak the Word of God. We can guard our pulpits so jealously that we fail to encourage young neophyte preachers and laypersons whom God is blessing in the Word. There is a basic sense in which the whole of the congregation is called to share in the office of proclamation which is held by Jesus Christ alone.

I remember with great pleasure the generosity of a gifted and consecrated layman who owned several factories. At Christmastime he would invite all of his employees to a party during non-working hours at which he would give his personal testimony and then ask his pastor to give a brief gospel message and appeal. Many and varied are the opportunities for proclamation in the stated services outside the church in the community, including special occasions such as weddings, funerals, etc. God has promised to bless His Word—and He does and He will.

THE SKILLS IN OUR COMMUNICATION

Humanly speaking, preaching is impossible. The whole process of preparation and delivery is futile apart from the guidance and unction of the Holy Spirit. A sermon is not merely the reading of a paper or preparing an essay or writing a treatise The sermon germinates out of deep absorption in the text of Scripture, grows into a form which communicates the central theme of the passage, and climaxes in an appeal to the will, heart and mind of the hearers respecting an appropriate response in worship and/or obedience. At every juncture and step, the preacher is dependent on the enabling of the Spirit of God.

The essential skill is to grasp the meaning of a Scriptural text in its context and translate that into a form that conveys its significance to hearers in our world today. Concerning teaching in regard to preaching, preaching is *application*. It is building a bridge between the Word and the world. As Sidney Greidanus so succinctly puts it:

> Since the message was first addressed to the early church, it requires explication; since that message needs to be addressed to a contemporary church, it requires application. The problem preachers face is how to integrate explication and application so that the whole sermon comes across as relevant communication.[1]

The interpreter must first find the main thrust or "big idea" of the preaching portion. This search takes into account the larger and immediate context, the literary genre, and the feeling tone of the passage. All of this needs to be reflected appropriately in the message. We do not decide what the text says; we try to *discover* what it says. A single, clear sentence which captures the meaning of the passage and states it principially is an indispensable tool in guiding the craftsman in the structuring of the sermon. The main points and subpoints must support the sermon sentence or proposition.

The main points should be cast into the present tense (requiring a subject and predicate); the development should follow the text so that the sermon is saying what the text says. Holding to the central idea of the passage, there should be continuous application, helpful illustration, and climactic conclusion.[2] The pictorial and illustrative are especially critical where there are listeners who are not that interested or listeners who are not that knowledgeable, which pretty well describes any congregation.

The preacher is not a soloist. The preacher is like the musician who has the score before him or her and then plays with abandon and skill without getting in the way of the composer's music. This involves entering not only into the thought but into the feeling of the music. Preaching without passion is not preaching at all. Someone described a sermon preached by Archibald Alexander: "He appeared absolutely overpowered by the truths he was presenting and his every feature was illuminated and glowing with the fire within."

Every aspect of this kind of preaching is hard work. A conspiracy of trifles in the parish will seek to distract and derail every preacher from the kind of concentration and dedication which are absolutely indispensable. There must be hours allocated, study habits developed, and personal discipline for this to happen. Much advance planning and praying will be required. Ample time for the internalization of the message (the development of the orascript) must be allowed. Saturday nights must be kept sacrosanct. We owe this to our Lord and to our people. Both urgency and artistry are required, and this involves a careful use of time.

The miracle of effective transmission and reception is wrought not by our gifts but by the Holy Ghost. As Professor Le Cerf used to say: "When you preach, you do not know what you do: you wield lightning!"

THE SUBJECTS OF OUR COMMUNICATION

There are so many broken hearts within our reach. So many around us are fighting difficult battles. This calls us from our aloofness and urges us to see the important interrelatedness between our preaching and our pastoral visitation and counseling. We will not be answering questions people are not asking if we are close to our people. The preaching moment becomes dialogical when we know and love our people. Ilse Joseph, the great violinist, expresses it this way: "I can sense a reciprocal contact with the audience."

The sensitive communicator will not overload. NBC has been widely criticized for its coverage of the 1988 Summer Olympics. In trying to show too much, they wound up showing almost nothing at all. Even Jesus had to say, "I have many things to say to you, but you cannot bear them now" (John 16:12). In dealing with the profound truths of the Christian faith, we must seek to speak plainly and clearly, recognizing that the danger in simplifying is distortion. Seek simplicity but distrust it.

Where are our listeners? In touching them where they are we need to remember that the exegesis of culture must follow the exegesis of the text. We severely acculturated western Christians are awash in our narcissism, our materialism, our hedonism. Instead of being "transformed by the renewing of our minds," we have been "conformed to this age" (Romans 12:2). George Lindbeck speaks accurately of the "dechristianization of the high culture of the west."

The word *secularism* refers to this age and describes the cultural drift in which we are engulfed. It is only fair to observe, however, that the western world is probably moving increasingly into what must be denominated a post-secular mind-set. As stated earlier, nature abhors a vacuum. The emptiness and existential loneliness of secularism have been appalling. The inquiring interest and curiosity of increasing numbers turning to evil supernaturalism, the New Age movement, and eastern religion all bespeak a shift which offers the Christian proclaimer new opportunity.

Though modern thinkers as a whole reject any notion of revealed truth—and even the idea of truth at all—or morality as such, we must not panic. We dare not move into an accommodation mode which jettisons the gospel. We must not give away the store in the name of relevant communication.

We are told, for example, that we should not speak of God as King because that is militaristic and triumphalistic. We are not to speak of God as Father because that is sexist and escapist. Nonsense. There is no special gospel for modern man. Christian proclaimers and missionaries have through the centuries confronted totally pagan and polytheistic cultures. Consider the earliest apologists. They used the Hebrew

Scriptures, they quoted God's Word, they argued from the fulfillment of Old Testament prophecy. They did not betray the gospel in a frenetic but ill-advised compulsion to please at any cost.

It is a harrowing hour for the Christian communicator in whatever setting. Gregory the Great said it so well for us: "It is for love of him that I do not spare myself in preaching him." May it be so with you and me.

CHAPTER 7

"Come, Let Us Bow Down in Worship"

The Pastor as Leader of Worship

Jesus, where'er Thy people meet
  There they behold Thy mercy-seat:
Where'er they seek Thee, Thou art found,
  And every place is hallowed ground.

Here may we prove the power of prayer,
  To strengthen faith and banish care;
To teach our faint desires to rise,
  And bring all heaven before our eyes.

(William Cowper)

The quickening of interest in the doctrine of the church in this century, with the attendant renaissance of focus on lay ministry, spiritual gifts, and the nature of true ecumenicity or inter-church relations, is also giving rise to a most positive and gratifying renewal of focus on worship in every stream of Christian tradition. Worship is not only personal and private, but it is the experience of the Christian community. Karl Barth did not overstate the case when he said, "Christian worship is the most momentous, the most urgent and the most glorious action that can take place in human life."

Leitzman was no less on target in arguing that "The heart of the Christian life is to be found in the act of public worship." One typical study indicated that of the thirteen major tasks of the pastor-teacher, the laity surveyed gave the task of leading divine worship higher priority than did the clergy. (However, both pegged it near the very top.)

Challenging the introversion of members of the human community is the worshiping community, which experiences and proclaims "the *mysterium tremendum*," the "beyond" which comes among us.

Worship is response to the presence of the living God among His people. The pastor-teacher has no higher a privilege than to guide the gathered church in an ever-deepening and more significant experience of worship.

WHAT IS TRUE WORSHIP?

The universality of the religious impulse bears testimony to the fact that human beings are worshiping creatures. The living God is looking for worshipers who will worship him "in spirit and truth" (John 4:24). The main Hebrew and Greek words translated "worship" mean "to bow down or prostrate oneself before God." Other verbs mean "to serve," and these are occasionally conjoined (e.g., Matthew 4:10). Worship is adoring response to Almighty God and the obedient submission of the whole person to God.

Robert Webber is an apt diagnostician when he observes, "There is a cancer at the heart of many churches—the failure to understand and practice worship."[1] How many persons at the average morning service called "Worship" do in fact worship? When theology reduces to sociology, worship flattens out to become oppressively and tragically horizontal. Then the appeal becomes, "Join us for worship—you will feel better." Worship becomes therapy, and this is a pathetic abdication.

Religionists for whom *God* is but a poetic word for human relationships must embark upon an endless quest for gimmicks. Jazz services, dancers gliding down the aisles hurling paper plates at the congregants, soda pop and potato chip services, etc. are desperate attempts to fill the vacuum. Much of this froth boils down to celebration of the self or worshiping the church (ecclesiolatry). Unfortunately, many conservatives shrink in outrage from such blasphemy only to revert to predictable, powerless worship forms. Many of our people are increasingly hungry for reality and vitality in worship, and we are losing many both to the liturgy of the right (the extremely high-church) and the liturgy of the left (the exceedingly unstructured or house-church in the renewal mode).

The point of proper beginning must be the recovery of a sense of what worship is. Here the pastor-teacher and the spiritual leadership of a congregation must give themselves to study and prayer. This calls for the formation of a worship commission to help plan and lead worship. Serious mining of the Biblical texts and careful attention to the theology of worship reflected in preaching and teaching will lay a foundation in understanding to be implemented in praxis.

Orthodoxy literally means "right praise." We are not talking about entertainment or folksiness or chumminess. Those of us from the more low-church, free-liturgy background have frequently permitted our worship to simply equate with pious congeniality, a good feeling, a tingling of the toes, all of which fails to acknowledge the transcendent dimension which is so crucial for worship. Calvin maintained that proper adoration is the prime purpose of worship.

William Temple gives us a splendid classic definition of worship:

> To worship God is to quicken the conscience by the holiness of God; to feed the mind with the truth of God; to purge the imagination by the beauty of God; to open the heart to the love of God; to devote the will to the purpose of God.

As Kierkegaard so magnificently put it: In worship, God is the audience, and we, His people, are the actors. Down with passivity and spectatorism. The pastor has an incredible opportunity to be a catalyst for the worship of God.

While worship is predicated on divine revelation (general revelation helps with the mood, but special revelation is necessary for the content), true worship is God-directed, Christ-centered, and Spirit-enabled. Our worship is mediated, and hence Paul Hoon is correct when he insists that "Worship, if done in response to anything other than the mystery of God in Christ, is idolatry."[2] To use the words of the Hartford Appeal: "We worship God because God is to be worshipped."

HOW SHALL WE BETTER WORSHIP?

If worship is the unqualified encounter of true Christian believers with the living God, and if the Isaiah 6 pattern is paradigmatic (adoration, confession, forgiveness, proclamation and dedication), what steps should the pastor-teacher take in seeking the enhancement and enrichment of the worship experience?

1) *The pastor-teacher must be dedicated personally to a deepening worship experience.* Sometimes we are so conscious of who is in the service and what we are going to do in the service that we ourselves don't worship. We must prepare to lead worship by genuinely worshiping. Sadly, many evangelical seminaries do not require a course in worship. Then we have make-up work to do in the rich Biblical materials, the many historical and theological works which can help us. It is impor-

tant to recognize that there is no evidence of a uniform liturgy in the early church. Yet certainly the ideals of spontaneity, simplicity, and spirituality were and are foremost.

2) *The pastor-teacher should encourage those in leadership to be part of the planning of worship.* Liturgy literally means "the work of the people." Diversely gifted people can make helpful contributions in the interest of varying and enriching the worship experience. Building the worship service around a theme is positive. The theme derives from the message and its text. The service can be organized variously from week to week and may involve components such as:

> We come to God.
> We speak to God.
> We listen to God speak.
> We respond to God.

3) *The pastor-teacher will foster more creative use of the essential ingredients within the service of worship.* Special attention will be given subsequently to the whole area of music in worship, a topic which is so nettlesome right now. Great care must be given to the public reading of Scripture. Pastors should model the effective public reading of the Word. Prayers present a perennial challenge to the pastor. We are always praying publicly—one of the most difficult things we do. The pastoral prayer is often a sermonette with the eyes closed. A variety of benedictions should be employed. This extending of the blessing should above all not be rote or routine. Use not only the Aaronic Benediction from Numbers 6:24-26 and the Apostolic Benediction from 2 Corinthians 13:14, but appropriately use 1 Timothy 1:17, Hebrews 13:20, 21, Jude 24, 25 or 1 Peter 5:10. You may want to sometimes preach a series of messages on Biblical benedictions.

4) *The pastor-teacher must become an avid student of the flow and movement of the worship service.* Browne Barr has made an astute observation in this regard, speaking of many worship services:

> I am appalled by how frequently they are like an amateur hour. One unattended problem is pace. The services drag painfully when they most need liveliness, as in prayers and hymns of joy and thanksgiving, and then leap ahead like a frightened deer when we most need time and quietness to confess our limitations or pray in silence. We are shot out of a time of meditation by a vigorous priestly "Amen" before we have had a

chance to sense any Holy Presence. Endless fussing with unnecessary microphones, tedious notice, an announcement by the presider and a long musical introduction for hymns already posted, choir processionals like traffic jams on a free-way—none of these hindrances could last a month if there were a team atmosphere and candid weekly critiques. But a professional is needed to bring this about, and this brings us to consider the minister not only as theologian and presider, but also as manager.[3]

Minimally this means the announcements must not be "show-time" to break the flow, nor should the grand-gallop to shake hands with other worshipers in the service be permitted to jettison all reverence and order. The erosion of all sense of mystery in our most holy faith is a conspicuous characteristic of our time. I used to enjoy escorting the third-graders of our Sunday school around the church and through the sanctuary on an annual worship visit. This became a beautiful opportunity for the pastor to initiate the very young into aspects of worship and form not understood.

WHERE ARE WE GOING IN WORSHIP?

Some very positive trends are emerging in the renascence of interest and thought about the worship experience of God's people.

1) We see a new emphasis on *the priority of worship*. Any congregation which is not talking about worship and is not consciously in quest of renewal in worship is definitely off the track. The rhythmic balance between worship and work is crucial. One without the other is doomed. The movement away from daily life and back into daily life is at the heart of spiritual health. Paul Scherer has wisely said, "Worship is that time when we bring the gods we have made to the God who has made us."[4] Most of the counseling we do will be done in the worship service. The word "ecstasy" means literally "to stand out of oneself" and should describe the result of the soul's preoccupation with the living God.

2) We see a new emphasis on *preparation for worship*. I am not talking about the introduction of ceremony for the sake of atmosphere or churchliness. I'm talking about leadership exercised to counteract the continuous intrusion of secularism and dedicated to fostering worship to the degree that we prepare orders of service as diligently as we prepare our sermons. Ushers need to be trained and briefed so as to abet

reverence. Worshipers should be trained to bow reverently when taking their places in the sanctuary. The atmosphere must not be like a hoedown. The bulletin should include aids to worship and present an attractive invitation to come and worship. Interpretive verses of Scripture, the use of different names for the components, and printed responses for the congregation require lead-time and prayerful thought. Preparation for baptismal services and Holy Communion is necessary if we are to be delivered from a debilitating sameness.

3) We see a new emphasis on *participation in the service of worship*. The use of responsive readings and creedal affirmations for occasional use will bring people away from being bystanders. The use of lay-readers can be encouraged. Testimonies and sharing times are now possible even in larger assemblies with the advent of the cordless microphone. What a beautiful time, perhaps on Thanksgiving Eve or Thanksgiving Day, it can be to take the roving mike among the saints to hear their praises to God. This is never in place of the Word of God. Concern for the highest quality in the service must always be balanced with the recognition that none of us is perfect. We want young and old to share their gifts. Good training programs are vital if participation is to be maximally beneficial.

4) We see new emphasis on the *special days and seasons of the church*. Baptism and the Lord's Supper have fallen on hard times in many a congregation. Strangled by unyielding custom and suffocated by formalism, we do not look forward to these special times of sharing as we ought. What may seem to be irrelevant to the world and its crying needs becomes most relevant when we recall P. T. Forsyth's sage comment, "The church is the only society with a fulcrum outside the world; and therefore the only one that can move the world." There is no more glorious a creative challenge to the pastor than to build Communion services through the church year with varying emphases—some very solemn (as on Maundy Thursday or Good Friday) and some very celebrative. Different settings and different times can immeasurably enlarge the blessedness of the sacred supper. It is veritably the antipasto of Heaven.[5]

The same is true for the great festivals of the church. An increasing number of low-church folk are responding positively today to the observance of the four Sundays before Christmas as the Advent Season, a unique opportunity to preach and proclaim the Incarnate Christ. After all, Christ Himself is the essence of worship. Precedent for Advent observance is as early as 380 A.D. and is all the more appealing as Christmas becomes increasingly secularized and commercialized.

The Lenten season, consisting of the forty weekdays and six Sundays before Holy Week, is a marvelous opportunity to orientate ourselves to the Cross of Christ. Strangely, few low-church congregations observe Pentecost at all. We give great play to the coming of Christ, but totally and inexcusably ignore the coming of the Holy Spirit in power on the seventh Sunday after Easter. Low-church as my own proclivities are, I have been enriched myself, and so have the people of God, by the addition of a collect of corporate confession before Communion. Careful preparation of prayers (while not reading them) calls for as much reliance on the Holy Spirit as the impromptu but often predictable spur-of-the-moment effort.

5) We see new emphasis on *the careful introduction of innovation.* Change is not easy for us, but there can be no progress without change. C. S. Lewis has a good word about novelty and its danger, in that it can turn our attention to the novelty and to the leader rather than to the Lord.[6] Great caution and wisdom need to be employed for the effective introduction of change elements. Explain them fully. Begin perhaps at an evening service. Don't overdo it, and be prepared to drop it if it isn't working well. Here we are talking about original liturgies, creedal recitation, a drama segment (on the Willow Creek model), prepared prayers by several people, sermon reaction panel, etc. If nothing new or fresh ever obtrudes, perhaps the fresh breezes of renewal are not being felt at all, and that would be most regrettable.

WHY IS MUSIC SUCH A TENSION IN THE CHURCH?

Singing to the Lord is an anticipation of the glories of Heaven when we will join with the saints of all the ages in magnifying and adoring the name of our God! Psalm 96:1, 2 instructs us as to how this is to be done. Igor Stravinsky, the famous composer, was correct when he observed: "The Church knows what the Psalmist knew: music praises God. Music is well or better able to praise Him than the building of the church and all its decoration; it is the church's greatest ornament." There is much about music and singing as worship in our Bibles, and the great blessing of it no one would deny.

Yet the fact is, we continue to experience painful and divisive tension over the style and kind of music used in the church. Recently Dr. David Rambo, president of the Christian and Missionary Alliance, wrote a letter to all of his workers, a portion of which was published in the denominational organ. He reported that at their recently concluded General Council "a distinguished pastor walked out of a weeknight service because the contemporary style of music offended him. Then on both Saturday and Sunday mornings a young woman left the services because she couldn't take 'those same old songs.'"[7]

President Rambo rightly expresses concern that our personal taste in music sometimes becomes the point of reference rather than the urgent need for seeking the reality of God in worship. Recognizing that we always face the danger of mere performance and exhibition whatever kind of music we prefer, we all need to broaden our tastes and sympathies and develop some tolerance for one another. I have my personal preference, which includes the great old God-centered hymns which are so theologically rich. Yet I have to came to terms with the fact that only 7 percent of the recorded music sold in our country is classical. The "post-hymnal age" into which we are moving is a fact of life.

My tastes in music are analogous to my love for the cadences of the King James Version of the Bible. Yet for anyone to believe that the King James is the original Bible is like believing that the "last years" of Jesus were spent in Britain with Joseph of Arimathea studying under Merlin in Avalon. The call is for understanding, openness and great growth and development in our desire for and experience of the worship of our God! Truly the late A. W. Tozer had reclaimed "the missing jewel" when he wrote: "I would rather worship God than do any other thing I know of in all this wide world."

> *We praise Thee, O God: we acknowledge Thee to be the Lord.*
>   *All the earth doth worship Thee, the Father everlasting.*
> *To Thee all angels cry aloud; the heavens and all the power*
>   *therein.*
>   *To Thee cherubim and seraphim continually cry:*
> *Holy, Holy, Holy, Lord God of Sabaoth.*
>   *Heaven and earth are full of the majesty of Thy glory.*
> *The glorious company of the apostles praise Thee.*
>   *The goodly fellowship of the prophets praise Thee.*
> *The noble army of martyrs praise Thee.*
>   *The holy Church, throughout all the world doth*
>   *acknowledge Thee,*
> *The Father of an infinite majesty;*
>   *Thine adorable, true and only Son;*
> *Also the Holy Spirit, the Comforter.*
>   (From the *Te Deum Laudamus*,
>   an ancient Christian hymn)

CHAPTER 8

"Whatever You Do . . . Do It All in the Name of the Lord Jesus"

The Pastor as Administrator

The church has accepted Y-F as their pastor. Needless to say he is impatient for the church to grow. His patience is being tried as he moves the congregation on in works of faith, labor of love and steadfastness of hope without undue fleshly pressure and ambition. He endeavors not to repeat the mistake of going ahead of the Holy Spirit in a frenzy of meetings and programs. Truly it is a narrow blade that divides the realm of walking in the Spirit and rushing by the flesh. (Letter from a young Malaysian pastor's wife)

Whatever your hand finds to do, do it with all your might. (Ecclesiastes 9:10)

A curse on him who is lax in doing the Lord's work. (Jeremiah 48:10)

All enterprise entails aspects of administration. Only an extremely Docetic view of the church, denying her true humanity, would challenge this. Some pastors have particular gifts and interests in "administry," while others tend to chafe under what they perceive to be a conspiracy of trifles and a mass of impressive trivia which distract from real ministry.

Lloyd Perry in his good treatment of administrative function defines administration as "working with and through people to get things done."[1] Luecke and Southard in their expert work integrating ministry and management contend that this is the most time-consuming work of pastors—and the least satisfying. They cite studies which indicate that administration is a major source of stress for clergy.[2]

The church after all is the largest network of voluntary associations in American society. The pastor of even a smaller congregation is the chief executive officer (CEO) of a fair-sized entity. The pastor must reject the philosophy, "You preach, we'll handle the business." The church is not a series of hermetically sealed compartments. Matters of finance and organization are as "spiritual" as prayer and Bible study. Whether the pastor's style in management is maximalist or minimalist (or in between), the pastor in shared leadership should seek to run a tight ship. All aspects of the affairs of Christ's church should be conducted honorably, efficiently and creditably for the glory of God. None should mistake incompetence for the way of the Cross.

THE BASICS

Administrative function must always be responsive to the basic philosophy of ministry and to the people of a congregation. Unlike corporate business, the bottom line is not profitability. Yet, modern capitalistic venture can teach us many things, as Jesus insisted: "For the people of this world are more shrewd in dealing with their own kind than are the people of the light" (Luke 16:8b). We are in debt to theorists and practitioners of modern management technique for many procedural improvements, but we must not worship at this shrine. The church is a unique genre. We must be cautious in the evaluation and employment of what "works well" in the marketplace.

The pastor needs to take a bifocal approach to effecting change. How shall we handle the difference between what is and what ought to be? The young pastor and the new pastor may be so eager for change that important human values are sacrificed precipitously, with exceedingly negative consequences. The Holy Spirit's own work in the believer's sanctification is gradual and progressive. We are involved in process. Sensitivity to people and the nature of group process in the specific community in which we work can obviate unfortunate negativity and conflict.

The approach "I say to one man 'Come, and he comes'" needs to yield to "Come now and let us reason together." When the situation is dreadful and unacceptable, we need to face it and try to understand the genesis and the factors responsible. Overall and long-range goals need to be set and then broken down into incremental steps for the amelioration of particular crises. Goals need to be specific, achievable and measurable.

Close attention to the instrument of governance—the constitution and bylaws—is imperative. The pastor should be an *ex officio* (not advisory) member of every committee and board—i.e., with the right of voice and vote. This is not to say the pastor will be responsible to attend every committee (which would be manifestly impossible and, with multiple staff, unnecessary), but it is to say that the spiritual leader is not excluded from any administrative or deliberative unit. Provision for limited terms and tenure can be an important encouragement in the development of new and fresh leadership.

Careful preparation of the agenda can cut down wasted time. Conscientious taking of good minutes and distribution of these minutes before the next meeting enhances shared experience. Organization of the office is crucial. A well-maintained central calendar of events to avoid embarrassing schedule conflicts, prompt issuance of visitors' letters weekly, attractive church bulletins and good communication, meticulously kept records of membership and pastoral acts are really not optional. The pastor's own promptness in handling correspondence and tending to details can set the pace and tone for the whole congregation.

THE BUDGET

The Bible has much to say about money and the handling of money. Some ministers are very uneasy about this area and consistently refuse to address it from the pulpit. Other ministers seem interested in money above all else. Studies show that those responsible for fiscal well-being in the church are unclear as to how their Christian beliefs relate to their task. Attention to this area must begin with a theology of Christian stewardship and with an ongoing, year-round stewardship education program. We need to teach children and youth, along with our own families, the basics of Christian stewardship.[3]

Crisis appeals and year-end ploys of desperation would better yield to training in regular, systematic patterns of giving. This is a spiritual duty for leadership. Customs differ widely, but many have found stewardship dinners and an accompanying opportunity for a faith promise to the Lord's work, or some variant of these, to provide a significant impetus for congregants to take serious stock of their spiritual responsibility with regard to their material means. What better check on the materialistic drift of our times than to practice proportionate giving as the New Testament lays it out (1 Corinthians 16:1-3). The tithe of the gross would seem to be the starting-point for Christian stewardship, for it is unimaginable for a believer under the New Covenant to do less than the believer under the Old Covenant. The pastor's own example here is not inconsequential.

The local church budget is the proposed plan for expenditures based on a realistic expectation of income. Participation in the formulation of the budget through hearings conducted by the leadership of the church or small-group input sessions through the congregation are essential for a sense of ownership on the part of the members. Local history and experience over a considerable period of time shape present practice and attitude toward the budget process and toward an annual commitment or canvass time. No approach or format keeps on working. Adaptations and thoughtful, creative innovations pay dividends.

Projection of income is the function of the number of giving units in the congregation. Unfortunately we cannot realistically count on even a tithe of our gross congregational income, but more like 6 to 7 percent. The rate of inflation needs to be taken into account and the addition of new members, not all of whom will move their full financial support to their new church immediately.

Five basic approaches to the kind of budget to be used can be cited:

1) *Recap budget.* This is really only the history of the previous year's experience.

2) *Designated budget.* Through the duplex envelope system, giving is specified.

3) *Unified budget.* All goes into the central pot to be divided by the percentage formula adopted at the annual budget advisory.

4) *Modified united budget.* Gifts go to designated funds, but inter-fund equalization guarantees expenditures in accord with the adopted percentages.

5) *Program budget.* This is a ministry-oriented budget with percentages allocated to the various branches of ministry, which sometimes seem arbitrary.[4]

The presentation and adoption of the annual budget are strengthened by clear, accurate exhibits of the previous year, experience to date, and the impression of great integrity in the handling of funds. Financial statements and regular reporting need to be top-drawer. Several responsible people need to count the offering (not during the service), and the cost of bonding such should be investigated. It is better for the pastor not to handle any monies except the discretionary aid or benevolence fund. All finances should be audited annually. Even the appearance of the slightest impropriety or a lack of care in honoring designations legitimately causes crises of confidence.

Voucher systems to control expenditures preclude many different people charging items to the church. This is the Lord's money, and carelessness in the church and its organizations or in a pastors' own personal finances can reflect grave discredit upon the Lord and His work. The managing of our finances testifies to what we really believe. Jeremiah's purchase of the field in Anathoth (Jeremiah 32) was a way of putting his money where his mouth was. How we handle our finances and allocate our giving are critical indices of our true spiritual state. Realism, faith and spiritual vision are hallmarks of good stewardship.

The personal giving records maintained by the church (for tax and other purposes) are strictly confidential. It is unwise and unnecessary to post personal giving amounts for general knowledge. I also believe it is imprudent for the pastor to inspect the giving records of the membership. Once I inadvertently saw such records, and I regretted it immediately. Many who were able to give were poor givers, and many who had little gave sacrificially. My attitude would have been better if I had not known the details.

More will be developed on stewardship in other contexts, particularly with regard to missions in the discussion of the missions conference and faith-promise pledging. The whole of the Christian life is an adventure in stewardship. We Americans who comprise 6 percent of the world's population and own one third of what is owned on this planet and annually consume half of what is consumed have an immense responsibility in this area. "To whom much is given, much shall be required" (Luke 12:48).

BUILDING PROGRAMS

The construction of additional physical facilities is no automatic panacea for lack of spiritual or numerical growth. Some pastors feel that a ministry in a local church during which there is no building program is deficient. More significantly, if only it could be said of us as was said of a pastor who never orbited in the higher spheres of ecclesiastical preferment: "He never served a congregation but what the spirit of revival touched the people during a season of that ministry."

The North American church has perhaps suffered from "an edifice complex" and has thought too highly of the physical buildings and structures. Yet long-term use of rental facilities in a community is expensive in its own way and fails to state to a community that there is a permanent commitment to ministry in that place. Astronomic building costs and prohibitive land prices in some areas are serious deterrents. Functional facilities are a great asset in ministry. Attractiveness and beauty are important criteria in what we do for our Lord.

We must be clear in realizing that a new structure or relocation guarantees nothing. Ministry builds the church of Christ under the sovereign Spirit, and physical structures are but one of many components (and by no means the chief). Careful and thoughtful consultation with architects should seek to make the physical structure itself expressive of the theology and worship of the congregation. The Communion table should not be pressed against a wall, but should be free-standing for the observance of the Lord's Supper, because it is not an altar but a table for fellowship at which we are guests of God. Here is where our theology needs to be embodied in the physical structures.

Some opinion circulates that a congregation should not on principle go into indebtedness. In our credit-type economy, there are few of us who would ever own a home were we unable to borrow funds. Similarly, no Scriptural *a priori* forbids prudent borrowing, though there is a point at which debt becomes so burdensome as to work at cross-purposes with current ministry needs. This is where a congregation needs to count the cost (Luke 14:28-30). Very possibly investment in personnel and programs to reach people should take higher priority. Also, extended time in a building program and its financing can drain much physical and spiritual energy from a congregation. This should all be calculated carefully.

Experience shows that the decision to proceed in a major program needs the strong support of the congregation. The pastor needs to be part of the deliberative process, but should not lead the charge or insist so strenuously that he lays his ministry on the line. The pastor's main contribution must be in fostering the spiritual dynamics essential throughout the building program. Firm insistence on high-quality amplification systems and not too much fabric in the sanctuary to absorb musical projection are special concerns for the pastor's focus. Superb resources are available for local churches in terms of guidebooks and manuals for future planning.[5]

BUSINESS MEETINGS

Business and committee meetings need not be drudgery, but do frequently become an endurance contest. Leadership should concentrate on developing the skills which will facilitate prompt, efficient and satisfying times for deliberation and decision-making. Our objective is to achieve consensus in both the smaller and the larger units of discussion and debate. To insist on unanimity is to make possible the tyranny of the minority. A single obtuse opinion cannot be allowed to thwart the will of the majority. The overt role of the pastor in the business meetings should not be dominant, nor should it be dormant.

Prior consultation and thorough airing of issues beforehand among the leaders should preclude too high a profile for the pastor in the meeting itself and will not jeopardize authentic discussion of the issues. There are major issues which clearly involve Scriptural principle, and here there can be no compromise. These are the rare but significant moments in which ministry is made or broken. But most of the issues we face are matters of judgment and wisdom, and these are not the monopoly of anyone or of a few. It is even beneficial for the pastor to lose on some of these lest he become dictatorial. It is also well to model for the congregation how a good loser behaves.

In the interest of order and fairness, to guarantee the will of the majority and the rights of the minority, assemblies are governed by rules of order. The United States Senate and the United States House of Representatives have their own rules of order. Many organizations stipulate *Robert's Rules of Order* as the guide for procedure. This is no undue concession to secularity, but simply the use, with any necessary adaptations, of a wise and considered instrument of great value.

Robert's Rules are not rigorously used in small committees but only principially. The larger the assembly, the more care and detail need to attach to procedure in the interests of fairness. If the presiding officer is shaky on procedure, a parliamentarian or advisor on procedure should be used. The pastor should basically master *Robert's Rules*. Conservatives have occasionally missed important junctures because they have been mute in a moment of crisis.

It is imperative to know the difference between a call for the question and moving the previous question (the latter of which immediately concludes the debate and requires a two-thirds vote). It is helpful to know how to use the debatable motion "to postpone indefinitely" as a trial balloon well before voting on the main motion.

Doing all for God's glory requires concern for the revivification of our church meetings. More thought, more planning, more prayer will mean more in attendance and more significant business conducted for the Kingdom.

BREAKTHROUGHS

Tremendous changes are revolutionizing management, and these impact the business of the church explosively. Resources are available to us of a kind and quality that are incredible. One firm makes available "Ministry Area Profiles" which describe the area within a five-mile radius of the church. This breakdown supplies population facts, demographic trends, lifestyle characteristics. Think of the value of this for church planting, evangelism and outreach, and building programmatic bridges to identifiable population segments.[6]

Computerization is offering incalculable benefits to the church. Advantages accrue in financial and attendance records, correspondence and sermons, retrieval systems for illustrations and data filing, new addresses and mailing lists. The purchase of the right system is a big decision, but possible adaptations are endless. One pastor in a relatively small congregation developed a system for discovering and deploying volunteers. A computer ministries file was compiled listing every position and office. This was correlated with a ministries interest survey of the membership. The result was a significant improvement in the numbers of volunteers absorbed and a greater effectiveness in their utilization.

Dull need not be the byword in the pastor's work as an administrator. Our fast-moving times present vast challenges, but these can be more than met through the technological and spiritual resources available for our use. God has not been napping in this hour of opportunity and harvest.

CHAPTER 9

"Comfort Ye, Comfort Ye My People"

The Pastor as Counselor

Canst thou not minister to a mind diseas'd
Pluck from the memory a rooted sorrow,
Raze out the written troubles of the brain,
And with some sweet oblivious antidote
Cleanse the stuff'd bosom of that perilous stuff
Which weighs upon the heart?
(William Shakespeare, *Macbeth*)

Ministry is people. The pastor is in serious trouble who said, "I would really love ministry if it weren't for people." Jesus ministered as the Great Physician to a wide array of individuals. Jesus invested so much of Himself in the rich young ruler, the young lawyer, Zacchaeus, the Samaritan woman by the well, the woman taken in adultery, etc.

The names of 110 different persons are mentioned in the Book of Acts. The Apostle Paul refers to ninety-nine different individuals by name in his epistles (see, for example, Romans 16:1-13). This contrasts sharply with certain intellectuals and self-styled beacon-lights of modern culture who love ideas and not people.[1] Sartre could say, "Hell is other people," and Bertrand Russell would boast, "I love mathematics because it is not human." Not so our Lord Jesus Christ and those who have followed Him and would follow Him today.

The morally firm but deeply compassionate concern for people which Jesus showed is well expressed in the words Matthew Arnold used of Goethe:

He took the suffering human race
He read each wound, each weakness clear;
And stuck his finger on the place,
And said: Thou ailest here and here.

WATCHING DIRECTIONS

The cure of souls has ever been the domain of the servants of Christ. While there has always been pastoral involvement in personal and family crisis, as in cases of illness and dying, there was very little systematic reflection on the pastoral role in such ministry. Richard Baxter plied his house to house catechetical instruction and urged it upon his compatriots in ministry. F. D. Schleiermacher (1768-1834), while seriously flawed by anti-supernatural bias, was one of the first to push practical theology to the fore and to press Christian concern for the community as a whole.[2]

The rise of modern clinical psychology and the development of a therapeutic society with great value attached to "feeling well" and "getting well" have made an immense impact upon the church and the expectation of the pastor-teacher and others who work in and through the church. Jesus Himself was a healer, and not all of the maladies He addressed were physical. Modern depth-psychology, emphasizing the mental and emotional underpinnings of physical well-being and a more holistic approach stressing the unity of personality, was not at all inconsistent with the Biblical concern for the whole person.

While some secular researchers limited themselves to a more experimental and statistical grid (as in the testings movement and in educational and social psychology), others moved with greater vigor to theories and worldviews in which they were increasingly hostile to Biblical presuppositions. Freud and Adler and the analysts generally viewed all religion as essentially neurotic. Carl Jung, while the son of a Protestant minister and speaking of the importance of a religious resolution for "modern man in search of the soul," differed little from his constantly quarreling colleagues in their disdain for revealed religion.

Carl Rogers, a refugee from evangelical upbringing, was helpful with his non-directive counseling techniques but was necessarily limited in the degree to which he could actually provide a model for helping people who are hopelessly enmeshed in sin. Departments and schools of psychology began to abound, and books with varying degrees of sophistication began to multiply up to the present time when conservative Christianity is awash in a glut of much "pop" psychology and some substantial work which evidences no serious integration with Biblical theology or orthodox systematics at all.

Some pastors are doing too much counseling, both in terms of the amount of time being spent and in terms of what is being attempted given their qualifications and experience. Several courses and a spate of books do not a counselor make. Too much evangelical preaching is overly laced with faddish psychological jargon. Self-esteem and self-love have become the bottom line, with sin and judgment being effectively dismissed. Thus much that passes for counseling is merely warmed-over secular theory. In this relatively virgin and fast-developing area of emotional and mental health care, there is a crying need for vigorous Biblical scholarship which will do some significant integration of theological, psychological and sociological data.

Predictably a strong revulsion against the psychologizing of Christian verities has arisen. Some stridently condemn all psychology. This is extreme because clearly psychology, the study of the inner life, is morally and theologically neutral, as is philosophy or anthropology or science itself. There is good theology and there is bad theology, and by the same token there is good psychology and there is bad psychology. A more reasonable critique by Jay Adams in terms of his "nouthetic psychology" has helpfully pointed the way to the centrality of the use of Scripture in counseling and the absolute necessity of facing the sin question. But unfortunately Adams's Van Tilian premise causes him to reject any insight from secular psychiatry.

This is to throw the baby out with the bathwater. We must appreciate a jewel even if it is in a hog's snout. We benefit from the findings of many a rascal whose worldview is far from being Christian. Viktor Frankl and his "logotherapy" do not derive from Christian presuppositions but nevertheless make a significant statement about the importance of a sense of purpose in life for survival, this coming from a survivor of Hitler's death camps. We can learn something from Erik Erikson about identity formation and Abraham Maslow's levels of human need.

Popularizers such as Paul Tournier, Gary Collins, Larry Crabb, Archibald Hart, Newton Maloney, James Dobson and Alan MacGinnis have much to offer the pastor who wants to understand and help anguished and suffering people. William Glasser's Reality Therapy certainly does not provide a Christian system, but does summon therapists and victims alike to the inescapable sense of personal responsibility for choices without which there is no such thing as ethical behavior or a system of morality. It is thus clear that pastors are facing a situation of excess on two sides: the danger of too much emphasis on psychology and counseling on the one hand, and the premature dismissal of the discipline on the other.

WISING UP TO LIMITATIONS

The question is not, shall the pastor counsel? Counseling is basically "(the) process of encouraging growth from within, which in the final analysis is the only true growth."[3] The pastor who is dedicated to fostering spiritual growth and health in all of the variegated situations and circumstances of life faces a never-ending challenge. The three basic skills required here, as Carl Rogers so well identifies them, are: *empathy*, or getting inside the world of the person; *caring or prizing*—i.e., affirming the worth of the person (cf. Matthew 10:29-31); and *genuineness*, being without pretension or affectation.[4]

The pastor who embodies these qualities and who communicates them in discourse and in terms of interpersonal relationship will lack for no opportunity to counsel. Filled with the wisdom of the Word of God and guided by the Holy Spirit, there is no reason why today's pastor cannot mediate substantive help and healing to troubled and bruised souls, as has always been the case. The spiritual shepherd has been the counselor through the ages. Study after study shows that people's first preference is for their spiritual leader in times of crisis.

Who is better qualified, as a rule, to share in significant discussions about guilt and the assurance of salvation or lack thereof? When people are wracked with doubt or ravaged by fear and anxiety of a specific or free-floating kind, is not the practitioner of souls a proper resource? In the ongoing nature of pastoral function, in preparation for marriage and in the interest of maximizing adjustment and preventing problems in a divorce-prone society, thorough and thoughtful premarital counseling is not optional. In connection with the birth of a baby and the rites of passage, the pastor faces a great teaching opportunity. Every pastor will do vocational counseling, and not only with the young—mid-career change is not uncommon, and mid-life crisis is less apt to be hidden today. The experience of death and dying requires the sensitive exercise of many skills (see Chapter 19 on the funeral).

Every pastor faces stressful family situations in the parish, and when calls for help are not forthcoming, spiritual leadership must prayerfully consider proper initiatives. Here is a call for the wisdom of Solomon. Chemical addiction and substance abuse frequently compound the complexity of life's tangles. It is no surprise that clergy are themselves subjects of depression, for everyone has moments (even hours) of blue funk. Many great figures of history have been melancholics. There are certainly clinical cases which need help, but perhaps we have unrealistically expected to live in a kind of perpetual euphoria.

This may be aided and abetted in a kind of effervescent church and preaching atmosphere in which we are to be "happy, happy, happy" all the time. Yet, there may be good and sufficient reasons at times for being downcast. One psychologist has written a helpful book entitled *The Right to Feel Bad*, in which she argues that depression has been overpsychologized and overmedicalized in our culture.[5]

The growing population of senior adults with the syndrome of physical, social, economic and spiritual issues common to these persons and their families is increasingly relying on the pastor's time and energy. Sexual identity issues pose challenges in our culture which are now blatant and overt whereas formerly they were most frequently covert. The local pastor now confronts within the active membership behavioral deviation of a kind not even identified by name previously.

Behavior disorders of a psychopathic variety wreak havoc within a circle of human tragedy beyond description. The compulsive sociopath, like a kleptomaniac or pyromaniac, are baffling aberrations. The widespread phenomenon of child sexual abuse or the cycle of marital abuse far exceed anything we previously thought possible. The highly neurotic can consume huge chunks of the pastor's time with the endless repetition of seemingly insoluble problems. A policy of deinstitutionalizing the mental hospitals of our country puts the pastor face to face with psychotic individuals, particularly in our large cities.

It is crystal-clear that any pastor who supposes or assumes that he can take the responsibility for counseling all persons needing help in all of these areas plus many others not chronicled here is himself or herself living in a world of unreality. In no previous generation of pastoral care have pastors been expected to shoulder such massive care obligations, and it is totally beyond the bounds of reason to expect any human being to do so now. Every pastor must do counseling, but no pastor can do all of the counseling.

WEIGHING OUR OPTIONS

Some of our most effective counseling can be done through the ongoing preaching and teaching ministries of the Word. The Scriptures, being God-breathed, are profitable and able to make the man or woman of God "perfectly adjusted for every good work" (2 Timothy 3:16, 17). The Psalmist explicitly says to God, "your statutes are my delight; they are my counselors" (Psalm 119:24). Our greatest asset as Biblical counselors is that we have the instruction book from the Creator and can face the brokenness of human existence from within an avowedly supernatural frame of reference. God is the healer; our Savior is the victor over all the hosts of darkness. (See Chapter 20 on healing and exorcism.)

The very presence of the man or woman of God may be an indescribable solace to the bereaved or suffering. Job's comforters teach us that we can talk too much, so cut the chatter. Albert Schweitzer related that when his father died in Gunsbach in the Alsace, the greatest comfort which came to him was his childhood friend putting his arm around his shoulders and silently walking with him from the cemetery to the village.

A movement has arisen in some quarters in the interests of training lay-counselors. Certain brothers and sisters among us have always ministered as advisors, nurturing friends and confidants. Some gifted for this ministry are in actual church leadership as elders or deacons/deaconesses, and some are not. Training programs, study courses and the like can help the pastor-teacher face the load of responsibility. Because of a special interest I have had in this area, I would occasionally offer as a Sunday school elective a course on Christianity and mental health. The crucial factor for the lay-counselor, as for any counselor including the pastor, is to recognize our limitations. We need to be sensitive as to when we should refer a person to a professional counselor/therapist.

Another very important therapeutic mechanism with great potential in the church is small group process. The existence of vital shepherding and support groups can be of immense blessing and value in a congregation. The lonely cry "No one cares for my soul" should never echo in the assembly of believers. However, not all small group experience has been positive in the church, and much care and prayer are required to sustain the viability of such a unit. Nevertheless, the small group process affords the possibility of a greater intimacy and accountability which can assist leadership in more adequately addressing the massive caseloads we face today.

The pastor can best handle brief therapy and short-range counseling needs. A contract or understanding about the counseling should be used. The pastor needs to reserve the right to make a referral at any time he deems advisable. Marriage counseling involving deep-seated and long-rooted problems may consume hours of time weekly. It may not even be desirable for the pastor to delve so deeply into these matters because this may jeopardize ministering to these parties in the normal course of pastoral ministry. The couple may also jockey to get the pastor to his or her respective position, with no evident desire for real reconciliation. Such futility is a dead-end.

Serious behavioral disorders, suicidal threats and behavior (always to be taken with the utmost seriousness), violence and masochism, serious hallucination and reality-denial may call for admission to a hospital and treatment by a psychiatrist. Needed medications can only be prescribed by a doctor. Most metropolitan areas in our country have Christian psychiatrists and psychotherapists who can be of prime assistance in a crisis. These costs are often high, but frequently adjustments are made in relation to the patient's ability to pay.

Referral is very difficult in geographically remote areas. It is further positively dangerous to make referrals to some professionals in the field who regard the Christian faith and moral scruples as antiquarian and neurotic. In situations where I have been desperate, I have made referral to a psychiatrist or therapist only after ascertaining that he or she (while not born-again as far as I could assess) nevertheless was a religious person or viewed religion as a positive factor in human experience. Great care and much caution must thus be used in making referrals. Most therapists are very willing to work with, discuss with, and keep in touch with the individual's spiritual counselor. At this point I suspect if I were drowning, I would rather have a Muslim who could swim than a Christian who could not swim. This is a very critical issue.

WORKING ON DISLOCATIONS

In whatever counseling the pastor engages, he must face the dynamics of transference and its attendant distortions (in which the counselee uses the counselor as a substitute or surrogate for someone else), or countertransference (in which the counselor's own personal problems become an integral part of what happens in the counseling). Spirit-sensitized and common-sense objectivity must alert us to the fact that if we personally have been hurt and scarred through alcohol abuse within our family experience, our whole approach to the alcohol abuser will be severely colored. Our own insecurities may make us exceedingly vulnerable to the creation of relationships of dependency which may be ego-flattering but which hinder spiritual growth and maturity.

The working premise of pastoral counseling is that Christ can heal and Christ can help. "With God nothing is impossible" (Luke 1:37). We must remember this when counseling thorny cases. For example, in today's climate of gay rights and gay marriages and religious bodies sanctioning gay clergy, we are facing a typical but exceedingly difficult problem. Clearly, homosexual and bisexual behavior is spreading to larger portions of society. In regard to, for example, the AIDS crisis, we need to give clear Biblical teaching to our congregations. Essentialist explanations for the origins of homosexual orientation are under fire by constructivists who argue (wrongly) that it is only society's definitions which challenge the counterculture's inevitable move to greater freedom and bisexuality.

For the Christian, sexual deviation from the Scriptural norm (be it homosexual or heterosexual) is unacceptable and sinful. Monogamous, heterosexual marriage is the norm for sexual expression, and all lust is sin. An accountability structure is necessary for a believer with same-sex orientation. Chastity is possible by the grace and power of God. Deeper therapy and healing are possible, but this area remains as one of the most difficult encountered in our times. The very environment in which we live encourages confusion.[6]

Few roles of the pastor-teacher are fraught with greater ambiguity and hazard than that role in which the pastor would seek to be, as Jesus was, a counselor (Isaiah 9:6).

CHAPTER 10

"Visit the Orphans and Widows in Their Affliction"

The Pastor as Minister to People

Midway this way of life we've bound upon,
I woke to find myself in a dark wood,
    Where the right road was wholly lost and gone.
        (Dante, *Inferno*, Canto I)

So they were scattered because there was no shepherd, and when they were scattered they became food for all the wild animals. My sheep wandered over all the mountains and on every high hill. They were scattered over the whole earth, and no one searched or looked for them. (Ezekiel 34:5, 6)

Jesus said, "Take care of my sheep." (John 21:16)

Pastoral care is more than pastoral counseling. Some of our parish ioners will never take the initiative to come to the pastor. Some are so reticent and retiring by nature that they will never grant admittance to what Yeats called "the rag and bone shop of the human heart." Others are beyond reach; the safety net of the fellowship has been ineffective. Even our Lord lost one like that, and Paul lamented Demas, the deserter. Other times we are dealing with "the mumps and measles of the soul," common but still dangerous.

It is not enough to invite people to come to us or to make our availability known. The incarnational principle summons us from pastoral passivity. Christ's life of diaconal service establishes the pattern of the shepherd going out after even one lost sheep. We are in a sense like waiters, at the beck and call of others. The Good Samaritan principle too requires our initiative. Luther was right in describing the pastor as "a perfectly dutiful servant, subject to all."[1]

THE SITUATION

The local church is to be an outpost of *shalom*. We are to be a network of reconciliation, what Trueblood called "the fellowship of the concerned." Pastoral care cannot properly function or flourish apart from the context of a community of faith which is willing to reach out to the disenfranchised and disinherited, the poor and the hurting. It is not the pastor who does this; rather the pastor along with many others is doing this.

In his monumental *A History of Pastoral Care in America*, E. Brooks Holifield traces the move from an absorbing concern about salvation in pastoral care to the present obsession with self-realization and self-fulfillment. He observes: "By following that movement toward an ideal of self-realization, one gains a better understanding of Protestantism's part in the formation of what Philip Rieff has called a therapeutic culture."[2] Contemporary evangelicalism has been more influenced by this cultural drift than we realize. Suffocating spiritual introversion and spiritual narcissism are doing us in.

No one has more acutely critiqued this "debilitating deference to psychological enterprise" than Richard John Neuhaus. He states the case well against a psychology of adjustment and adaptation and against a continuing emphasis on meeting "needs" rather than forming character. Reconciliation is not resignation or a negotiated settlement, nor is it conformation (cf. Romans 12:2).[3]

Yet the hour is ripe for doing what the church has been ordered and equipped to do: to be conduits of the love of Jesus Christ through the Holy Spirit. We have more than good advice—we have the Good News. Times of cultural transition are times of spiritual openness. The fact that one in ten Americans is caught up in the New Age movement shows that we are living in post-secular days when people are reaching out frantically for some spiritual dimension. The American longing for belonging is shown in our being such "joiners." High-tech times afford opportunity for high touch.

As Mona pled in Thornton Wilder's *Our Town*, "Mother, look at me as if you see me." This is the scarcely repressed cry of our neighbors and must be addressed by the New Testament pattern: "Day after day, in the temple courts and from house to house, they never stopped teaching and proclaiming the good news that Jesus is the Christ" (Acts 5:42).

EVANGELIZATION

We have already recognized the primacy of the evangelistic imperative in the mission of the church. The pastor must "Do the work of an evangelist" (2 Timothy 4:5). While feeding and nurturing the flock, the pastor must appropriately address the unconverted from the pulpit. We must beware of an implicit universalism which assumes that everyone present is in a right relationship to God through Christ. The issuance of the public invitation or the public pledge heightens the awareness of the people of God that those outside of Christ are eternally lost. Nothing is more encouraging than the conversion of the lost and their being added to the church.

Every church needs a regular program of parish evangelism in which it is patently recognized that more than the pastor should do evangelism. Evangelistic Bible studies have been effective in many places. Churches Alive and the Lay Witness Movement have ignited some congregations. My own experience with Evangelism Explosion has been very positive. Training, standing alongside of, and sending out believers to do evangelism can be the most exciting thing that happens in a church.

But the pastor has got to be with it or the effort will prematurely subside into occasional spasms of well-intentioned futility. The pastor needs to be a winner of souls. Every pastoral function, be it counseling, hospital visitation or the conducting of a funeral, offers opportunity to talk with unsaved people about the Savior.

When pastors call upon prospective members or newcomers, they will often find a made-to-order opening for a presentation of the gospel. We must allow neither congeniality nor fear to deter us from asking, "What do you think of Christ?" We can too easily beat around the bush and shilly-shally and miss our God-given responsibility. I remember praying with an eighty-eight-year-old man to receive Christ who had lived in bitterness and rejection since his early years. At long last the Holy Spirit brought him under a deep spirit of conviction, and he was fruit ripe for the picking.

Every pastor should give clear priority to the making of specifically evangelistic calls.

VISITATION

The preceding underscores the urgent necessity of visitation by the pastor. Our Lord Jesus is the heavenly visitor, as Dr. Luke records: "The dayspring from on high has visited us" (Luke 1:78). In His searching parable our Lord speaks of visiting those who are in prison (Matthew 25:36). "To visit the orphans and the widows in their affliction" (James 1:27) means to look after them, to give them care.

Traditional pastoral visitation is one of the common casualties of the modern era and its emphases. Pastors are making many fewer calls. Hectic schedules and much counseling conspire against the availability of time. Access to apartments in many neighborhoods is difficult if not impossible. So many wives are working in the daytime. Ministers' spouses are also employed and cannot visit along with their partners. Although one third of the married women in our society are homemakers, it is not seemly or appropriate to visit them when their husbands are not home. The reasons visitation is difficult are many and have proved persuasive to many practitioners, resulting in a marked decline in visitation by pastors.

Despite the difficulties and inconveniences, every pastor needs to do some visiting. If we are going to preach relevantly, even the preaching pastor of an exceedingly large parish needs to do this. Hospital calls and nursing homes can be visited in the afternoon hours. Senior citizens are generally home. Probably one night weekly should be devoted to new member enlistment calls, evangelistic calls, and specific troubleshooting calls. There is a case to be made for making prior appointments when moving through a geographic area in the interests of economy of time and expense.

Visiting the sick and the dying is an art to be cultivated. Since 1937 and Cabot and Dicks's *The Art of Ministering to the Sick*, many fine treatments have been written to assist all who enter the hospital or hospice in the name of the Lord Jesus Christ. Most large city hospitals have clergy parking areas or validation of parking. Many times the hospital chaplain's office can provide a hospital census with room numbers, and a place to hang one's coat. It is well to check with the hospital as to the status of a patient before making a trip, since we often learn of admissions and dismissals after the event, to our embarrassment. A current hospital census is critical for the pastor.

Some basic suggestions for visiting in the hospital include:

1) While clergy may visit during other than stated hours (with the exception of coronary care and maternity), it is always wise to check

with the charge nurse at the nursing station about a patient's readiness for a visit. This is especially true if the door to the room is closed. No visit should be attempted while the doctor is making his rounds in the room.

2) The pastor should enter the room warmly but not jauntily—or, as one has said, as if he were going to stay all day but in fact stays only briefly. One should not squeeze the patient's hands or sit on the bed. Visits need not be long to be helpful, but should depend on the condition of the patient.

3) The pastor should not give medical counsel or advice even if asked. It is advisable and proper to speak to the physician about the case, especially in terminal illness. Pre-operation calls are critical, and checking in with the family of a patient in surgery can be a most profitable ministry of comfort.

4) In giving a brief Scripture and word of prayer, the pastor can include the other patients in a multiple-bed room (with their permission). There may be unusual instances of hostility or family estrangement where it would be unwise to read Scripture or to pray without the permission of the patient. Even when the patient seems comatose, the pastor should not hesitate to share Scripture and pray. More is heard than we sometimes realize (which is a good reason not to discuss the patient's situation with others while in the room). Care should be taken to always leave a calling card with a little note even if the person is asleep in order that the relatives and friends can be assured that pastoral ministry is being extended to their loved one. We must not forget to include the family of those who are ill in our circle of concern. This is a draining and demanding time for them and may involve varieties of guilt and/or anxiety.

5) While one wants to be heard, we must beware of automatically assuming that the ill can't hear us sufficiently and thus actually speak too loudly. In dealing with victims of a stroke, we must allow them to speak haltingly. Give them a chance even if it is painful. (One such victim complained after his pastor's visit that the pastor never allowed him to complete a single sentence during the entire visit.)

6) Keep good records of the visit, recording the Scripture used and any brief notes which can be of subsequent help.

7) Generally speaking I have found the following axiom true: if in doubt, go. Better to err on the side of making an unnecessary call than to miss an essential one. The funeral is easier if we have been dutiful and faithful.

Few of our problem areas in visitation are unique to our time. It would be helpful for the ministering pastor to dip regularly into the the priceless anthologies edited by Thomas Oden for samples of pastoral experience in the care of the sick, the dysfunctional family and the dying.[4]

There are additionally critical visits to be made in relation to church discipline which will be dealt with in Chapter 14. The pastor and his family should not only be on the receiving end of hospitality, but should, as they are able, reciprocate with simple but tasteful hospitality in relation to staff and officiary and other groupings in the church. My wife and I recall with delight a dinner we shared with a group of our elderly widowers. Priceless!

CONFRONTATION

Occasionally there arises the need to confront one of the sheep of the flock on a matter of particular urgency. This is called an intervention. It may arise out of a call for help from an abused spouse, troubled parents or frantic friends and is not unrelated to church discipline. It may, for example, involve a feud which is polarizing a congregation in its efforts to mediate a rift within a family. The peril here is that both sides may turn on the mediator (which is another good reason to counsel with the spiritual leadership of the church before, after and during these crises).

The classical intervention involves the coming together of the principal figures in a person's life who insist on a remedial course in direct and unexpected confrontation with the subject of concern. This is high risk, but generally we have erred in backing away from confrontation and failing to face unraveling situations. Such avoidance brings grave consequences. We can so easily be trapped into merely descriptive nonevaluative feedback which essentially says little more than "I experience the following feeling when you . . ." There is a place for that mode, but the ambassador of Christ needs to grasp the thistle firmly on occasion. This should not be done as a Lone Ranger, but in tandem with praying leadership. Regardless of how difficult this is, it needs to be done.[5]

In all that we have said about ministering to people in need, we have properly emphasized what we give and share, but it is equally true that those who care for souls learn more and more. Every person has a story. Human nature and experience never cease to yield fascinating treasures and insights for physicians of souls.

VARIATION

One of the abounding and never-ending joys of the parish pastor is the opportunity to work with a variegated population. The professor or teacher tends to work with a more limited strand, but not so the pastor.

The pastor has contact, for example, with children. The undershepherd should emulate the Chief Shepherd in being a friend of children. This means recognizing and acknowledging them. Remembering a child's name is a very special gift of affirmation to him or her. In several parishes I pastored I sent birthday cards to the children as well as to the adults of the congregation.

The rites of passage give us special opportunities with children. Visits to their Sunday school departments on occasion communicate concern. The Children's Pulpit in the morning service is another opportunity to gather these precious ones around. We must not despise even one of these little ones. While the bulk of this responsibility rests on the Christian Education Department and the Sunday school, the pastor should relish touches of ministry to the children.[6]

Vacation Bible school or day camp may allow some visits with the children during the less-demanding summer season. While our own children are growing up, we feel closer to the children in the church. The same is true for the youth. Many fellowships encourage the pastor to take a week at one of the summer youth camps. These are rich opportunities to sit where they sit.

Other varied opportunities also exist. The pastor may choose to take the college class for a quarter or to speak at a singles' retreat. Various kinds of support groups for parents without partners, those recovering from cancer, those struggling with sexual identity or coming off addictions of various kinds—these all present opportunity for occasional ministry.

The poor and economically disadvantaged need the attention of the church. In every community there are pockets of poverty. Indigents off the street will present themselves in some settings. The giving of meal tickets to a local eatery is far preferable to the giving of cash. A clothes closet can be a gracious ministry. Judicious use of a deacons' fund or a benevolence fund is a very strategic expression of Christian love. The Bible has much to say about the poor and our ministering to them in a way which does not demean them but which genuinely helps them and expresses Christ's love.

Immigrants in the eighties exceed in number the immigrants of the first decade of this century, which has up to now represented the greatest influx to these shores. But these new ethnic enclaves open up ministries on a breathtaking scale.

The rich resources of our senior citizens are a treasure as the proportion of those over sixty-five markedly increases. So many of these retirees have so much to offer Christ and His church in this country and abroad. What they possess in experience and spiritual maturity in many cases is staggering. They are embroiled in physical, social, financial and emotional change, but it is a foolish church which simply puts them on the shelf.

Almost every congregation has a group of "keenagers" or senior saints, and if the pastor can go along once in a while for one of their meetings or bus trips, he will encounter a choice chance for building rapport and conversing in a more unstructured setting.[7]

Having luxuriated in the infinite variety of persons with whom the pastor has spiritual opportunity and concourse, we must not be blind to the fact that there are those we cannot help. It was so even with our Lord. Like doctors, there are patients we lose. Like attorneys, there are cases we do not win. There are those who even in the face of sincere effort on our part will only criticize. In this there is sorrow and keen disappointment, but it too will pass.

The best prayer for the pastor to pray is:

Lord Jesus, make me humble; Lord Jesus, keep me human; Lord Jesus, make me holy. Then, Lord Jesus, help me to forget myself, in the joy of being a slave of Christ and a servant of God's people and a minister of your gospel, all my future days.

III
Relationships

CHAPTER 11

"As for Me and
My House . . ."

The Pastor and the Family

A Christian family is a mobile blown by the gentle breeze of
the Holy Spirit. This is not a romantic idea; it is in accordance
with what the Bible teaches is possible. Each member of the
family, as he or she is born again, is indwelt by the Holy Spirit.
If this takes place, one can picture . . . the Christian family as
constantly changing from month to month, year to year, with
the mix never the same—age-wise, interest-wise, talent-wise,
intellect-wise—never static, with always new fascination in
discovering new points of communication as human beings are
growing and developing. A mobile—blown by the breeze of
the Holy Spirit. (Edith Schaeffer in *What Is a Family?*)[1]

He will turn the hearts of the fathers to their children, and the
hearts of the children to their fathers; or else I will come and
strike the land with a curse. (Malachi 4:6)

God sets the lonely in families. (Psalm 68:6a)

Christian ministry in the church is always for and within the context of God's purpose for the family. The family, after all, was the first
divinely ordained institution to be established. Divine wisdom personified "rejoices in his whole world and delights in mankind"
(Proverbs 8:31).

The relationship of Adam and Eve in the Garden is prototypical for
the subsequent experience of the race. The Biblical pattern is the
monogamous, permanent union of a man and a woman in marriage.
Although this ideal has been violated and challenged, it is the rule of
God. Polygamy as widely practiced through history or serial polygamy
as generally accepted in our times is an abrogation of the divine order.

The inviolability and indissolubility of the marriage covenant are seen in Scripture as paradigmatic of the union between Christ and His church (Ephesians 5:25-33). The experience of family is used as an analogy of the relationships within the church of Jesus Christ (Ephesians 3:14, 15). The equality of the sexes and yet the diversity of role and function are in clear evidence from the beginning (Genesis 2:23, 24). Three of the Ten Commandments bear specifically on the family (the fifth, seventh and tenth). The Biblical narratives provide abundant positive and negative models of family life.

The appropriate fulfillment of God's purpose for the family clearly extends beyond providing for the physical, emotional and intellectual needs of the children, necessary as these are. The supreme responsibility of the parents is for the spiritual impacting of the lives of their children (Deuteronomy 6:4-9). Reforms in the days of Ezra and Nehemiah reflected great concern for the integrity of the family. Psalms 127 and 128 echo what God intends for the family in veritable rhapsodies of celebration.

It is not too strong to say that "Jesus reaffirms the original charter of the monogamic family (Matthew 19:1-12; Mark 10:2-12)."[2] The New Testament builds on the Old Testament's pattern for family life and the relationship between husband and wife, parents and children and the like. Timothy's sincere faith lived first in his grandmother and then in his mother and then in his own heart (2 Timothy 1:5), and this vital transmission was achieved in that "from infancy [he] had known the holy Scriptures which are able to make you wise for salvation through faith in Christ Jesus" (2 Timothy 3:15). Christian ministry through the church is seen therefore as virtually symbiotic with the Christian family.

THE AGONY OF THE MODERN FAMILY

The passing of the centuries has seen tribal organization yield to clans and in more modern times the emergence of the extended family. But emigration and now extensive geographic mobility in North America have undercut the extended family, so that we have the dominance of the nuclear family, which consists of the father and the mother and the children. With drastically shifting economic factors and climatic conditions in the sun-belt drawing more and more of the senior adult population, the larger family is increasingly dispersed, resulting in less intergenerational reinforcement of values in our culture. This is only the beginning of pressures which are clearly leading the family unit toward serious disintegration.

The more serious and threatening agents of destabilization of the family derive from the tragic moral and spiritual drift of our culture as a whole. The Apostle Paul spoke of the perilous and terrible times which would increasingly obtain as the age draws toward a close (2 Timothy 3:1ff.). Conformity to our age leaves us awash in what Paul sketches: "lovers of themselves, lovers of money, disobedient to parents, without natural affection, without self control, lovers of pleasure rather than lovers of God, having a form of godliness but denying its power" (2 Timothy 3:2-5). This is an apt and accurate characterization of our society gone amok.

"When the foundations are being destroyed, what can the righteous do?" (Psalm 11:3). Well do I remember the couple who wanted to change the marriage vows in their wedding service from "as long as we both shall live" to "as long as we both shall love." Low commitment within marriage is one piece with deficient levels of commitment in every other sector of human existence. Clearly the incidence of divorce has risen sharply within our ranks, and studies show that a third of clergy marriages are in serious trouble as well. While we must grapple with the issue of divorce in Chapter 18 in dealing with the wedding we must never lose sight of God's own words: "I hate divorce" (Malachi 2:16). The dissolution of a marriage covenant wreaks havoc in the lives of all concerned, especially in the lives of the children who are torn and confused in the painful process.

With marriage itself at such risk, the corollary concomitants of spouse abuse and child abuse are on the rise. One of six women was sexually abused as a child or young girl. By the year 2000, 50 percent of the children in our country will be in single-parent homes. The fallout of the moral drift of our times beggars description. In 1958, 80 percent rejected sex before marriage. By 1978, 80 percent accepted sex before marriage without condemnation. The deferral of gratification is not a popular message today, and we see the consequent results and fruit of this all around us. Teenage pregnancy has risen sharply, and the percentage of children born out of wedlock boggles the mind. Our television-made children are glutted with violence, marital infidelity and crudity to the point of virtual insensitivity to the moral norms of our Judeo-Christian heritage.

We are no longer content to keep up with the Joneses—we want to be the Joneses with whom everyone else tries to keep up! More and more mothers are working out of the home (some because of stringent and legitimate necessity), and this situation puts additional pressure on the family under siege. Then again, half of the mothers in America are in the home but are often made to feel as if their nerve has failed because they are not out in the marketplace. Clergy spouses are not at all exempt from these prevailing currents in the larger cultural context.

We have actually reached the juncture where there is *de facto* redefinition of the family in our country. This redefinition is in terms of function rather than structure. Unmarried heterosexual couples and single-sex liaisons are to have the recognition and the rights accorded to married partners, some say. This is more than a reaction to a changing environment; it is the promotion of a new social agenda. What this agenda includes (government-sponsored day-care centers advocated on the premise that children are better off without their mothers; children's suffrage; etc.) raises many dilemmas for the Christian family in relation to education and nurture.

The sinister reality of the AIDS epidemic, the abortuaries which have proliferated since *Roe v. Wade*, the rise of youth suicide, the tragedy of child abuse all tear the fabric of the contemporary family. The wail and cry of untold anguish and suffering beat upon our eardrums. The whole educational system and the nation's health and future are tied into the strengthening of the family in America. What can the church and Christians do?

A STRATEGY FOR THE CHRISTIAN FAMILY

The necessity for cultural nonconformity is nowhere more clear than in relation to the Christian family. "It is time for judgment to begin with the family of God" (1 Peter 4:17). What kind of a strategy should be implemented?

1) *Christian leaders need to lead.* The National Association of Evangelicals has insightfully urged that the recovery of the Christian family must start with Christian leaders and their families. Sadly, sometimes we are more concerned about other families than we are about our own. The NAE Task Force on the Family identified several reasons for the reluctance of Christian leaders to initiate strong family-life programs in the local church. These include:

a) A sense of inadequacy as they view their own families.

b) The difficulty of making their own families' legitimate needs primary over the needs of other families (a point to which we shall return below).

c) The expectation that they be ideal models (life in the piranha bowl) instead of seeing themselves as fellow-strugglers dealing with family pressures. Local churches need to be sensitized to the key role leaders assume in this regard and to free up expectation levels in order to allow leaders time to fulfill their own family obligations.

2) *Congregations need to be rich resource centers for family development.* Study groups and Sunday school classes need to feature helps for marriages and families. Dr. James Dobson and his organization are giving rich support in this last decade of the century. Campus Crusade's Homebuilders Project recognizes the crisis nature of the current situation.[3] A plethora of superb publications, videos and film series are available for home and church use. Biblical preaching and teaching must address the issues in most practical ways. Prudence will dictate the most advantageous times and places. Central city churches with large numbers of singles and senior citizens will want to feature these concerns in such a way as not to weary or bore large congregational segments with the irrelevant and/or the personally painful.

Strangely, the church has often been a culprit by overscheduling that disrupts family life or by programming which divides the family. Intergenerational care-groups address this need. Local churches need to be centers for the solidarity of the family and aid-stations for the dysfunctional family. Larger congregations need special support groups for parents without partners and a whole range of specific needs. Smaller churches need to network for common needs which no one of them is able to address alone. Most denominations have special programs to help local churches face these challenges.

3) *Parents need to be encouraged to establish and maintain a family altar.* Very few Christian families today are practicing any kind of family worship such as Bobby Burns immortalized in *The Cotters' Saturday Night.* The combination of conflicting schedules and immense time pressures have induced most Christians to give up altogether. This is disastrous. Significant parental responsibility in Christian nurture is essential; the Sunday school and the church proper cannot carry the whole burden. As one who was converted in family worship, I cherish memories of opening the Word of God and hearing the fervent prayers of my parents. Very attenuated and almost garbled rote prayers at mealtime offer little awareness of the majesty of Him with whom we have to do. Bible story times and the maximizing of teaching opportunities at the festivals and high days in the church year can have major impact on little children. What natural times for instruction these seasons provide. My mother's prayer times with me before I left for school every

day have been an unforgettable legacy. Shall we have burden for others and not minister to our own households?

4) *Specific local and national issues need to be addressed by the Christian community.* In the next chapter I shall make a case for balanced Christian activism, and here I shall argue that there are family life issues which require articulate, uncompromising address at local, state and national levels. For example, John Ankerberg reports that taxpayer monies in the amount of $437,690 were expended on a government report entitled "AIDS, Sexual Behavior and Intravenous Drug Use." The conclusion of the report is to the effect that "one of the biggest impediments to combat AIDS is the Christian faith" and our view that homosexual behavior is sinful.[4] Such nonsense calls for a wave of protest and vigorous resolution.

5) *Marriage and family counseling requires careful strategizing by the spiritual leadership of every church.* Maximum utilization of local and regional support structures is mandatory. Preventative steps need to be taken in establishing a strong premarital counseling program (see Chapter 18). The pastor-teacher and other spiritual leaders need to share these responsibilities, for the load is too great for any one person, no matter what his level of competence. Marriage counseling, the single life, parental counseling and marital crisis counseling are big-ticket items in all communities. We must be ready to help.

THE PRIORITY OF THE PASTOR'S FAMILY

The pressure to be a model family and to have a model marriage seems to be a sore point with an increasingly large group of clergy and spouses. Yet there is an inescapable and inevitable necessity for the Christian leader to be "an example to the believers" (1 Timothy 4:12). All Christians are to be examples. All parents have the responsibility of being models to their families. All Christian leaders have the same high calling in relation to their flocks. Paul said to the Corinthians in a kind of holy audacity, "Follow my example, as I follow the example of Christ" (1 Corinthians 11:1). None of us is sufficient for this, "but our sufficiency is of God."

The role of the clergy spouse has quite recently become far less traditional. More clergy spouses are employed. Congregations are much more flexible in what they require of the spouse. One study found that clergy spouses identify three chief difficulties: 1) unrealistic expectations by the congregation (which in many cases are self-imposed; 2) loneliness replacing lack of privacy as a focus of concern; 3) lack of urgent purpose in the local church.[5] In no profession is the spouse so deeply involved as in the ministry. This offers an immense opportunity, but it also inflicts a heavy burden.

The recurring complaint and the gnawing frustration for pastor, spouse and family appears to be that they must ever take second-place to the church and the needs of the people in the church. While churches may be relaxing on the unique role identifications for the pastor's spouse and children, the whole question of the pastor's prioritization must now command our attention. We all recognize the complexity of the issue and would pray with Paul that we might "always be able to recognize the highest and the best" (Philippians 1:10).

Most younger clergy, tortured by the horror stories of parental neglect in the parsonage, are attempting to head off this disaster by asserting, often with some vehemence, God first, family second, church third. There is a woodenness and brittleness in this formulation which ultimately proves less than helpful. Rather than a vertical listing of priorities (or even a horizontal listing), several have commended the figure of a wheel hub with spokes. At the center the Lord Jesus. Christ is to be above all and totally supreme (Colossians 1:18). The Lordship of Jesus Christ entails "seeking first the kingdom of God" (Matthew 6:33). No one of us can please everyone, and it is the sense of Christ's primacy in all which will deliver us from the tyranny of the bleating of the sheep. All must be subject to Christ.

Emanating from this indisputable hub is a series of spokes. In progress and forward movement, emphasis will fall on each one of them in a balanced and even way, to the neglect of none. Each must yield regularly, but each will have its turn. I would propose the priorities as all subject to Christ but requiring fair and even emphasis:

1) *Human lives in need.* There will be occasions when every other second-tier priority must yield to an emergency at the hospital or some grave crisis. Actually many professions require extended absences from the home, as in the case of over-the-road truckers, construction workers, etc. Shift-workers have peculiar schedules. The minister who sets his own schedule has considerable advantage over the worker on the time clock. It was not difficult for me to arrange my schedule so as to attend my sons' athletic games, for example. But there are also times when everything must give way to human life in need.

2) *Duties at church.* Other involvements must never be allowed to become more engrossing for us than the local church which has called and supports us. To work only forty hours a week is to fail to recognize that many laypersons work their forty-plus hours and then put in

much extra time for the Lord. Ministers should work forty hours plus for the Lord as do their laity.

3) *The family.* There will be times when all else must yield to the family. I remember when I scheduled a funeral for an unheard-of Sunday afternoon because I had promised my wife and children a particular outing. The family demands its due. To assume the responsibility of a family necessitates our fulfilling that responsibility. Handling and balancing the unique stressors in this area requires much careful discussion.[6]

4) *Careful use of time.* Jowett used to say, "It is never the supremely busy persons who have no time." Jesus was always at leisure for individuals. We are to redeem the time, which means we are not to fritter and waste time fiddling around with the inconsequential. Do what needs to be done now!

5) *Our own physical health and mental well-being.* A regimen of physical exercise and healthy diversion of stress agents is absolutely essential. This is a priority. We also need to keep a sense of humor and not always take ourselves with the utmost of seriousness.

6) *Necessary support structures.* Some accountability structure is important. Certain denominational or fellowship groups provide such structures. Each of us needs a Barnabas to encourage us, a Timothy whom we can encourage, and an Epaphroditus who is a "buddy."

The minister's own marriage and family life can enable or cripple. The renewal and revitalization of these primary relationships is foundational for our ministry for and effectiveness in relating to families. As we wrestle with how to put all of these things together, the prophet's question to Hezekiah is germane: "What did they see in your house?" (2 Kings 20:15).

CHAPTER 12

"Hold Out the Word of Life"

The Pastor and the Community

My ear is pain'd
My soul is sick with every day's report
Of wrong and outrage with which earth is filled.
(Author unknown)

"You are the salt of the earth. But if the salt loses its saltiness, how can it be made salty again? It is no longer good for anything, except to be thrown out and trampled by men. You are the light of the world. A city on a hill cannot be hidden. Neither do people light a lamp and put it under a bowl. Instead they put it on its stand, and it gives light to everyone in the house. In the same way, let your light shine before men, that they may see your good deeds and praise your Father in heaven." (Matthew 5:14-16)

Christian ministry is conducted within the context of another divinely established institution—government at various levels in society (Romans 13). We do not minister in a vacuum. The structures of society and the texture of culture have immense bearing on the lives of the people who constitute the church and effect the tone of ministry to those outside of Christ. Thus Paul urges "requests, prayers, intercession and thanksgiving for everyone—for kings and all those in authority, that we may live peaceful and quiet lives in all godliness and holiness" (1 Timothy 2:1, 2).

The 5.2 billion of us on Planet Earth are living in the most radical period of change the world has ever seen. Old values and certainties are crumbling. Whole systems are collapsing (as in the Soviet Union and Eastern Europe). What next? Rapid population growth continues, with 87 percent of the births nonwhite. By 2000 73 percent of the populace will live in the great urban centers. The economic, social, moral and spiritual implications of all this tend to stun the mind.

How shall we relate to this flux and ferment? God's purpose has always been to create "a people that are his very own, eager to do what is good" (Titus 2:14b). The separation of His people is never with an objective of isolation (John 17:14-19). The figures used to characterize the people of God are often figures of penetration (see, for example, Matthew 5:14-16). Salt and light cut through and exert influence. The candle in the house and the city on the hill make a major impact.

THE PERIL OF INWARDNESS

God's ancient covenant people displayed a tendency toward spiritual introversion. Israel was chosen (according to the principle of concentration) in order to impact the whole world (Genesis 12:1, 2; Isaiah 43:10ff.). This vision dissipated in a narrow nationalism and deep-seated prejudice (cf. the book of Jonah). Even though concern for the poor and for strangers in the land was deep-dyed in Israel, the nation disintegrated in spiritual inertia and a colossal failure of nerve.

Jesus, like a refreshing breeze from Heaven, summoned His followers out of the maze of legalism and the haze of spiritual myopia to become the people of God in the world. This entails a primary loyalty and allegiance to God (the first and great commandment) and an empathetic and profound concern for our neighbors (the second commandment). In all of this, as C. S. Lewis insisted, "Jesus Christ must be overwhelmingly first!"

The church through the centuries has frequently been able to fight off excessive inwardness and to influence culture positively. When the church has become the state, she has frequently been corrupted by political power (an ever-present danger, as Lord Acton well warned). Actually Bible-believing Christians were at the growing edge of much social change in the last century (as in Wilberforce's and Shaftesbury's successful efforts for the abolition of slavery in Britain and similarly in a broad range of issues in our own country, as Timothy Smith of Johns Hopkins and others have amply documented).

In this century liberals and the ecumenical movement have often espoused an agenda of social action which totally jettisons the historic gospel of salvation. The blatant end-product of this tragic betrayal was seen at a political conclave where an ordained minister of considerable national prominence "apologized to all present for possibly offending anyone by referring to God in his invocation."[1]

Although evangelicals tended to take seriously Carl F. H. Henry's call for a more balanced involvement (as first issued in his *The Uneasy Conscience of Modern Fundamentalism*), the spectre of conservative arousal on a number of pivotal issues does not indicate any significant impact or a track record of much solid achievement.

The chief problem is evangelical capitulation to the narcissistic culture of our times. Instead of being a militant, suffering, protesting minority as Kierkegaard urged, the church has tended to be a toothless and amiable supporter of the *status quo*. Toynbee argued that self-love is the universal religion of mankind. Insensitivity and a granite indifference fostered by affluence and a dedication to maintaining the comfort zone are the prime obstacles not only to the fulfillment of the Great Commission in our time, but also to the fulfillment of the broader cultural mandate given to the church.

The symbol of this acculturation is an evangelical book entitled *How to Be Happy Though Rich*, with the author perched on a Rolls-Royce on the dustjacket telling us how he accepted Christ and then, "using biblical principles," got rich. Such phenomena explain why instead of changing our world we are being changed by our world.

THE PROFILE OF INVOLVEMENT

The church has a position and a witness on every issue having to do with fairness, morality and justice. The application of Biblical preaching, the exploration of issues in Sunday school and adult study groups, the availability of relevant reading materials through the church library are all essential. Many denominations and the National Association of Evangelicals publish resolutions regarding many of these issues. Every local assembly should have a Christian citizenship or social concerns commission to alert the membership to such issues and to process the involvement of members in particular areas.

A broad front of issues is particularly compelling in our time. The murder of the unborn is a contemporary holocaust. The issue is not really individual freedom, but societal murder. All environmental issues have Christian implications, but the moral poisoning of America through pornography is especially urgent. Issues having to do with our schools are paramount. Some in conscience have opted for home schooling or Christian schools, but we must not fully abandon public education and its concerns. MADD (Mothers Against Drunk Driving) has reminded us of the tragic toll of addictions in our society. We must do more than protest evil—we must propose reasonable and prudent alternatives. If the water is flowing out of the bathtub upstairs, we need to do more than mop up the floor—we need to turn off the faucet.

The evident bankruptcy of Marxism and socialism in our day do not afford us the luxury of avoiding hard questions about the pockets of poverty in our own nation. There is an aching permanent underclass in our country. Many among the lower one third in our society do not vote. The urban ghettos are showing "the lack of a critical mass of stable, achievement-oriented families that once provided neighborhood cohesion."[2] The results are inadequate prenatal care, premature child-bearing, high drop-out rates and long-term welfare dependency. A pro-life stand must include concern for the quality of life for those who are already born as well as a burden for those who are unborn.

On all of these issues there will be legitimate differences of opinion as to the best ways and means of address. What should the role of the church be, and what should the role of individual members within the church be? Christians have not been of one mind on the sanctuary movement for illegal immigrants, the anti-war and anti-nuclear movements, and many other contemporary issues. The existence of these differences is not ground for avoiding the issues, but rather challenges us to handle differences with Christian grace.

The church must not become directly involved in partisan politics. To do so jeopardizes the traditional tax-exempt status of the church and also produces more serious consequences. Members should be encouraged to become involved in the political party of their persuasion. In a state with the caucus system, our Christian citizenship commission encouraged participation of the members in the political process and sponsored a post-caucus rally in which reports were given from the two main political parties. Several members went on to county and state conventions and addressed the Christian agenda within these forums. This kind of involvement should be viewed as a special stewardship for certain members. We do not need to see the local church as capturing all of the involvement and energy of all of our members.

Evangelicals have always been conspicuous in support of the rescue missions in our cities. Cooperative food pantries and clothing cupboards are not uncommon. Massive infusions of relief are appropriate for the world's hungry and disaster-struck. The cup of cold water given in Jesus' name is hardly optional. The basic situation is as follows: Sitting around the Lord's Table are twelve Christians. Eight are colored (black, brown, yellow, red, mixed race) and four are white. Three whites and one colored (the elite who cooperate with the whites in poor countries) start the meal by taking all of the chicken, most of the vegetables and most of the rice. All that remains for the seven colored and the one white are some unequal portions of rice and some leftovers so that some of them remain hungry. After the meal, the remains from the plates of the three whites and one colored are discarded. The rich also have a beverage with their meal; the others have only the small cup which follows the the Lord's Supper. *Can any of us accede to this as being in any sense Christian?*

Increasingly believers will feel self-consciously and deliberately at variance with the trends and tenor of our times. The bias of the media is relentless. So the *New York Times* advises Catholic bishops "not to persist in their quaint belief that people should not engage in illicit sexual intercourse."[3] The fact is, Hollywood is against religion.[4] In a very real sense we are not shocked or surprised, but neither should we be duped. "Love not the world," the Scripture warns (1 John 2:15). "Friendship with the world is enmity against God" (James 4:4) is hardly palatable to our tastes, but it is the truth. We are not to retreat from the fray, nor are we simply to rail at what is out of joint. Early Christians turned the world upside-down, which is only to say they turned it right-side-up.

"Eternal vigilance is the price of liberty" has been the watchword from the days of our founding fathers. If the Community Chest or United Fund includes Planned Parenthood among its recipients, they should be challenged. If the YWCA offers a course on "Lesbian Relationships" (as it has actually done), we must publicly protest. Our confrontations should not be strident or raucous, but they must be firm, intelligent and shrewd. The fact is, humanism is a religion, but we do not want it to become the *de facto* state-supported religion of our nation.

A PHILOSOPHY OF INVESTMENT

"Alive in Christ and alert to our world" is the path the old pietists marked out. The pastor-teacher should not be a one- issue messenger, though there is also the danger of spreading ourselves too thin. The more activistic need to beware of enjoying community issues and activities more than parish responsibilities. Differences in individual styles in these matters must be allowed in the local church. One person cannot become involved in everything. Jesus didn't (Luke 12:13, 14), and Paul didn't. (For example, neither of them launched a crusade against the pernicious wrong of slavery, although the gospel soon brought an end to it.) Where shall we make our personal and leadership invest-ments of time and strength? Several areas invite consideration:

l) *The immediate neighborhood.* The pastor's family gives a testi-mony and witness to the neighborhood. Christ-like relationships are important. While we felt uncomfortable at the noisy, late-hour block parties, we enjoyed inviting neighbors in for Christmas cookies and coffee. We felt an important value was at stake in projecting Christian congeniality to those who lived nearby. The PTA is an excellent oppor-tunity for Christian parents. Whatever the venue for our children's socialization and education, we have the opportunity and the duty to relate to those who take leadership in this crucial societal responsibil-ity. When living in a parsonage and therefore not paying property taxes, we felt less a part of the functioning community. An advantage of own-ing one's own home is the larger stake one has in all community endeavor.

2) *The larger community.* There is a case to be made for the pastor's identification with a service club in the community. I have been both a Kiwanian and a Rotarian. The weekly meetings give an opportunity for informative conversation, and the programs are often enlightening. It is imperative that the pastor interface with other than church members. Special service projects afford an excellent opportunity to get to know business leaders, government officials and other neighbors. Some pre-fer Toastmasters or some such activity. My experience has been that the members of the congregation are pleased if their pastor has some visi-bility in the community. The only publicly elected office I ever held was a term on an urban redevelopment council representing the area in which the church was located. One year I served as clergy representa-tive for a community services organization.

3) *Denominational duty.* Although denominational loyalty is increasingly passé in American church life, independence has its own peculiar challenges (in the matter of continuity patterns, ministerial supply and a sense of the larger body). Clergy members of denomina-tional fellowships need to "pay their dues" if their voices are to be heard and their influence felt. The "never-show" pastor gives his local church a black eye needlessly. Though personally quite conservative, I never lacked any opportunity to serve my denomination at the local, district conference or national level. There is something special about the larger fellowship of brothers and sisters. We can well understand the Apostle Paul's reaction upon meeting the delegation from Rome: "At the sight of these men Paul thanked God and was encouraged" (Acts 28:15).

4) *The religious community.* We need to go beyond our own

denominational gatherings. In my last parish I was part of four clergy groups. No one can attend every meeting of every group, but benefits come from these associations. The broader ministerial association was occasionally exasperating, but it also provided programs and speakers of religious significance. Meeting other evangelical ministers gave opportunity for fellowship with those of like mind. The downtown clergy group was very representative (rabbis, priests and ministers) and was a vehicle of action. This group addressed the issues of the downtown area and if inclined (as on sauna/massage parlor advertising in the newspaper) could get action because the influence-makers of the city belonged to the parishes represented. Politics is the art of the possible. How fascinating to watch this happen. I also participated in Good Neighbor Fellowship, composed of black and white congregations in our immediate area. What beautiful times we had, and what thrilling projects we had (such as an evangelistic series with a gifted black evangelist).

5) While the pastor must exclude partisan *politics* from the pulpit, this does not mean he cannot be active in the party of choice. I was a precinct chairman for my party and enjoyed every minute of it.

6) *Special issues* thrust themselves front and center and absorb attention and energy for a period of time. My own focus over the years would intermittently include Christian-Jewish relations because of my interest in the state of Israel and my protesting of anti-Semitism whenever it reared its ugly head. This gave wonderful access to rabbis and synagogues. Other issues I have faced include liquor control and all substance abuse, abortion and abortuaries in our community, and the combating of cults and false teaching through a local cooperative agency which maintained its own literature depository and quarterly publication.

In all of these enterprises we represent Christ and His church. We may even make common cause with unbelievers in some specific objective (as in right-to-life activity), but we must be cautious of extremists and ideologues. Above all, we must be wary of any arrogance in representing our Master. Hit lists, rating scales, simplistic answers to complex problems, shrill and strident rhetoric will only frighten thoughtful people and minorities and will also damage our just pursuits.

A PROGRAM FOR INVITATION

However fired-up we become and however fervent our zeal in any of these areas of concern, we must not fall into the trap which has enveloped so many who have gone on before. Namely, we must not lose the priority of the saving gospel of Christ. This, after all, is what we uniquely offer to lost humanity. Horace Bushnell was correct when he maintained that "the soul of reform is the reform of the soul." A plethora of community involvements is no substitute for a workable and working program of evangelism into the community. Evangelism Explosion is not everyone's cup of tea, but it is an approach to touching a community for Christ which I have seen excite a congregation in a remarkable way.

Biblically this is not an either/or issue. It is both/and. How exciting to see the gospel let loose in a community and people coming to Christ, and then Christians, as growing and maturing disciples, following their Savior in the penetration of a society for Christ.

CHAPTER 13

"Servants of the Church" and "Fellow-workers"

The Pastor and Team Ministry

After the brief thanksgiving Paul sets about trying to brace the resolution of his young disciple, and in particular encourages him to be ready to endure suffering for the gospel's sake. The note of anxiety which pervades the passage springs partly from the awareness that Timothy's inexperience and natural timidity need stiffening, but even more from his consciousness of the weighty responsibilities which must shortly devolve upon him. Even so he is able to point to the divine commission given in ordination, to the example of his own endurance, and to the new life bestowed on men through Christ, as compelling motives for courageous exertion. (J. N. D. Kelly on 1 Timothy 1:6-14)[1]

If Timothy comes, see to it that he has nothing to fear while he is with you, for he is carrying on the work of the Lord, just as I am. No one, then, should refuse to accept him. Send him on his way in peace so that he may return to me. I am expecting him along with the brothers. (1 Corinthians 16:10, 11)

Christian ministry is always seen as shared ministry in the New Testament. We can only feel great uneasiness when Christian leaders make such statements as, "A laity-led, layman-led, deacon-led church will be a weak church anywhere on God's earth. The pastor is the ruler of the church. There is no other thing than that in the Bible." In point of fact, something entirely different from this is everywhere seen in the Bible. Jesus deputized the seventy. Jesus gave immense time and effort to the training of the twelve for the work to be entrusted to them. There was a division of labor in the apostolate.[2]

The Apostle Paul was a super-aggressive leader, but worked with a team in implementing his church-planting strategy. Certainly he held a divinely appointed office (Romans 15:17ff.), but clearly he saw the church as a functioning organism with many diverse parts working in harmony. Paul gathered a ministering team around him. Among his coworkers were Timothy, Titus, Dr. Luke, Barnabas, Silas, John Mark, etc. A key team member in relation to Colosse was Epaphras, in relation to Ephesus Tychicus, and in relation to Philippi Epaphroditus. Priscilla and Aquila were pivotal in several situations as well. Occasionally Paul was lonely, but he was not a loner.

Ministry in the local church involves synchronization of the entire body, but also specialized staff ministries for an increasing number of local assemblies. Almost all ministers will function as part of a ministering team during part, if not all, of their careers. Relatively small congregations are making an investment in a second staff person, often a minister to youth. Ministers of discipleship and evangelism are in great demand also, perhaps more than ministers of Christian education. Our interest here is in the critical facets of effective team ministry in the local church.

THE BIBLICAL AND PHILOSOPHICAL FOUNDATION

Almost every Christian leader views himself or herself as a team person. Yet high levels of frustration and disappointment are widespread. In my own experience of ministry in the local church, staff ministry and relationships were both the highest and most fulfilling *and* the most difficult and depressing experiences. Scapegoating is fairly common, and junior staff members are frequently seen as dispensable lambs to be offered in order to assuage an undercurrent of discontent. The scar tissue and permanent damage of such manifest unfairness are incalculable.

The ministering staff is to model the pilgrimage, to be the church in microcosm. A congregation soon knows how relationships are progressing in the staff. If the staff is feuding and fussing, the congregation is demoralized.

The pattern for both staff and congregation is 1 Corinthians 12. Here in Paul's classic discussion of the spiritual gifts is the recognition that within divinely intended diversity there is a real unity (cf. Ephesians 4:1-6). The church is not a mass of similar particles, like a heap of sand or a pool of water. The church is not like a living swarm of antagonistic individuals, like a cage of beasts. The church is a body established by the Holy Spirit and uniting many insignificant elements to form a mysterious essence which is of inestimable worth.

Instead of harmonious functioning, Paul hears of grumbling in the Corinthian church. The truth is, dissatisfaction with one's unique endowments and placement is spiritual high treason. Humbler and lesser-noticed parts perform vital if unseen functions (think of your body's heart, liver, intestines). God compounds and mixes the diverse components (12:24), establishing a certain equilibrium in the body. His purpose is that there should be no schism or cleft in the Body of Christ. The members are to have mutual care for one another in recognition of the fact that God has assigned each to his or her own place for the over-all health and well-being of the organism. Do we really believe this? We subscribe to the concept theoretically, but find its validity more problematic when in a pinch or under pressure.

The ministering staff needs to exemplify and personify what a helping and healing body is. It is imperative that we who are in team ministry steep ourselves in the meaning and implications of 1 Corinthians 12, 13, 14.[3]

MAXIMAL AND OPTIMAL FUNCTION

Some systems analysis is desirable. A system is a set of parts coordinated to accomplish a set of goals. The emphasis in systems analysis is on the interconnectedness and interrelationships of the various components. Congregational planning and goal setting must include careful consideration of staff needs. Overloading the pastor-teacher will have a deleterious effect on the whole organism. "If one part suffers, every other part suffers with it" (1 Corinthians 12:26).

The general rule of thumb is that one staff member is needed for every two hundred members, even when a networking of lay-care is in existence. The question is, should generalists be added to the staff and all pastoral function be divided cross-sectionally, or should specialists be added to the staff with specific expertise in certain desired fields? The direction for a specific local congregation in this decision must be the function of some careful systems analysis as described above.

Occasionally the idea of co-pastors presents itself. The fact is, every team needs a leader. This is true in the family, in business, in athletics, in government. The senior pastor should be *primus inter pares* (first among equals). Where there is no formal recognition of the leader, then someone *de facto* becomes the leader. It seems, therefore, wise to give formal recognition to the leader as such and thus relieve any uncertainty or needless befuddlement which could be injurious to healthy function.

There seems to be a growing sense among some that they are called to be the "second pastor." These persons do not aspire to the rigors of a heavy preaching load but see their contribution to be chiefly in the areas of administration, visitation, counseling or teaching. Clearly if the expectation is that the senior pastor be primarily the preaching pastor, it would be a serious blunder for a person with a great compulsion to preach to move into the second slot on that staff no matter how cordial and congenial the prospects of relationship may be.

The associate pastor should complement the senior pastor. Special challenges exist for the associate pastor when the senior pastor is either exceedingly effective or exceedingly ineffective. This role is clearly one of the most "complex, ambiguous and demanding roles" in the local church. The carefully written job description needs to stake out special turf for the associate pastor, building on the individual's strengths.

Absolutely essential for effective staff function is the real experience of *koinonia* within the staff. This requires regular staff meetings of both formal nuts-and-bolts business and informal, less-structured times of heart-to-heart sharing. Open communication is imperative. Team leaders who are deficient in communicational and interpersonal skills need help (and may even need help to see that they have such lacks). Honesty and candor are *sine non qua*.

With a ministering staff of eight, we felt at our church that we needed a regular Monday morning review and report time to make assignments and touch base on a variety of situations. The whole secretarial staff met with us for devotions before morning coffee on a daily basis, and on Wednesdays the custodial, parking lot and day-care persons joined with us. *Esprit* requires some relaxed times together.

Monthly or quarterly we would meet for casual conversation. Various staff persons would lead in the discussion of a book we were reading together. These were genuine growth times when we sought to interact on central issues and get to know each other in some depth. Staff retreats pay dividends in consequent camaraderie and good morale as well.

Letters of call to staff members should include encouragement to attend area conferences and denominational assemblies. Every staff member should be allowed to attend one major meeting annually for professional enrichment. This is the kind of thoughtful investment by a congregation that comes back to bless manyfold. Arrangements for ongoing study and degree work (when possible) should be given positive consideration. Local congregations should not think only of what can be derived from a staff member, but in what ways the congregation can minister to that staff member. Many a small church has had a critical ministry in the early stages of the development of a burgeoning servant of Christ. Some who come to us are diamonds in the rough—shall we not grow together?

Many a senior pastor wrestles with a substantial ego problem. The "Peter Principle" (rising to the level of our own incompetence) impales many a pastor-teacher. But genuine team-ministry is satisfying and fulfilling for everyone involved. The willingness to be vulnerable with each other and the openness to express our hearts with impunity are crucial. Lao-tzu, a wise man of ancient China, observed: "When the work of the best rulers is done, their task accomplished, the people all remark, 'We have done it ourselves.'"[4] How much more preferable is this than the infernal "Credit, credit, who is going to get the credit?" charade so prevalent among us. Vance Packard's *The Status Seekers* is unfortunately a fairly accurate description of the church.

Two perceptive Lutheran ministers have prepared what they term "A Survival Manual for Clergy Seeking Maturity in Ministry."[5] Their proposals are predicated on the premise that "Despite the pious things they say, at any given time less than 5% of any group of people in the church is operating with purely Christian motivation. The other 95% is asking 'What's in it for me?'" The ministering team needs to pattern what the Cross and Christian discipleship really mean. This is a significant challenge for all of us.

ESSENTIAL AND VITAL NEGOTIATION

In interviewing for a staff situation, certain in-depth soundings are necessary. Not only does the church profile need careful scrutiny, but the self-image of other staff members needs evaluation by the prospective pastor. I would always encourage candidates to have lunch or an informal conference with the other staff members in addition to the usual interviews with the search committee and responsible boards charged with making recommendations along with the pastor.

What is the general climate in the congregation? What is the expectation of the church? Some combination positions (for example, youth and music) are notorious killers. Is the church expecting two for the price of one? What do you pick up from the senior pastor—is it "Everybody is perfect here" or "It's O.K. to grow here"?

A very important reading has to do with the pastor's leadership style. In looking as objectively as we can at ourselves, how will we fare given this particular pastor's *modus operandi*? Brown has given us a most helpful analysis of the basic leadership styles:[6]

1. PRIEST DEVELOPER	2. BISHOP-EXECUTIVE
(Person Centered)	(Modern Executive)
3. DISCIPLE-COLLEAGUE	4. PROPHET-DIRECTOR
(Collegiality)	(Task-Oriented)

In style 1, there is low task support but high socio-emotional support. In style 2, there is both high task support and high socio-emotional support. In style 3 there is both low task support and low socio-emotional support. And in style 4, there is high task support but low socio-emotional support. The team leader needs insight into his style. Team members need to seek objectivity as to their own needs. Kenneth Blanchard in *One Minute Management* helpfully points out that there needs to be a dynamic in the relationship which is able to both recognize what is needed now in terms of support and what the stages of growth should entail.[7] As persons mature and develop, the kind and amount of support will vary.

The choice of a senior pastor by a congregation needs to be the function of a careful self-study and analysis of where the congregation is presently and where it needs to go. The gifts of a candidate are critical, but the track record and style of staff leadership are also crucial. There are many different kinds of leadership gifts, and a wise congregation both seeks the mind of the Spirit and engages in careful analysis as to what the paramount needs of the congregation are at this time.[8] This is all part of the negotiation which should take place in fitting candidates to positions.

CONFLICT RESOLUTION

"Live in harmony with one another" is our ideal (Romans 12:16a). But the experience of the apostolic band and of Paul himself warn us to expect interpersonal problems. So the apostle says, "If it is possible, as far as it depends on you, live at peace with everyone" (Romans 12:18). In Chapter 21 we shall deal with conflict management in the church proper, but here we must address conflict resolution in the staff itself.

The senior pastor must set a tone of basic loyalty for the ministering staff. It is all too easy to give ear to complaints and criticisms directed at staff associates and thus deflect any legitimate self-blame. The senior pastor needs to give the message loud and clear that he stands with staff except in cases of moral turpitude (which needs to be handled in the New Testament way; cf. Matthew 18:15-17) or in cases of gross incompetence.

Preventative maintenance in staff relationship and function can get on top of situations before they become festering problems. Accountability is a Biblical concept and of great importance in ministry. Every staff member (including the senior pastor) should set annual personal goals for ministry. In dialogue with the Pastoral Relations Committee (consisting of key board chairpersons) or some such constitutional provision, staff members should meet for an annual accounting of progress or lack of same. Allowing staff to interface with key leadership (not only with the senior pastor) can vent tensions and difficulties before they reach the eruptive stage of irreparable harm.

Conflict can be of several kinds: 1) Intrapersonal; i.e., something in the staff member's own family, finance or personal life is causing problems and hindering effectiveness. 2) Interpersonal; i.e., there is a problem with another staff person or members and constituents of the congregation. Or 3) substantive; there are serious differences of opinion or direction with regard to facts, methods, goals or values. In the case of the latter we may have a situation which affects the ministry negatively.

In the next chapter we shall deal with church discipline, but for now let us say that a staff member needs to be treated like any member if discipline is required. Resolution of conflicts requires confrontation without condemnation. The facts must be gathered before any judgments can be made. Nothing is more difficult for a church to handle than irreconcilable differences among staff members or moral or behavioral problems within the staff. The handling of these issues makes a statement to the congregation that is very important.

No one would argue for weak or inept leadership. A tongue-tied quarterback serves no one advantageously. But decisiveness should not translate into dominance. In recent years there have been a number of superb treatments of the multiple staff in its various aspects.[9] There are encouraging signs of greater thoughtfulness and farsightedness in many congregations these days as we are becoming better acclimated to both the pluses and the perils of team ministries in our churches.

CHAPTER 14

"Are You Not to Judge Those Inside?"

The Pastor and the Unruly

When Christ calls a man, he bids him come and die. . . . Cheap grace is the deadly enemy of our Church. We are fighting today for costly grace . . . [cheap grace] is the grace which amounts to the justification of sin, without the justification of the repentant sinner who departs from sin and from whom sin departs . . . the following of Christ is not the achievement or merit of a select few, but the divine command to all Christians without distinction. . . . Unbelief thrives on cheap grace, for it is determined to persist in disobedience. . . . All along the line we are trying to evade the obligation of single-minded, literal obedience. (Dietrich Bonhoeffer, *The Cost of Discipleship*)[1]

When Jesus invites us, "Come to Me . . . follow Me . . . learn of Me," He is proposing a radically new lifestyle which is to be conspicuous in the world and always characteristic of His people. Rather than cloning the soft and self-indulgent lifestyle which is gnawing away at the vitals of western civilization, Christians are to be vigorously countercultural.

Pace-setters in athletics, education and business recognize that in all human endeavor disciplined application is imperative. Musicians and artists must give themselves to a regimen of diligent practice or their giftedness becomes irrelevant. Still, the drift of our culture toward undisciplined living is threatening to swamp our society in a morass of mediocrity.

Paul argues that God has given us "a spirit of self-discipline" (2 Timothy 1:7). Recent books such as Richard Foster's *Celebration of Discipline* and Dallas Willard's *The Spirit of the Disciplines* underscore a renewed recognition that authentic discipleship requires disciplined living.

The Bible makes plain that the integrity of family life depends on the maintenance of careful and consistent discipline. A generation ago James Dobson's *Dare to Discipline* stirred many Christian parents to see that there must be a definition of limits or the family will fall apart in the turbulence of permissiveness now engulfing us.

God Himself is a disciplinarian. "God disciplines us for our own good, that we may share in his holiness" (Hebrews 12:10). Within God's forever family, the church, the exercise of discipline is not optional but obligatory. The health of the body hinges in no small degree on the timely treatment of the incursions of disease and disability which, if unaddressed, increasingly hinder normal function. The pastor-teacher is not the administrator of discipline, for that is the prerogative of the assembly of the believers and/or their designated representatives. But the pastor-teacher has the solemn responsibility of raising awareness levels through the teaching ministry and fostering a climate in which discipline can be courageous and constructive.

THE DIVINE CHARTER

While theonomists and dominion theologians are mistaken in their insistence that the legislation for Israel is directly applicable to the church, nonetheless we can see a significant statement of principle in the necessary discipline of Achan (Joshua 7). Certainly there are the tares which will mingle with the wheat until the Eschaton. The pure church is the ideal toward which we seek to move, always realizing that our reach will exceed our grasp. Jesus did not immediately expel Judas Iscariot, but worked with him most graciously and with great magnanimity, even in the upper room and in the garden where Jesus was arrested. But the old leaven had to be purged, and another had to take his place.

Jay Adams's very helpful *Handbook of Church Discipline*[2] begins with an important chapter on "Preventive Discipline." Corrective discipline will be most effectively implemented in an environment of genuine Christian caring and concern. Where the "one another's" are flourishing, the more public discipline in the assembly as a whole becomes the logical and loving extension of the more personal interrelationships already extant in the believing community. Adams builds his model for discipline on Matthew 18:15-17, a model which begins with a preliminary step of self-discipline (cf. 1 Corinthians 9:25).[3]

The most thorough and provocative treatment of the four subsequent steps, in my judgment, is that of J. Carl Laney in his indispensable *A Guide to Church Discipline*.[4] The careful study and discussion of such a volume by church leadership will be conducive to the creation of a climate where effective discipline prevails.

The four steps are: 1) *Private reproof*, 18:15. Laney quotes Finney: "If you see your neighbor sin, and you pass by and neglect to reprove him, it is just as cruel as if you should see his house on fire, and pass by and not warn him of it."[5] How natural this is in a setting where the saints are confessing their sins to each other (James 5:16). This confrontation is to be personal and private. Both the offended and the offender have responsibilities (cf. Matthew 5:23, 24). Public confession should not be pressed unless there is clear negative impact upon others. Church history bears ample witness to the dangers of overemphasis on public confession in doubtful cases.

2) *Private conference*, 18:16. In Old Testament terms, the addition of two or three witnesses (cf. Numbers 25:30; Deuteronomy 17:6; 19:15) was clearly to safeguard against extremely idiosyncratic bias. But the witnesses here described are obviously included to add solemnity to the confrontation and to provide resources if more public steps are necessary.

3) *Public announcement*, 18:17. A flagrant offense, such as the incest in 1 Corinthians 5, was generally known, and I think Adams is right that discipline then begins with the congregation's procedure as outlined in its constitution and bylaws, based on the Scripture. Courts of law are concerned that congregations follow "due process," and this is guaranteed by a clear statement of procedure. These matters should not be handled in public services but in a closed meeting of the membership. The congregation will want to be satisfied that its spiritual leaders have followed a reasonable course and have exhausted every possible recourse.

4) *Public exclusion*, 18:17b. This is excommunication from the assembly. Ray Stedman argues that the admonition means to regard the recalcitrant as a non-Christian rather than to excommunicate, but this is a moot point because in the church to be a non-Christian is to be excluded.[6] This last step is always taken with extreme reluctance and with tears. Certainly our purpose is to seek the purity of the church (1 Corinthians 5:6-8) and to discourage others from sinning (Acts 5:11; 1 Timothy 5:20), as well as to maintain the testimony of the church before the world (1 Peter 2:12). But assuredly we have as a prime objective the restoration of the offending brother or sister (Galatians 6:1). Our goal is restoration, not retribution.

In fact, in 2 Corinthians Paul becomes very concerned about the man who had been "delivered to Satan" (the case is outlined in 1

Corinthians 5). Apparently he had become penitent but was finding reinstatement problematic (see 2 Corinthians 2:6-8).[7] Serious study of the verb "restore" is a great help, and emphasis on "in a spirit of gentleness, looking to yourself, lest you too be tempted" (Galatians 6:1) will help us avoid some of the dangerous pitfalls along this necessary path.

THE DIFFICULT CHALLENGES

Congregations need help and encouragement in this critical area. One recent study of 439 pastors indicated that "50% acknowledged situations in their ministry where discipline would have been appropriate but no action was taken." Many fellowships have provided practical help and material for congregations and pastors exercised to take appropriate action.[8]

What is the scope and sweep of discipline in the local church? What is the range of appropriate and necessary concern? Three areas need address:

1) *Moral and ethical problems.* To some degree our churches were earlier relatively sheltered from certain societal pathology, or at least we tended to repress it and keep it in the closet. Now the full force of the gale of immorality beats mercilessly upon all our congregations. Small-town and rural America are facing it as surely as the cities and suburbs of North America. Some counsel caution or inaction because of the delicacy of some of these matters. Fallout from families which prefer to be left alone in their misery prevents action in some cases. But the passage of time seldom ameliorates these situations. It is better to fail in honest attempt than to default with inertia.

2) *Doctrinal issues.* There is such a thing as sound doctrine; truth is not a circle which encompasses all error. This is not to say there are no areas where earnest believers have differed or that there are not areas unaddressed by Scripture. But when we come to the great foundation blocks of Biblical truth, "the faith once for all delivered to the saints" (Jude 3), we must address error, the teaching of error, or a lack of Christian spirit in handling the controversial areas. Passages like Galatians 1:8 and Titus 1:9 and 3:10, 11 urge us to resist defection and avoid apostasy. Fidelity to confessional standards must be maintained.

3) *Relational concerns.* Dissension among members and feuding factions can quickly cripple the spiritual resilience of a congregation and lead to possible schism. Second Thessalonians 3:6, 14, 15 portray the chronic troublemaker who must be confronted with the nasty business engendered by a poison tongue, a factious spirit and a malevolent dis-

position. Rather than allowing some mean-spirited Diotrephes (3 John 9) to tyrannize staff and leaders at will, spiritual leadership needs to meet with such individuals and prescribe a course of reconciliation and healing. Where members go to law with each other, the truth of 1 Corinthians 6 needs to be laid down kindly and firmly. There are bullies in the church who prey upon rather than pray for those who are weak and vulnerable.

Not infrequently in serious confrontation a member will choose to withdraw rather than to proceed with the steps of Scriptural discipline, the idea being that if the member resigns, the congregation no longer has any jurisdiction over him or her. However, pastoral *concerns* do not cease with the termination of membership. I would say to anyone with such a spirit, "We are going to keep on loving you and praying for you." The fact is, removal from membership need not always be bilateral (in the cases of death or inactivity, for instance). If a person is totally unresponsive, there is nothing else we can do. But some groups have historically practiced "shunning" in a manner which goes beyond anything authorized in the New Testament.

Does discipline ever extend beyond the membership? Jay Adams emphatically insists that non-members are never the subjects of discipline.[9] But in many communions the approach to membership is so conservative that many worship regularly who are not members, and yet in the sight of the community they are clearly identified with that local congregation. Should they be included in the above categories, failure to discipline them brings scandal to the church. There may be exclusion from the Lord's Table for a period of time, which can make a statement to the community about a non-member or a member if there are church court proceedings of a serious nature. Violation of a civil court order on harassment should not be permitted on the premises of a worshiping assembly.

What to do when a spiritual leader falls into sin involves us not only in what the Scriptures explicitly say to this point, but in procedures in the courts of the church and the ordaining body. John White and Ken Blue address this sensitive matter with skill and finesse in their fine treatment *Healing the Wounded.*[10] Examples of fallen leaders abound in Scripture. High position and great responsibility must not be allowed to hamstring or delay discipline. The question will come back to haunt us: what did you know and when did you know it?[11]

The issue of "church hoppers" and communication of sensitive information between congregations sometimes get lost in a rush to obtain new members from among the floating ribs in the Body of

Christ. It may be flattering to ministerial egos to have these new atten-
dees among us, but are they in fact refugees from discipline elsewhere?
A courteous call may well save us from mountains of grief.

THE DIRE CHANGES

In the general uprush of renewed interest in the church, spiritual gifts,
new modes of governance and all of the concomitants, we have seen a
renewal of interest in discipline in the local church. Many congregations
which had never experienced discipline have been encouraged to
explore and in a growing number of instances to administer Scriptural
discipline. Unfortunately, living in an extremely litigious society as we
do, lawsuits and threats of lawsuits have begun to have a dampening
effect upon the exercise of discipline in many congregations.

There is a related issue as to whether or not the judiciary ought to
interfere in matters of discipline in ecclesiastical bodies. In a very
insightful piece on this issue, Ralph Mawdsley cites the United States
Supreme Court case *Watson v. Jones* (1871):

> The right to organize voluntary religious associations to assist
> in the expression and dissemination of any religious doctrine,
> and to create tribunals for the decision of controverted ques-
> tions of faith, and for the ecclesiastical government of all the
> individual members, congregations and officers with the gen-
> eral association is unquestioned. All who unite themselves to
> such a body do so with an implied consent to this government,
> and are bound to submit to it.[12]

But even where a proviso is included in the instrument of governance that members agree not to sue the church, the courts are admit-
ting cases which they adjudge to involve civil rights, such as invasion of
privacy or unreasonable publicity. In the *Quinn v. Church of Christ of
Collinsville, OK* case, some basic good-sense canons of consistency and
confidentiality were violated by the church leadership in publicly sharing unnecessary details and in promulgating these matters to four other
churches. The result was heavy compensatory and punitive damages
against the church, with an out-of-court settlement.

The fact that we have made past mistakes or that we face a veritable minefield in getting hold of what are many times very complex
issues must not deter us from doing what the Head of the church has
asked us to do. The living Christ says: "Those whom I love I rebuke and

discipline" (Revelation 3:19). The prospect of litigation is not pleasant. Where matters can be adjudicated in a Christian conciliation system (such as is maintained by the Christian Legal Society), this would be desirable. Currently a number of suits are under appeal in various parts of the country.

Another area related to this is the seemingly new trend toward clergy malpractice suits. Laws in thirteen states require a pastor to divulge information about suspected child abuse. Historically the confidentiality of the confessional has been on a par with the medical and legal profession's client relations.[13] *Time* magazine carried an ad entitled, "Even the clergy can't escape the lawsuit crisis."

The precedent-setting *Walter and Maria Rally v. Grace Community Church of Sun Valley, CA* is one in which the pastors of the church were accused of incompetence in their counseling because the Rallys' twenty-four-year-old son committed suicide. The judge dismissed the case, but his ruling was overturned by the Court of Appeals. The position of the church has been upheld by the California Supreme Court, and the United States Supreme Court has let that stand. These have been most heartening developments.

The situation with regard to counseling should encourage churches to evaluate just who is doing the counseling in the church and to explore the still quite reasonable cost of clergy malpractice insurance. Possibly potential counselees should be encouraged to sign arbitration agreements before entering counseling. Trouble-spots to watch are: the danger of suicide, premature termination, and failure to make a referral.

"It is time for judgment to begin with the family of God" (1 Peter 4:16). The church needs to have its own house in order. We do not want to be policed by government, but we are sometimes showing an indisposition and an inability to police ourselves.

A very significant volume treating these issues is Lynn R. Buzzard and Thomas S. Brandon, Jr., *Church Discipline and the Courts* (Wheaton, IL: Tyndale, 1987).

The matter under discussion is the nurture of the people of God. R. C. Sproul has put it well: "The church is called not only to a ministry of reconciliation, but a ministry of nurture to those within her gates. Part of that nurture includes church discipline."[14] Although this is one of the more nettlesome areas in our common life today, we have no alternative but to take Biblical precept and example to heart and say with the Apostle Paul, "I press on toward the mark of the high calling of God in Christ Jesus."

CHAPTER 15

"There Are Many Parts, but One Body"

The Pastor and the Vitality of the Body

They devoted themselves to the apostles' teaching and to the fellowship, to the breaking of bread and to prayer. . . . Every day they continued to meet together in the temple courts. They broke bread in their homes and ate together with glad and sincere hearts, praising God and enjoying the favor of all the people. And the Lord added to their number daily those who were being saved. (Acts 2:42, 46, 47)

If all the members were just like me,
What kind of a church would my church be?

The way the chief executive officer actually behaves is crucial for the survival of organizational renewal and change activities. It is his behavior (and subsequently that of other officers) that ultimately does or does not confirm the idea that organizational development is necessary and credible. (*Harvard Business Review*)

In what relationship does the pastor-teacher stand to the growth and development of genuine fellowship in the Body of Christ? Our exaggerated individualism and our cultural narcissism militate against the experience of real community. There are many lonely people and fringe persons among us. Church members are like ships passing in the night. The first graduating class from the University of Colorado consisted of one student who chose as the class motto: "United we stand, divided we fall."

The New Testament word which describes what our common experience is to be is *koinonia* or fellowship (1 Corinthians 1:9; 1 John 1:3, 7). This word is used of the closest of relationships, including a marriage contract in the days of Augustus. It bespeaks reciprocity, an active participation where the result depends on the cooperation of the receiver as well as the action of the giver. This is a unity which the Holy Spirit fosters and preserves (2 Corinthians 13:14; Philippians 2:1). It is exemplified in the breaking of bread in the Holy Communion (1 Corinthians 10:16, 17) and is expressed in generosity and giving (Romans 12:13; Hebrews 13:16; 1 Timothy 6:18). A new name is given to this new phenomenon—"the fellowship" (Acts 2:42).

Peter Wagner and others have well pointed out that every believer needs vital fellowship at three levels: 1) *the cell*—the small group, providing a kinship circle; 2) *the congregation* of fifty to two hundred or more for worship and teaching; 3) *the celebration level* where everyone comes together. Small congregations realize this third level in denominational district gatherings, and we all experience it in an interchurch concert of prayer or an evangelistic crusade. There are times when we need a sense of being part of a larger segment of the people of God.

Pragmatically speaking, work gets done when people work together with that elusive element of *esprit* pervading the group. The fact is, one ant can move 232 grams in six hours, but two ants can move 785 grams in six hours. One horse can pull four tons, but two horses can pull twenty-two tons. The nature of this spiritual "togetherness," set forth in the New Testament, is magnificently described in a study book, Gene Getz's *Building Up One Another*. What are to be the foci of the pastor-teacher's vision for the revitalization of the body?

DEVELOPING LEADERS

The prevalence of intensely active ministers and passively supporting laity is lethal for the experience of true *koinonia*. If small group experience is to be more than the pooling of ignorance and mawkish sentimentalism, there must be a networking of competent and skilled persons who are willing and able to take initiative. Clearly the early church had a plurality of ministering leaders.

How can the vicious cycle of passivity be broken? The pastor-teacher should be discipling leaders on a one-on-one basis. No pastor can possibly do this with more than two persons at a time. I usually liked to work with one younger and one more mature, established leader. Those discipled will themselves become disciplers. As time progresses, the pool of those able to lead increases.[1]

But to achieve geometric multiplication at a faster and more intense rate, the pastor-teacher needs to use existing small groups as leadership training cells. Every existing church board or committee should be engaged in a serious study and development program (beginning with a group study of Gene Getz's book, by way of example[2]). While small groups have a leveling effect such that people will produce at about the same level as others in the group, existing Sunday school classes can represent a beginning point in settings where small groups don't seem to work. Other congregations have gone to house churches or area shepherding groups.

The pastor-teacher sets the tone for significant movement and organizational renewal. Is renewal a *pro forma* interest, or is it genuinely a priority? Models of interdependence need to be developed. The pastor must practice the art of affirming people, not whipping them. Leadership in the final analysis is Christlikeness. Using a "from the bottom up" rather than "from the top down" kind of approach and seeking input and broader ownership for policy and implementation will aid that participation which is at the center of *koinonia*.

Coordinated planning would minimally require an annual leaders' night when all boards and committees and commissions convene for instruction, information and informal brainstorming. This is how good new ideas are put forth and how people feel involved in the process. Leadership retreats can be exceedingly productive if creatively planned and projected. Sometimes the best investment a congregation can make is to send several couples to a key national seminar or institute. This can potentially rejuvenate thinking patterns and move previously negative minds to a more positive mode.

Leadership analysis should seek to determine present and future need for leaders and workers. Where will there be gaps? Potential leaders need to be identified, then enlisted for training. Serious losses ensue when untrained leaders are thrust forward. New leaders and workers need to be recruited for specific positions and then supported in those positions, not abandoned to a sink-or-swim status. Providing continuing in-service training and development opportunities is critical for a positive outcome.

Every effort must be made to encourage creative thinking. The pastor-teacher must be concerned about the creation of a climate in which new ideas and approaches are not instantly stifled. We need to begin to receive input from younger people earlier than is usually done. My old pastor took great risks with me as a very young person, but this was pivotal for me. More creative use of women is long overdue in many of our churches. More attention should be paid to spiritual giftedness in the believing community than to other incidental factors of a secular nature. The growing number of senior adults can make a rich contribution for their own as well as the congregation's welfare. This whole area of leadership development must represent an urgent burden for every conscientious and dutiful undershepherd.

ENLISTING NEW MEMBERS

The infusion of new blood is absolutely essential to the vitality of the Body. Nothing is more heartening to the morale of the Body than to see the unconverted coming to Christ and then being added to the fellowship. Biological growth is natural, and transfer growth in a highly mobile society is to be expected, but new-convert growth should be the main source of numerical enhancement. Proximity to a college or university, bridges to some special ethnic or population segment, opportunity with service personnel from a nearby base, development of an effective cradle roll program, evangelistic Bible studies—all these provide open doors of opportunity. Are there people who need Christ? They are our mission field. The cults and the New Agers are busy, and we must be busy also. Accessions to the Body on profession of faith are the inevitable outcome of *koinonia* in the New Testament sense (Acts 2:47).

In some of our church traditions, we have become so cautious and so conservative in enlisting new members that by any standard too many people who should be in the membership are on the sidelines. It would almost seem that in some cases keeping the voting membership small is part of a strategy to maintain control. One sister said to me years ago, "Pastor, I liked our church when it was small years ago. I don't know about all these new people." New insecurities are bred as the result of growth. Since the maintenance of a membership roll is imperative in the interests of church order, we ought to accord membership the importance it deserves. People who are not members too easily fall back on the excuse that "I don't belong."

Some congregations are waiting too long to encourage believing young people to join. A category of "associate member" can be useful where state laws regarding the age for voting are a problem or where college and university students would like to become involved but do not want to move their membership from their home church. Where membership in the church is required for singing in the choir or teaching Sunday school, interviews with the diaconate can be used to process eligible persons who for valid reasons do not seek membership.

The first step in enlisting new members is to welcome newcomers. We shall speak in Chapter 23 about the developing situation in communication and publicity for the local church. Every local church should have a well-trained cadre of greeters welcoming the worshipers to every service. The ushers have their own critical function, but these are in addition to identifiable greeters in the foyers of the church. Actual recognition of guests in the public service can often be embarrassing, and "handshaking" extravaganzas can be disruptive to the flow of worship. The ministry of hospitality is a very special ministry for some in the congregation but certainly one in which all should become involved at some level.

Registration of all worshipers is important. The guest book will get less than 10 percent of the newcomers, and cards in the pews will not do too much better. But if every worshiper registers, some 80 percent of the newcomers will do the same. Possible check-off lists requesting information about various pastoral services, giving prayer requests, making reservations for Wednesday family night suppers, as well as giving other information for the church office, make all of the work and bother more than worthwhile. In my last parish we had more than twenty-five persons annually indicate that they wanted to receive Christ on the friendship sheet which was passed down the row. One obvious advantage in the use of the tablet for the ritual of friendship is that it reminded the other people in the row of the names and status of their neighbors.

Follow-up contacts should be prompt. Every newcomer should receive a personalized letter early in the week following the worship experience. Careful sorting of the names should discard casual visitors from neighboring churches and persons who are known not to be real prospects. Lay visits or Evangelism Explosion team visits should be considered. In some cases there needs to be a visit from one of the pastoral staff. In rural and small-town America, where well-known family and denominational lines make visits assume significance of a special kind, care must be taken. In urban centers it is not always possible to make visits in apartment buildings without appointments, and sometimes the only viable means of real contact is to encourage some member to move into the large complex as a means of entry.

The following data from The Institute for American Church

Growth in Pasadena, California are of interest: 6 to 8 percent of our newcomers walk in off the street; 8 to 10 percent are attracted by the pastor; 3 to 4 percent come because special needs are being met through the church; 1 to 2 percent come through some visitation program; 3 to 4 percent come through the Sunday school; .0005 percent come because of an evangelistic meeting or TV program; 70 to 80 percent come because they are brought by a relative, neighbor or friend. These facts have encouraged many congregations to use a Visitor's Sunday when special efforts are made for everyone to invite newcomers.

It is important also to note, as Lyle Schaller has pointed out, that in 1952 seven of eight members in denominational churches had been born into that church. Now "The average Protestant church is finding that, out of its last 20 adult new members, three are former Catholics, six are transferring from . . . another Protestant denomination . . . three have had no previous church affiliation, and only eight are coming from a sister church of the same denomination." This means that if something vital and alive is happening in our congregation, we have a chance to attract a healthy pool of prospects.

The idea of a coffee time following the morning service is especially important for congregations with large numbers of visitors. Special receptions and dinners for students and singles can also be advisable as part of an overall strategy to enlist newcomers.

PROCESSING NEW MEMBERS

Church membership is an important union and like marriage ought not to be entered into hastily or unadvisedly, but reverently and in the fear of God. Most congregations have recognized the importance of membership and require membership inquiry classes or communicant's classes to assist prospective members in their decision and to improve the quality and texture of the ensuing membership tie. Other assemblies are not receiving church letters of transfer other than as a matter of record or commendation of character.

A sequence of classes with helpful discussion and the distribution of informative material can be conducted during the Sunday school hour or before the evening service or on a weeknight. The sessions should include a careful presentation of the requirements of membership and what it means to be a Christian; the history of the denomination and consideration of the doctrinal and behavioral standards; and the history and structure of the local church. Various church leaders can make enlightening presentations which can be of inestimable help to newcomers. Not infrequently class discussions disclose that a prospective member may not in fact be a Christian or may have some serious problems in the area of the assurance of salvation. This becomes an open door for ministry and counsel.

The next step becomes the interviewing process. Each church will have its own custom and procedure. Some conduct interviews with the whole diaconate and others will utilize a membership committee to hear the testimonies. In some traditions testimonies are given to the whole congregation at a quarterly meeting or a special meeting called expressly for this purpose. The presiding pastor can assist the very shy and inarticulate by asking direct questions. In one congregation which we served, the new-member candidates met with the deacons at the parsonage for a fellowship hour. This more relaxed setting also gave the pastor and his wife the opportunity to extend Christian hospitality to the whole class of prospects.

The initiatory process is completed by offering the right hand of fellowship and then receiving new members at the next Communion service. This should be done with a gracious spirit and with symbols of inclusion and welcome appropriate to the fellowship and its traditions. These are precious occasions and should be hallowed and cherished in the body. There is a subjective tone which sensitive spiritual leadership will seek to make an integral part of this whole process in the interests of building true *koinonia*.

INTEGRATING NEW MEMBERS

Adding new members to the roll is just the beginning. These new members need to be welcomed into the hearts and homes of the congregation. All of them can begin to do some task in the common effort (although one should not be too hasty in thrusting newcomers into large leadership roles). A talent survey should be made in every congregation on a regular basis, and all new members should have an opportunity to indicate the areas of service and activity in which they are inclined to find participation. Some churches hold an annual new members' banquet to show special honor to newcomers and to give them the opportunity to mingle with the officiary of the church. Sometimes pictures of the new members are posted in the narthex or included in the parish paper.

Pastoral follow-up is needed, particularly in some cases. Some pastors send birthday greetings to all members; some make a brief phone call on the person's birthday. We need to keep some tab on our new members. They are vulnerable and susceptible in their newness and need nurturing. In some situations sponsors might well be appointed to especially shepherd the newcomers.

Care must be taken to introduce new members into existing small group structures and home Bible studies or appropriate Sunday school classes. In one parish we served, it seemed one whole younger age group was at loose ends, so we began a Mariners program, widely used in the Presbyterian Church. The group was divided into mutual interest "ships" which would meet monthly. The whole "fleet" would meet quarterly. This was a useful program to help us develop relationships in an age group which needed focus and direction. Some have used "Dinners for Eight" as a simpler approach to the same problem.

The problem we particularly face in fast-growing local situations with regard to the church roll is that so many roll in and then roll out. The existence and maintenance of true *koinonia* in the local church continues to be a major concern in the local church today. Relationships tend to be very superficial and shallow. Many seek anonymity in mega-churches which must develop an infrastructure of sub-groups to reach out to those living in spiritual isolation. In other more traditional and older communities, a long history with much intermarriage of families makes newcomers feel like outsiders. North Americans generally have a great longing for belonging. In the impersonality and alienation of our times Christian churches ought to offer islands of caring and compassion—indeed a "divine society" which is without parallel.

IV

Rites

CHAPTER 16

"The Household of Faith"

Baptism and the Presentation of Children

The difficulty arises from the modern wrong conception of the New Testament meaning of the word "baptism," that it is a mere rite, an act to be done, at the best, because one believes in Jesus. The New Testament writers never separate it from the faith which it embodies and expresses. It is the fixed sign for faith, just as any appropriate order of letters in a word is the sign of an idea. The sign stands for the thing and is constantly used for the thing. Hence Paul can say that Christ was "put on" in baptism (Galatians 3:27), and Peter does not hesitate to declare that "baptism does also now save us" (I Peter 3:21). (James M. Stifler)[1]

All the chief Christian doctrines are involved in the theology of baptism. (Alec Vidler)

For baptism, however understood and administered, holds a place never far from the cutting edge of the church's impact upon the wider community. (David F. Wright)[2]

An integral and by no means incidental part of pastoral function has to do with the administration of the sacraments or ordinances, which for Protestants are two in number: baptism and the Lord's Supper. They are the visible enactment of the gospel and represent God's gracious accommodation to our physical being in that all five physical senses become doors of teaching and understanding. The word *sacrament* literally means "a thing set apart as sacred" or "a military oath of obedience as administered by the commander."[3] Later *sacrament* was understood as "a visible word or an outward and visible sign of an inward and spiritual grace."[4] Because of certain very negative his-

141

torical connotations, the word *sacrament* carries too much freight for some, who prefer the word *ordinance*, which is translated in the New Testament as "institution," "arrangement" and "tradition."

In contrast with the seven sacraments of the Roman Catholic Church, Protestants following the Reformers have seen but two, insisting on the following criteria: 1) The sacrament must have the authority of the Lord Himself. 2) It should utilize a physical emblem, such as water or the bread or the cup. Quakers and the Salvation Army have tended to spiritualize baptism and the Lord's Supper, and ultradispensationalists have argued that neither is valid for this church age, although some in the Grace-truth movement have allowed the observance of the Lord's Supper.

Some believers have taken the position that "the towel and basin," or footwashing, should be practiced regularly since ostensibly both of the above criteria are met (see John 13:1-16). In this instance, however, the wisdom of the church as a whole down through the ages has been that footwashing was clearly a cultural matter appropriate in Jesus' day given the footwear and composition of paths and roadways in that ancient time. We most meaningfully follow Christ's example of humility and self-emptying by expressing the mind of Christ within the self-seeking and self-serving culture of our time, which is so obsessed with looking out for Number One.

Sadly, these visible witnesses to the unity of the Body of Christ have through the ages been the subject of most vicious and sometimes violent controversy and conflict. It is imperative that the pastor-teacher delve deeply into the theology of accepted practice in his communion and that clear, careful instruction be given to the flock in a spirit of Christian love. More civil and Christian discussion of the issues seems to be taking place today.[5]

THE MANDATE FOR BAPTISM

There is a great gap between our doctrine of baptism and our practice of baptism. The danger here is that the practice can so easily become cultural or traditional and we can for all practical purposes come to view baptism as *ex opere operato* (i.e., the water of baptism contains and confers grace), which is very close to the Roman view.

Augustine observed: "Our Lord Jesus Christ hath knit together a company of new people by sacraments, most few in number, most easy to be kept, most excellent in signification."[6] The background of the Christian practice of baptism is well stated by Bromiley: "Christian baptism has its origin with the baptism of John, and especially with the baptism of Jesus by John, and the taking up of baptism by Jesus and his disciples."[7]

John's baptism was an extension of Jewish proselyte baptism. Proselyte baptism among the Jews was more than ceremonial ablution, for it involved elaborate catechetical preparation. The candidate would recite commandments while covered with water to the loins or neck. Usually a new name, selected from the Scriptures, was given at this time. Proselyte baptism was by immersion, and interestingly circumcision was also required.

The revolutionary note in John the Baptist's summons was his insistence that only real repentance and submission to a baptism of repentance would suffice to bring a person (in his day, a Jew) into right relationship with the Messiah. John's baptism, as White puts it, was "initiation into the eschatological fulfillment, into the Messianic Age, and into the prepared Messianic community, the nucleus of the coming kingdom."[8]

Jesus used the word "baptism" in referring to His own passion (Matthew 20:22) and instituted baptism in the context of His death and resurrection (Matthew 28:18-20). Concerning references to baptism in Romans 6, we can only conclude that in the early church the coincidence of the baptizing work of the Holy Spirit initiating the new believer into the Body of Christ (1 Corinthians 12.13) and the experience of water baptism are so close as to be meant simultaneously in that chapter. Baptism everywhere in the New Testament is closely identified with the experience of new life in Christ (cf. Acts 2:38; 8:35, 36; etc.). Baptism was never optional or unimportant in the apostolic church. An unbaptized Christian would be as incongruous as an uncircumcised Pharisee!

Just recently the Church of Sweden decided to study for the following two years the question of whether baptism should be a condition of membership. Those opposing the baptismal requirement argue that "openness in the church must be emphasized: the church must not be open just for the few pious but there must be a multitude of ways to approach the church."[9] At issue here is the meaning of inclusion in the Body of Christ. Is everyone a part of the Body of Christ? Or is not repentance-faith-baptism the way of initiation for all?

Some even object to the relevancy or authenticity of Christ's command to baptize. In Matthew 28:19 the command of Christ to make disciples is basic, with baptism and teaching being coincident. Meticulous scholarship has grappled with the issues here, supports the genuineness of the text and asserts that "The Matthean statement that the Lord gave a command to baptize has the support of the fact that the practice of the Church from the earliest days is inexplicable without such a command."[10] Paul's comment in 1 Corinthians 1:17 is to be seen as putting two tasks in their order of relative importance, not as abrogating the practice of baptism.

THE MODE OF BAPTISM

When and how should baptism be administered? Many Christians have felt that what circumcision and the Passover were under the Old Covenant, baptism and the Lord's Supper are under the New Covenant. Baptism then, it is argued, can be given to the children of believing parents as a sign of God's prevenient grace, for even before they know of Christ's death and resurrection His love has acted on their behalf.[11]

Does this mean that unbaptized babies are lost? Joachim Jeremias has argued that infant baptism was practiced in the early church,[12] but Kurt Aland, an avowed paedo-baptist, has answered him point by point.[13] Aland holds that no evidence for infant baptism exists earlier than the third century and that the practice is not deduced from Scriptural records, but is built on theological grounds. The household baptisms in the New Testament do not countermand this.[14]

The association of baptism with the cleansing of sins (Acts 22:16; 1 Corinthians 6:11; Hebrews 10:22, 23; 1 Peter 3:21), which is entirely the work of God in those who believe, and the association of baptism with the gift of the Holy Spirit (Acts 8:16, 17; 10:47; 11:15, 16; 19:1-7; Titus 3:5), who is given to those who believe, have been used to support the position that water baptism is the sign of God's saving grace and should legitimately be given only to those who believe.

The concern for a clear understanding of how baptism relates to conversion is necessary for all Christians. Baptism may afford a false sense of security and become a substitute for genuine saving faith regardless of when it is administered or how. John Baillie shows how believer's baptism belongs most consistently and logically to those who believe in a gathered church with its insistence on conversion and faith as prerequisite to membership.[15]

Karl Barth followed his eldest son, Markus, in abandoning infant baptism in the interest of an "essentially missionary and mature church." The strong move in many European countries against indiscriminate infant baptism is a reflection of this same basic concern.

Whenever and however we baptize, we must give thoughtful and careful instruction prior to baptism. We need to teach and preach concerning the meaning of this sacrament. Candidates for baptism should be thoroughly examined. In some cultures a period of probation is required before baptism because of what baptism represents as a real break with the old life in that culture.

Some sprinkle or pour; others use immersion in a church baptistery, lake, river or swimming pool. The amount of water is probably not the critical factor in the final analysis, although even Bromiley concedes that "Most of the Reformers allowed that immersion was in some way best calculated to bring out the meaning of the sign (Romans 6:4)."[16] Similarly, the Reformers insisted that "baptism must never be administered privately in the home, or even in a semi-private service in church,"[17] but in the context of the corporate worship of the people of God.

THE METHODOLOGY OF BAPTISM

Baptism should always be administered with great reverence and appropriate dignity. Appropriate certificates should be prepared and signed in advance. Arrangements should be made and overseen with the help of deacons and deaconesses. These are high moments for the person to be baptized and for the family, as well as for the congregation. There is no room here for anything which smacks of the careless or the casual, but there should rather be a warm, caring disposition on the part of the pastor. Baptism should always be in the name of the Triune God. Personalization of the experience only enhances its significance for all.

Baptism of infants by sprinkling or pouring should be done in the context of appropriate Scripture emphasizing the Biblical covenant (for example, Acts 2:38, 39). Godparents or sponsors are used in many cases. Such persons assume no legal obligation but promise to encourage and pray for the parents.

Sometimes candidates for immersion are troubled and anxious in anticipation of their experience. The candidates' class can do much to allay that anxiety and to focus on the meaning and great joy of following the Lord in the waters of baptism. If the baptism is to be outdoors, great care needs to be taken in examining all of the physical features of the situation. When baptizing in moving water such as a river, the candidates should always be baptized against the current.

There is great advantage in having the candidates wear baptismal robes, which can be old choir robes or inexpensively made gowns.

Swim apparel can be worn underneath. Men, of course, can wear casual pants and white shirts. Full regalia is available for the pastor-teacher, but I have never worn other than pants and white shirt.

The pastor on entering the water should introduce the baptisms with appropriate words of Scripture, and then the candidates should be led into the water. "An integral part of baptism in the New Testament is the candidate's act of faith."[18] A confession of faith or personal testimony should be elicited by the pastor. Extreme caution should be employed if there is any microphone or amplification being used lest the candidate reach forward nervously and take hold of the microphone.

When positioned appropriately, the candidate may either clasp both hands over the midriff or place one hand over the nose (persons with fear of water may prefer to do the latter) and then just relax while buckling the knees as the pastor lowers him or her into the water. Very tall individuals or generously proportioned persons really pose no serious problem because they are buoyant in the water. Usually I say, "Upon your profession of faith and in obedience to Christ's command, I baptize you, my brother (or, my sister), in the name of the Father and of the Son and of the Holy Spirit." As I lift them out of the water, I ordinarily say, "Buried with Him in baptism, raised to walk in newness of life."

The blessing of the baptismal service rises out of the joyful testimony of the believer and the fruit of obedience to Christ's command. While very young children should not be baptized until they really understand the meaning of this service in relation to their own experience of salvation, people of all ages testify to the meaningfulness of this ancient ceremony. The question of rebaptism as an adult believer is a vexed issue in some quarters, but if the pastor is to be the pastor to all of the people in the congregation, he will need to respect the conscience and conviction of the person seeking adult baptism.

A fascinating treatise by John Bunyan is entitled: *Differences in Judgment About Water Baptism, No Bar to Communion* (1673). He laments the fact that the water of baptism has become "A wall of division." I would not diminish vigorous conviction on baptism, but do welcome a more irenic searching out of the meaning of these things. What must be especially alarming in all of this is what appears to be a growing apathy on the issue and practice. This is sub-Biblical and is but another reflection of passivity and a drift toward indifference among us.

THE MEANING OF THE PRESENTATION
OF LITTLE CHILDREN

Little children are precious to the Lord whether or not they are baptized. We would wish for more divine revelation on the matter of infant salvation. The sacramentarian believes that the water of baptism washes away original sin (and is then left with limbo or some such place for the unbaptized). John Calvin seems ambivalent at times, sometimes limiting salvation to the children of the elect but at other times seeming to suggest that God saves all infants who die by divine fiat (which constitutes a serious problem if this means some gain Heaven apart from the finished work of Jesus Christ). Many Wesleyans have built on a suggestion from Romans 5:12-21 that Christ's work removed the guilt of Adam's transgression for all, thus making each person accountable for his or her own actual sin. Thus infants who die prematurely or the mentally deficient or fetuses are saved eternally through the merits of Christ's blood.

Reflective of this certainty of Christ's love for children and responsive to the fact that our Lord was Himself presented in the Temple by Mary and Joseph (Luke 2:22), the custom has grown in many quarters to present or dedicate little children to the Lord in the presence of the congregation. The narrative about Jesus blessing the little children (Mark 10:13ff.) is described by Jeremias as "pre-sacramental."[19]

The Paulicians, a somewhat heretical sect with roots back to the sixth century in Asia Minor, used a thanksgiving service for their children which has been described as "a moving service of thanksgiving, parental vows, naming and prayerful dedication."[20] Something akin to this took root in the nineteenth century in some Baptist circles. The example of Hannah bringing Samuel to the Lord (1 Samuel 1:11, 22, 28) and the general principle of dedicating valuable and precious objects and places to the Lord's use would seem to be precedent for parents of faith. I do not think this compromises our position on baptism, but only recognizes that the children of believing parents are set apart to God (cf. 1 Corinthians 7:14).

Some pastors like to hold the infant (but these little ones don't always like to be held in strange arms), and others have pleasant customs to encourage bonding of various kinds. The keys are appropriate Scripture, questions and vows for the parents, and a prayer for God's outpoured blessing on this little life. The Bible abounds with choice verses for such an occasion. One of my favorites is: "All your sons will be taught by the Lord, and great will be your children's peace" (Isaiah 54:13).

We desire above all else that our children become believers when they reach moral accountability and come to the age of understanding. Of this Jonathan Edwards movingly spoke in his "Farewell Sermon": "Every Christian family ought to be, as it were, a little church, consecrated to Christ, and wholly influenced and governed by His rules." Surrounded by God's people and upheld by prayer, we shall take courage in seeking to preserve and present our children as part of "the household of faith."

CHAPTER 17

"Proclaiming the Lord's Death Until He Comes"

The Lord's Supper

The highest cannot be spoken, it can only be acted. . . .
(Goethe)

The cup of blessing which we bless, is it not a communion of the blood of Christ? The bread we break, is it not a communion of the body of Christ; seeing that we, who are many, are one bread, one body; for we all partake of the one bread. (1 Corinthians 10:16, 17)

My God, and is Thy table spread?
And does Thy cup with love o'erflow?
Thither be all Thy children led,
And let them all its sweetness know.

Hail, sacred feast, which Jesus makes!
Rich banquet of His flesh and blood!
Thrice happy he who here partakes
That sacred stream, that heavenly food!
(Philip Doddridge)

While the New Testament gives only sparse details with respect to the practice of baptism, it gives considerably more to the practice of observing the Lord's Supper. While the Lord's Supper is basically eating the bread and drinking the cup in remembrance of Christ and His death, the sacrament or ordinance is linked with the liturgical meal celebrated annually by the Jews at Passover (Luke 22:15, 16).[1] Jesus is, then, the true Paschal Lamb, the antitype of the whole sacrificial system of the Old Testament (cf. Exodus 12:1-13; John 1:29; 1 Corinthians 5:7, 8).

The four New Testament accounts of the Lord's Supper (Matthew 26:26-30; Mark 14:22-26; Luke 22:14-20; 1 Corinthians 11:23-26) supply us with the essential parameters. Like baptism, the elements in Communion are *verba visibilis* ("visible words"), to use Augustine's terms. They are signs and seals, like wedding rings. The proper emphasis is on the breaking of the bread, signifying Christ's body, and the fruit of the vine, signifying the shedding of Christ's blood. As Bromiley well insists:

> The cross and the passion are the real action underlying the external sign, and the Lord's Supper is a witness and a reflection of this basic work, an enacted, visible and tangible sign to bring home its truth and reality to the participants.[2]

The memorial meal was most frequently called the "Eucharist" in early church history (meaning "praise" or "thanksgiving"). There was seldom a gathering without the breaking of bread. Early on it was part of a proper meal (just as Jesus appended the first supper to the Passover observance), but gradually it became a ritual meal in its own right because of the abuse of the *Agape* or Love Feast.

Early precursors of subsequent misunderstanding can be seen in Irenaeus' use of the word "altar" with respect to Communion and Origen's speaking of "bloodless sacrifice," as well as the increasing tendency to import the whole system of Jewish priesthood as the context for its observance. The Reformers repudiated the serious metaphysical obfuscations of the medieval church, but understood aspects of the practice variously. Calvin urged a weekly Eucharist, and Zwingli instituted a sitting Communion. Outside of Scripture, it was in Strasbourg that the term "Lord's Supper" was first used.

The Holy Communion is unspeakably precious to the believer and is veritably "the medicine of the soul." Sadly, it has been the subject of so much tragic division and debate. Surely as regrettable, the observance of Communion is often routinized and slipshod, lacking proper reverence and understanding. The pastor-teacher must lead the congregation in recovering the mystery and meaning of this gift to Christ's church.

THEOLOGICAL DIVERSITY

Quality Bible exposition and careful theological interpretation are indispensable for the proper observance of the Lord's Supper. Luther's consubstantial view (stressing the ubiquity of Christ) clashed resoundingly with Zwingli's more "memorialist" conviction, while Calvin held a middle position which emphasized the Holy Spirit's mediation of the presence of Christ in a real way. Clearly the Supper had Messianic significance and anticipates eschatologically the Messianic banquet.

As Cullmann well pointed out, Christian worship is the focal point of the tension between the "now" and the "not yet" of Christian faith and experience.[3] Thus Communion is seen as the festive banquet, "the antepast of heaven," the Maranatha meal of the people of God, the meal of faith before the Day dawns.

The core of the meaning of the Supper is then to be seen as:

1) *A commemoration of the death and passion of the Lord Jesus.* "This do in remembrance of me." We remember the scenes of His passion, "the very dying form of one who suffered there for me."

> *According to Thy gracious word,*
> *In meek humility,*
> *This will I do, my dying Lord,*
> *I will remember Thee.*
> (James Montgomery)

2) *A communion with the living Christ and with other believers.* We are not a "Dead Poet's Society," but rather have the unspeakable privilege of fellowshiping friend with friend in vital and real contact with the Christ "who was dead but is now alive forevermore" (Revelation 1:18).

3) *A covenant with our God.* The people of God are under "the blood of the everlasting covenant" (Hebrews 13:20). Just as in days of old when the making of a covenant was followed by a meal which included the pledging of life and loyalty (cf. Genesis 26:30; 31:54; 2 Samuel 3:20; etc.), so "the new covenant" (Jeremiah 31:1-34) is now "ratified by Jesus in a meal at the Supper."[4]

In just what respect the presence of Christ is manifested and made known will be expressed variously in different traditions. Some will prefer a more mystical understanding, as did the old Moravians who spoke about "living in the wounds of Jesus." Anglicans have historically sought a compromise understanding such as is reflected in Cranmer's denial that Christ is present in the sacrament in the same sense as in the Incarnation, yet opposing the notion that a generalized presence was enough. There is a special and real presence, he argued.[5]

An encouraging development has been the movement toward

greater agreement among Protestants regarding the Lord's Supper.[6] This must never be achieved, however, at the price of indifference to the fundamental theological issues which undergird our celebration of the Lord's Supper.

LITURGICAL COMMENTARY

While evidence for a uniform liturgy in the early centuries cannot be found, we see various elements included along with the Lord's Supper, going back to Justin Martyr. These are: reading of Scripture, singing, taking an offering, the people's amen, confession of faith, the kiss of peace, prayers and preaching. There really should be a sermon, an opening of the Word, before the observance of the Supper. As Dr. Van Oosterzee remarked, "Christianity is par excellence the religion of the Word."

The idea of the Lord's Supper as an appendage to a regular service is hard to reconcile with good practice. The whole service should be a Communion service, with the completion of the ministry of the Word experienced in the sacramental meal. Calvin rightly maintained that "The sacrament standeth not without the Word." Often in the projection of a series, we can come to texts which are most appropriate for Communion Sunday. At other times, special teaching messages can be used to treat aspects of the Supper or related implications.

"The liturgy of the upper room"—i.e., elements of the actual Supper itself—should include the presentation of the elements, the prayer of thanksgiving and consecration (and in more high-church circles, the Epiclesis or invocation of the Holy Spirit), the manual art of breaking the bread and taking the cup, and then the delivery and the reception.

It is crucial to bear in mind that this is the Lord's Table. Jesus Christ is the Host and in some sense also the food. He is the one who breaks and pours; we are to take and eat. This is essential nutrition for the inner person, the soul. Necessarily the meal is for believers only. The admonition to examine ourselves and partake worthily should be emphasized (1 Corinthians 11:28, 29). Of course, in the final analysis our worthiness is found only in Christ.

There may well be instances when believers should not partake of the elements. As Bromiley correctly observes, "It is obviously improper that Christians should come to communion if they are willfully unrepentant in respect to certain sins, especially in their relations with fellow-Christians."[7]

Children and youth need an instruction or confirmation class so they can discern the Lord's body. Minimally, children who have received Christ should sit with their parents and should be instructed by their parents before coming to the Table of the Lord.

The frequency of the celebration of the Holy Communion differs markedly. In many traditions the observance is monthly, in some quarterly, and in some annually. Many believers have a great hunger for the Supper. In one congregation where the custom was for quarterly Communion, a provision was made for a more frequent observance in the Prayer Chapel in a service before the Sunday school hour. This was a rich and rewarding time of sharing and worship.

Varying methods for the distribution of the elements are also to be found. Usually the elements are matzos or wafers, while some prefer to break a whole loaf of bread. The use of unfermented grape juice is preferable out of deference to any believers who have had problems with alcoholism. This is also a compassionate recognition of the serious problems we have in our culture with addiction. In general the elements have been served from the aisles, with each worshiper serving his or her neighbor or each person being served by the server who holds the elements until all are served. The latter is called simultaneous Communion and may necessitate sitting every other row. The former emphasizes the priesthood of all believers and the latter the unity of the Body of Christ.

Ordinarily the servers and the officiating pastors should be served last, but no one should serve himself or herself. All believers are guests at the table and should be served. Some traditions limit the Communion observance to a stated service of public worship. While some seem to break bread on almost every possible occasion (at camp, minister's meetings, etc.), great care must be exercised to ensure the awareness that these signs and emblems are most meaningfully shared in the life of a local congregation of believers. Portable Communion ware is available to extend the fellowship of the local congregation to shut-ins and the institutionalized, lest they be deprived of the blessing and joy of the Supper.

Preparation for coming to the Table enhances and enriches the whole experience of Communion. Minimally this requires the thoughtful choice of hymns and music which are conducive to the Supper and which join with the motif of the sermon. Reminders of the upcoming service and notices in the parish publication can further alert communicants to ready their own hearts and minds for a more meaningful and more worshipful observance. Matthew Henry's *A Communicant's Companion* was typical of materials used in previous generations but is not available today. Andrew Murray's superb little piece *The Lord's Table* recommends readings for the week before the Supper, the Communion Sabbath itself, and the week after the Supper.[8]

Many younger people in our congregations are not satisfied with the *ad hoc* atmosphere in Communion. While they appreciate participative involvement, they also want dignity and decorum. Our congregations have their hoary traditions in all of these matters and often service books which are helpful.[9] There is some real advantage in planning each Communion service to be slightly different and unique within the basic givens. We fight the enervating inroads of sameness and tedium and must confront a serious cultural drift if we are to foster concentration in the remembrance of our Lord.

PRACTICAL CONSISTENCY

Careful attention needs to be paid to doctrinal and theological statements made in conjunction with our Communion practice. For example, in many churches of the Reformation the Communion table is pushed against the wall, necessitating the pastor's turning his back on the congregation to minister the elements. This makes the table a *de facto* altar and the pastor a priest. Bromiley is correct in insisting: "The fact that by nature the Lord's Supper is a meal and not a sacrifice means that it is properly administered at a table and not an altar."[10]

The placement of the table on a level with the congregation for the observance of the Supper also reinforces the idea that it is not an elevated altar, but a table for fellowship around which we gather as the Lord's family at a memorial meal. We need to think through our theology and must insist that our observance be in harmony with our common conviction as to what indeed this all means.

In a very thoughtful treatment, William Willimon urges that we pay close attention to our leadership of these rites. Movements and gestures should all have significance and should be seen by every worshiper.[11] However, greater attention to what we do does not mean we prolong the service and make it tedious. Every believer is to take and eat. "No one else can take for us; each must eat and drink for himself (or herself)."[12] A most significant theological statement is being made in offering Communion in all these ways. This is what we need to think through carefully.

In some congregations Communion is served directly from the table as communicants walk forward in groups. No doctrinal canon is violated here. In addition, there may be special times, such as Christmas or New Year's Eve, when families will come at various times during an announced hour for worship and Communion.

Particular pains should be taken to preserve some sense of divine transcendence in the observance of Holy Communion. There is immanence in and through the incarnation of the Lord Jesus Christ, but there is also the greatness of Him with whom we have to do and the awesomeness of approaching Him. Some (not all) contemporary Christian music, if it is all we use, is most forgettable and trivial. We can soon be in Peter Berger's "world without windows," with no sense of mystery. Trendiness too often triumphs among us.

I have heard of one group which observed Communion with potato chips and Pepsi as the elements. I doubt this was the Lord's Supper. Our practice must portray our theological principles.

DESIRABLE VARIETY

Yet leadership must be concerned to seek some sense of variety within the bounds of propriety. It is the total predictability of our forms that threatens the serious substance of our content. The very shifting of themes within the church year should open a variety of appropriate moods in Communion. Certainly Maundy Thursday and Good Friday services of the Holy Communion are sombre and solemn. But there are also times when the note of jubilation should be sounded. "This is the joyful feast of the people of God" is not an inappropriate refrain. "The Lord's Supper is a feast celebrating life. It looks forward to the day when 'men and women shall come from east and west and from north and south and sit at table in the kingdom of God.'"[13]

Variation in serving patterns can be positive. Vocal music as a variant with the organ is a good change. Calvin and Knox both read Scripture during the serving of the elements. On occasion the Communion can be used in connection with a meal. The service could be held in a Fellowship Hall sitting around tables with the one loaf. Even among the more liturgical, the trend (because of health anxieties) is not to use the common cup but rather small cups filled from a large chalice.

Some have used Communion in homes with chairs in a circle. Small-group Communion expresses a special nuance of fellowship, especially in a larger church. We have already described a Communion procedure in which the communicants come forward to be served. Some will administer Communion at the evening service as a change. Local situations open opportunities for creative adaptation within faithful adherence to doctrinal symbols.

A great aid to leadership is to break new trails in our thinking about the significance of the Supper. Although the two writers I am about to quote come from entirely different camps liturgically, I have personally benefited greatly from reading Martin Marty's *The Lord's Supper* and Geoffrey Wainwright's *Eucharist and Eschatology*.[14] Regarding the eucharistic assembly and the company of Heaven, Wainwright comments: "the bread and the wine become the firstfruits of that renewed creation which will be so entirely submitted to the divine lordship that it will enjoy total penetration by the divine glory while yet remaining distinct from the transcendent God it worships."[15] Then he quotes from the richness of Charles Wesley:

> *Author of life divine, who hast a table spread,*
> *Furnished with mystic wine and everlasting bread,*
> *Preserve the life Thyself hast given,*
> *And feed and train us up for heaven.*
> *AMEN AND AMEN.*

CHAPTER 18

"The Two Will Become One Flesh"

The Wedding

Heirs together of the grace of life. (1 Peter 3:7)

To be happy at home is the ultimate result of all ambition. (Samuel Johnson)

Love is strong as death. Many waters cannot quench love, neither can the floods drown it. (Song of Solomon 8:6, 7)

WHAT IS MARRIAGE?
It is sharing and caring,
Giving and forgiving,
Loving and being loved,
Walking hand in hand,
Talking heart to heart,
Seeing through each other's eyes—
Laughing together,
Weeping together,
Praying together,
And ALWAYS trusting
And believing
And thanking God
For each other.

Helen Steiner Rice

By virtue of call and custom the pastor-teacher is uniquely involved and privileged to minister in the high moments of human life and experience. Who beside the pastor is so integral a part in all of the major rites of passage—birth, dedication, baptism, marriage, death?

As the officiant at weddings in such a variety of circumstances and situations, the pastor has the opportunity to make a substantial contribution for Christ in the building of strong Christian homes. Though the divorce rate fluctuates somewhat in relation to economic and other factors, the divorce rate has doubled since 1966. A marriage formed today has no more than a fifty percent chance of survival. It is estimated that half the children born in recent decades will spend part of their childhood with only one of their natural parents. No-fault divorce now prevails with its incalculable fallout of suffering and anguish.

Children of divorce bear lifelong scars. The average divorced woman's standard of living declines 73 percent in the year following her divorce. The breaking of a marriage exacts a frightening physical, emotional and spiritual toll on its victims. The survival rate for second marriages plummets to 36 percent. Individuals and society suffer because of divorce. Further, our God hates divorce (Malachi 2:16).

The pastor-teacher stands in a strategic gap to challenge the erosion of the family and to be God's watchman on the wall with regard to a ballooning crisis. Because marriage is a creation mandate, the pastor serves as an agent of the state under the laws governing marriage. Each state has its own code. Even the matter of who may officiate at a wedding is stipulated in law. A minister newly arrived in an area is well-advised to check local provisos. In some states ministerial credentials need to be on file with the court clerk in the county of residence. In any event, marriages can be performed only when duly authorized by the issuance of a license. Ministers ought to promptly and carefully handle all paperwork in connection with the solemnizing of a marriage.

But above all the pastor-teacher represents the Lord Jesus Christ. The minister is not obligated to perform any wedding which in his judgment is not Scripturally based. We function in this role on behalf of Christ and His gospel.

PREPARING THE HEARTS

In an effort to stave off the rising divorce rate, many Roman Catholic dioceses are requiring at least a six-month notice and a period of preparation before a church wedding. Quick weddings find only occasional justification. The "tying of the knot" should be the last climactic step of a careful and thoughtful process of preparation for marriage.

Every congregation should develop a "Church Policy for

Weddings." This statement should treat the availability of facilities and services as well as the terms. Who officiates at weddings? Who can play the musical instruments? What about reception facilities? Is any wedding allowed after 4 P. M. on Saturday? What about the use of alcoholic beverages? What is the policy on an honorarium for the officiating pastor? If these matters are addressed and spelled out, consistent practice will emerge.

The policy document should mandate premarital counseling for every person to be married in the church. Perhaps a sliding scale for the number of required sessions is best, considering that generally eighteen-year-olds require considerably more time and attention than middle-aged persons with considerable education. In some cases five or six sessions will be best, while in other cases fewer sessions will suffice.

Perhaps the use of premarital testing can provide a foundation for practical and helpful counseling sessions. Pastors can develop skills in administering Taylor-Johnson, or the Family History Analysis, or Prepare II (Premarital Personal and Relationship Evaluation).

The pastor must never marry an unbeliever to a believer. Such a mixed marriage is contrary to the clear teaching of both the Old and New Testaments. How could the blessing of Almighty God be sought on a marriage He has forbidden? Marrying two unbelievers can provide opportunity for witness, though a problem arises if one of the persons receives Christ in the course of counseling. All of this presupposes clear Biblical preaching and teaching on the nature of Christian marriage. Youth need to be prepared over the years of their upbringing in home and church for this most critical and important step and relationship.

The so-called "shotgun" wedding in which the bride is pregnant should not call for the suspension of the regular rules for a wedding. A couple who are not truly compatible and whose long-range prospects are not very positive should be encouraged to think about more than just saving face or salvaging respectability. Even secular books on etiquette indicate that such a wedding should not be a large public one, but rather a private ceremony with only close family and friends. How we handle these very sensitive matters must involve us in a consideration of what kind of statement we are making to our youth and to the larger community concerning our views of Christ and His commandments.

Sessions with the pastor will include planning for the wedding. Some excellent resources are available.[1] Counseling should cover the Biblical and spiritual foundations for Christian marriage; patterns for effective communication; human sexuality in God's plan; areas for dialogue before marriage, such as family planning and birth control; a philosophy of child-rearing; the handling of finances and the accrual of debt. Reading assignments should be given in carefully chosen books.[2] Only under the most unusual circumstances should this counseling be done just before the wedding. Ample time and deliberate, unhurried discussion are essential if we are to significantly prepare couples for marriage in these complex times.

FACING THE HURTS

Fractured and fissured relationships confront us with difficult decision-making in determining who should properly be married. The pastor is not wise who plays Lone Ranger in this area. The pastor needs the counsel, wisdom and united support of the diaconate or elders when a tough call has to be made. If there is a wedding the pastor cannot in conscience perform, the pastor again needs the backing of the spiritual leadership to bear the immense and very unfair pressure which may be thrown upon him.

The remarriage of divorced people and the status of divorced persons with respect to church office and spiritual leadership are issues of considerable controversy and difference of opinion within the Christian community. Each local church should seek to come to a general position on these matters from within which specific cases can find consistent address. These matters were controversial even in Jesus' day. Divorce may not be the unforgivable sin to be sure, but in the church it does seem to be an unforgettable sin.

Beyond any doubt the Scripture sees marriage as being for life (Matthew 5:32, 33; 1 Corinthians 7:10-16; and the other passages). Jesus goes back to Moses, when marriage was declared to be indissoluble. Yet Moses allowed for divorce because of the hard hearts of the people. Some argue categorically that there can be no divorce and hence no remarriage of divorced persons (Bill Gothard, Paul Steele, Charles Ryrie, etc.),[3] while others argue on the basis of the exceptive clause in the Gospels and the Pauline privilege of 1 Corinthians 7 that when grounds for divorce do in fact exist the remarriage of the innocent party is permitted (John Murray, Jay Adams,[4] Richard DeHaan, George W. Peters,[5] etc.).

This is clearly a vexed point. The concept of "innocent party" is not easy, and yet it stands as a witness for the person who has not broken the marriage covenant. If the exception validly applies to the marriage, it necessarily applies to the issue of the remarriage of the innocent party.[6]

What about a divorce which takes place years before conversion? Romans 7:1-4 is part of an important Pauline discussion of the relationship of the believer to the Law and hence must not be used as chapter and verse in the discussion of divorce and remarriage.[7]

As far as "the husband of one wife" requirement for spiritual leaders is concerned (see 1 Timothy 3:2), some argue that this neither forbids remarriage after the death of the spouse nor remarriage after divorce for either the innocent or guilty party.[8] This is a matter which merits the most careful study in every local church. Often denominational positioning on these issues can be of immense aid in formulating local policy, but should never supplant the necessity for serious discussion and inquiry at the local level of implementation.

With the rise of the incidence of divorce among us, the urgent need for more compassionately and effectively addressing the issues of pastoral care is clear. One fellowship gives sensitive guidance when it recommends:

> When a marriage has ended in failure and there has been true repentance, there is forgiveness and the moral onus is past. When steps are taken to understand the dynamics that went into the failure of the previous marriage, and forgiveness is experienced, then that person may consider the possibility of marriage. . . . The pastor, after wise and thorough counselling, may then choose to conduct the marriage service.[9]

Both the text and the tone here are helpful.

ESTABLISHING THE HOME

The wedding itself is not primarily a performance or a spectacle of opulence. It is first and foremost a service for the worship of God in which family and friends gather joyfully around the wedded couple and commend them to God in their journey through life together as husband and wife. This understanding should be keynoted at the rehearsal. An orderly, thorough and pleasant rehearsal is essential to a meaningful wedding ceremony.

Some churches utilize a wedding hostess to advantage, but in any case the pastor should commence the rehearsal with prayer and with a clear agenda which has grown out of discussions with the couple in the course of counseling. While the rehearsal may follow the groom's dinner, there is advantage in holding the rehearsal first and the more relaxing time afterwards with its important bonding between the two families, many of whose members may not have extensive subsequent contacts because of geography.

Beginning the wedding on time is a courtesy to all and is facilitated by setting the pre-service picture-taking sufficiently early (an increasingly popular custom which allows the wedded pair to be more involved in the reception to follow). Having the organist begin the prelude twenty to thirty minutes before the wedding, using a sufficient number of ushers, and having several guest registries also assists punctuality.

The basic ingredients of the wedding ceremony are (with many common variations and local customs):

> The Prelude
> Candlelighting
> Escorting Parents and Grandparents into the Wedding Locale
> Special Music
> The Processional
> The Betrothal (Greeting questions to bride and groom, etc.)
> Congregational Hymn
> Wedding Homily
> Wedding Vows and Exchange of Rings
> Wedding Prayer—Special Music
> Pronouncement
> Unity Candle—Special Music (optional)
> Benediction
> Presentation
> Recessional

After the bedlam of bizarre wedding practices out of the sixties and early seventies, there has been a very strong move back to more traditional weddings. Yet we have emerged enriched with the conviction that all weddings should not be carbon copies, but rather each wedding service should carefully and creatively reflect the personality and uniqueness of each couple. The pastor can greatly enhance the meaningfulness and memorability of each wedding and thereby contribute significantly to the durability of the relationship.[10]

The question of whether the bride or groom should sing at the wedding or memorize their vows gets to the heart of what the wedding really is intended to be. In some cases everyone will be more relaxed without this. Very young and inexperienced children acting as ring-bearers and flower girls are sentimental favorites but are often distracting and disruptive. The serving of Communion to the wedded couple during the service seriously violates Protestant principles. Far better would be a Communion service for believers in the wedding party in a chapel or parlor of the church before the wedding proper.

The pastor and his family will want to give a gift to the wedded couple, but in the interest of practical consistency it is a good idea to present the same gift to each couple (perhaps a helpful book of daily devotional readings for the first weeks of marriage). This should be presented on the night of the rehearsal so it can be taken along as part of the trousseau for the honeymoon. Christian marriage should be Christian from the beginning.

SHARING THE HOMILY

One of the pastor's very special investments in the wedding is the wedding homily shared in the course of the service. If the average service proper is about thirty to thirty-five minutes long, the wedding homily should last about five minutes. There should be clear focus on a nugget of Scripture briefly expounded.

The homily should be warm and friendly, articulating Biblical principles for the newlyweds and for all married persons present. The homily should be personalized and Christ-honoring and should give a brief statement about how a person is rightly related to God through the Savior. The use of a text such as "Other foundation can no one lay than that which is laid, even Jesus Christ our Lord" (1 Corinthians 3:11) sets forth basic truth for marriage and for all of life. Thus we can commend our Savior to everyone present.

The homily should be optimistic in tone (this is not the time or place to belabor the decline and dissolution of the traditional family). Speak to the couple, but include in your reference truth for everyone in the congregation.

FUELING HOPES

Certainly one of the greatest blessings to be experienced in this life is to live in a happy, harmonious Christian home. Principal Raney, the Scottish divine, when going through a very difficult and stress-filled time in his career, was asked by a friend how he was making it. He replied, "What carries me through is the grace of my God and a happy

Christian home." Weddings both large and small afford the pastor-teacher incomparable opportunity to share in the profoundest experience of human existence and to contribute to the permanency and vitality of relationships which are foundational to everything we hope for in the church and in society.

This is why the celebration of wedding anniversaries are so significant. We need to highlight and honor those who reach fifty years of marriage (more and more common nowadays), those who are reaching sixty and even seventy years of marriage, etc. One couple I know who came to Christ through Evangelism Explosion wanted to publicly renew their marriage vows. What a moving time after a midweek service for the whole congregation to surround this couple with expressions of their love.

> Whom God has joined together, let no one put asunder.
> (Matthew 19:6)

WEDDING CEREMONY PROCEDURE

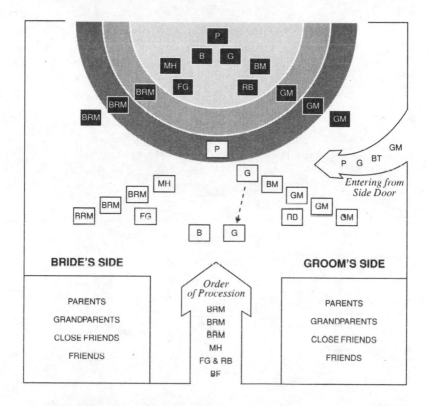

BRIDE'S SIDE

PARENTS
GRANDPARENTS
CLOSE FRIENDS
FRIENDS

GROOM'S SIDE

PARENTS
GRANDPARENTS
CLOSE FRIENDS
FRIENDS

Order of Procession

BRM
BRM
BRM
MH
FG & RB
BF

USHERING PROTOCOL
1. Groom's Grandparents
   Paternal 1st
   Maternal 2nd
2. Bride's Grandparents
   Paternal 1st
   Maternal 2nd
3. Groom's Parents
4. Bride's Mother

(Usher out in reverse order)

ALTERNATE PLAN
Pastor, Groom and Best Man from side door.

Bridesmaid and Groomsman process from back in pairs and stand together on alternating sides of altar.

KEY

Position for 1st stage of ceremony: questions and parental consent	Position for 2nd stage of ceremony: homily and vows

P	Pastor
B	Bride
G	Groom
BF	Bride with Father
FG	Flower girl
MH	Maid (Matron) of Honor
BRM	Bridesmaid
BM	Bestman
GM	Groomsman
RB	Ring-bearer

CHAPTER 19

"Man Is Destined to Die Once"

The Funeral

Death has been swallowed up in victory. . . . Where, O death, is your victory? Where, O death, is your sting? The sting of death is sin, and the power of sin is the law. But thanks be to God! He gives us the victory through our Lord Jesus Christ. (1 Corinthians 15:54b-57)

Life is real and life is earnest
And the grave is not its goal—
Dust thou art, to dust returnest,
Was not spoken of the soul.

(Henry Wadsworth Longfellow)

Let dissolution come when it will, it can do the Christian no harm, for it will be but a passage out of a prison into a palace; out of a sea of troubles into a haven of rest; out of a crowd of enemies, to an innumerable company of true, loving, and faithful friends; out of shame, reproach and contempt, into exceeding great and eternal glory. (John Bunyan)

We do not want you to be ignorant about those who fall asleep, or to grieve like the rest of men, who have no hope. (1 Thessalonians 4:13)

The pastor-teacher is continually plunged into the the difficult experiences of human existence, one of the most traumatic of which is death. Here we confront our own mortality and the brevity and transiency of all life. We are at any moment but a step from death. The ambulance siren, the news bulletin about today's plane crash, the day's obituaries—all remind us of the utter inevitability of death.

While George Bernard Shaw used to say that no young man really believes he is going to die, the fact is that this dread visitor does not respect persons but rather comes for young and old, rich and poor.[1] In all denominations and within all philosophies of health, the mortality rate is running at 100 percent. Every day we turn a page in the book of our lives, and not one of us knows how many pages remain.

Death is called in Scripture "the last enemy" (1 Corinthians 15:26). Even in cases of long terminal illness, death is a shock. We can never become accustomed to it because it contravenes the original intention of the Creator. The life-urge is very deep-dyed within us. Death is the result of sin in the race, a physical sign of human estrangement from God (cf. Genesis 3:3; Romans 5:13-31).

We properly revel in life but find ourselves encased in a chrysalis of clay, a mortal coil which often elicits from us Augustine's question: is ours a living death or a dying life? Throughout church history Christians have often reflected on death, as for example in Jeremy Taylor's *Holy Dying*. But our culture prefers to deny death, to use euphemisms which avoid facing the reality of death.[2] The Christian communicator needs to help people prepare for death, not only in terms of their eternal destiny, but in the sense of coming to terms with the issues surrounding death and separation from loved ones. Most Americans have life insurance and provide for accident and health contingencies. Pastors need to encourage people of all ages to prepare for the experience of death.

DEATH: THE EVENT

What the death of the organism really is, and when and how death occur, are matters of serious medical discussion and scientific inquiry.[3] Vexed ethical issues are being raised as life-support systems are able to prolong a vegetative existence which can scarcely be called human. The pastor may well be part of family discussions with a medical team on whether extraordinary methods of extending "life" should be abandoned for a brain-dead patient. Many personal and emotional factors must be weighed carefully. For the Christian "to depart and be with Christ is far better" (Philippians 1:33), but this magnificent hope does not preclude the anguish of painful decision-making.

When news comes of a death, the pastor is well-advised to attempt an immediate personal contact. I have never regretted going to the bereaved as soon as possible. Sometimes notification does not come until later through the mortician. So much depends on the relationship of the deceased to the church and innumerable individual scenarios. At this stage the pastor's function is to be a comforting and strengthening presence in the shock of death. It is not necessary to say much. There is a right time for Scripture sentences and brief ejaculatory prayers. The bereaved will already be going over and over the last circumstances and the immediate situation, and this is altogether normal.

There is great advantage in meeting with the family at the funeral home for the planning of the memorial service. Customs and traditions vary considerably from city to rural and from one part of the country to another. In large metropolitan areas the visitation the night before is much more significant than the service itself because of the logistical problems of people taking a full day from work for the funeral. The church is the ideal place for the funeral of a member of the congregation, but a service in a mortuary is preferred by some because of greater privacy for the mourners and more convenient logistics.

Many times the issue of an autopsy has to be faced with the family, and the wisdom of medical data needs to be weighed by some family members as against the whole idea of a postmortem examination of the body. The vast majority of funeral directors are honorable and upright professionals, but occasionally a surviving spouse needs to be guarded against overspending for a funeral service which becomes a vehicle for the assuaging of guilt, true or false in nature. Funerals come in all price ranges, but they do represent one of the most significant capital outlays made in life, next only to automobile and residence.

Funerals are a rite of cultural passage, and the customs in a community should not be thoughtlessly flouted. People sometimes pay heavily for such deviations in terms of guilt and regret. Fortunately more and more people are prearranging many aspects of their funeral and burial, indicating elements they wish included in the funeral service. The pastor needs to be prepared to gently lead in the identification of the components of the service, the interment and graveside service, and a fellowship hour following at the church or home. The latter is a very important kind of personal reentry into the familiar circle of loved ones and friends and should not be avoided.

The coming of the family to view the body before the visitation is an especially difficult time, and the pastor can have a significant ministry if it is possible to share in that experience. A special little family service conducted by the pastor is becoming more common, and brief remarks at the visitation are occasionally in order when the funeral itself will be small. A special service for very young children can also be very helpful. The viewing of the body may be a very positive teaching time for children, but very young children at the funeral service itself can become problematic. Clearly there are many inappropriate pastoral functions in conjunction with death. But who can better be helpful when the "king of terrors" stalks abroad than the representatives of the living Lord Jesus Christ?

GRIEF: THE EXPERIENCE

All who minister to the dying and the bereaved need to understand something of the psycho-dynamics of grief. Grief has been defined as "a whole cluster of adjustments, apprehensions and uncertainties that strike life in its forward progress and make it difficult to reorganize and redirect the energies of life."[4] The exact form of the grief experience and its progression are impossible to predict. Some very frail souls seem to find the most unusual resources and maintain balance and resilience beyond anything we would have imagined. Other more stalwart individuals of whom we might have predicted great sturdiness never seem to recover total equilibrium after the death of a dear one.

Paul Irion in his classic treatment cites as common experiences of the bereaved tearfulness, bewilderment and loneliness, fear, ambivalence, hostility, guilt, idealization.[5] Underreaction is perhaps a greater danger than overreaction. There is a cycle of grief work which must be accomplished. We all need to work through the loss in our own way. We must allow and indeed encourage expression, not suppression. Being stoic and strong may be seen by some Christians as part of their spiritual duty and testimony. It is dangerous to stifle grief and sorrow, because in all likelihood they will come back later to haunt us and demand payment.

While no law (human or divine) requires the embalming and viewing of the body, there is immense psychological and emotional help for us in coming to terms with the fact that death has in fact occurred. Certainly there are cases when long terminal illness or death in an accident or fire makes the viewing of the body questionable or impossible. Death denial is so persistent a problem, however, that at least some family members ought to inspect the remains and bear witness to the actuality of death. In some cultures one family member remains at the grave to actually witness the covering of the grave.

For this reason a visitation time prior to the service or the night previous with the casket open for viewing becomes a significant part of reality acceptance. The whole cycle of grief involves holistic experience—physical, emotional, spiritual. Weakness, anger, and a bizarre sense of unreality are not uncommon. Such phenomena in varying degrees will normally continue for months and occasionally for several years. Holidays and high days in the church year will pose particular crises; birthdays and anniversaries are especially difficult. The entire social milieu changes upon the death of a loved one, and innumerable tasks of arranging Social Security and pension benefits, disposing of effects, considering alterations in living arrangements all press in unrelentingly upon those already physically, emotionally and spiritually drained.

It is little wonder that strong support systems are necessary in the family and in the church. Certain anniversaries of the death and funeral should be carefully noted by the pastor. A visit, card or phone call on such days afford an unsurpassed opportunity for the sensitive pastor to share the ministry of the Word and prayer.

A very live issue on the contemporary scene has to do with the increasing move toward cremation in our culture. Many cultures have practiced cremation, especially where limited burial space made disposition of the body difficult. In the increasing mobility of our society and with its lack of roots, the appeal of the old family burial plot is lessening. On the North Shore of Chicago where we live one third of the "burials" are cremations. Some Christians have compunctions about cremation, feeling it represents a violation of the body as the "temple of the Holy Spirit" (1 Corinthians 3:16). Actually it would appear that cremation is just the hastening of the natural process through calcination. Again, if any aspect of cremation represents a problem to the survivors, it would be a serious mistake. Disposition of the "cremains" can also represent a problem. Certainly cremation does not pose any problem for God in the resurrection.

COMFORT: THE EXPRESSION

The funeral service should not be long, and the committal service at the grave is rapidly becoming attenuated or for the family only. A church funeral for the believer should include congregational singing and will be a little longer than that held elsewhere. (A service in a mortuary should generally be half an hour in length with about fifteen minutes for the message.)

Happy is the pastor who can personalize the funeral through a real acquaintance with the deceased. Some timely phone calls to old friends can further enrich the preacher's preparation. The funeral for a believer takes on an entirely different tone and is the occasion for properly affirming the centralities of Christian faith and conviction. While this personalization is desirable and helpful and an obituary is necessary, the focus should move to Christ and the hope of the gospel.

Flowery eulogies are risky since family members may have unflattering knowledge unknown to others.

A typical order of service is as follows:

> Prelude
> Scripture Sentences and the Call to Worship
> Hymn
> Special Music
> Scripture Lesson
> Special Music
> Obituary
> Sermon
> Closing Prayer and Benediction

The funeral message should use a brief text as the focus of meditation. Every funeral message should make the way of salvation plain. The facing of eternity at death is one of the signal opportunities for the Christian proclaimer to share the Good News of Jesus Christ to people who are more than ordinarily reflective about spiritual things.

John Ruskin once said, "Of all the pulpits from which the human voice goes forth, there is none from which it reaches so far as from the grave." Now is the time to quietly but confidently herald Christian certainties about the life hereafter in sharp contrast to the speculations of those without divine revelation as we have it in Holy Scripture.[6] Scrounging about for evidence of life after death from near-death experiences is flimsy and unsatisfying. Here is where probing study of what Scripture teaches can be shared meaningfully. The Bible does not tell us a lot about Heaven (perhaps because then we would do little but think about it), but there is rich and sufficient disclosure that will bring immense comfort to the grieving believer.[7]

In younger suburban congregations there will not be many funerals. In older central-city and small-town congregations there may be numerous funerals. The pastor is advised to develop a funeral notebook in which seminal thoughts and texts are placed as in a plant nursery.

Then when the critical moment of need suddenly comes, the preacher can take a stroll into the greenhouse and see which seedlings are promising and appropriate. Numerous practical helps are available to prime the pump.[8] Our message is for the living—and what a choice opportunity we have.

The graveside service, with the pastor always standing at the foot of the casket, offers us additional opportunity to share portions of Scripture and prayers, concluding with a brief committal to God. Traditionally dirt or sand have been used in this ritual: "Earth to earth, ashes to ashes, dust to dust." I like to use a single red or white rose, but this is a matter of personal preference.

DIFFICULT CASES: THE EXCEPTIONAL[9]

Every pastor sometimes faces a particularly nettlesome funeral. Twisted and distorted human lives come to an end, as do all human lives. Sometimes we do not even know or have never met the persons whose last rites we share. Yet even such a difficult situation gives us an opportunity to share Christ, and if the survivors do not want this, they should seek another clergyman because we dare not deny what we are. Difficult cases may include the following:

1) *The unbeliever.* We must never try to preach anyone into the Kingdom. We must commit all of whom we have doubt or no knowledge into the hands of God who always does justly. "Will not the Judge of all the earth do right?" (Genesis 18:25b). Appropriate address concerning God's available strength and grace can be made to the survivors, but a good word for Jesus Christ as Savior and Lord also needs to be spoken. Even in the funeral of a rascal, we need to faithfully point to the Savior.

Not a few preachers today are facing funeral services for victims of AIDS. We may or may not know anything about the spiritual state of the deceased, but will find a very special context for the sharing of the Good News of God's grace. (Regarding AIDS we must remember that hemophiliacs and others can contract this dread disease through transfusions and accidental infection.)

2) *The suicide.* The tragic spiral of calamity and the suspension of rational process leading to suicide is unspeakably sad and lays heavy guilt and stigma on the survivors. The unfounded sentiment that all suicides are damned reflects a sub-Biblical understanding as to what constitutes the basis of a right relationship with God. In the case of the suicide of a believer, we can face the tormenting questions of the sur-

viving family from the standpoint of God's love from which we cannot be severed (cf. Romans 8:31-39). In the instance of an unbeliever's suicide, we can invite all present to cast themselves upon God, from whom alone we can find solace.

3) *The infant.* The funeral of a little infant or fetus becomes indescribably difficult as in many cases the mother cannot be present. Usually this is a very small service, often only a graveside service. Many funeral directors donate the little casket. Scripture does not really address the matter of infant salvation directly, but in most theological systems (apart from the highly sacramental) all infants are believed to go to Heaven, not having consciously rejected Christ. The reading of comforting and strengthening Scriptures, along with compassionate prayer, constitute this brief service.

The situations for ministry in "the shadow of death" are as various as can be imagined. I have never conducted a funeral, even if only the undertaker and myself were present, but what tears came to my eyes and what a lump was in my throat as I contemplated the mysteries of life and death. Yet how privileged and rich are we who proclaim the living Christ, the One who tunneled through the grave and now exclaims, "I was dead but now am alive forever and forever!" (Revelation 1:18).

CHAPTER 20

"The Prayer Offered in Faith Will Make the Sick Person Well"

Anointing for Healing and Exorcism

If all hearts were open and all desires known—as they would be if people showed their souls—how many gapings, sighings, clenched fists, knotted brows, broad grins, and red eyes would we see in the market-place. (Thomas Hardy in his diary for August 8, 1908)

Is any one of you sick? He should call the elders of the church to pray over him and anoint him with oil in the name of the Lord. (James 5:14)

Remember not, Lord Christ, our offenses, nor the offenses of our forefathers; neither reward us according to our sins. Spare us, good Lord, spare thy people, whom thou hast redeemed with thy most precious blood, and by thy mercy preserve us for ever.

    From all evil and wickedness; from sin; from the crafts and assaults of the devil; and from everlasting damnation, GOOD LORD, DELIVER US. ("The Great Litany," *The Book of Common Prayer*)

A primary focus of the ministry of the pastor-teacher is the care and cure of souls. While essentially spiritual in nature because the human predicament is basically spiritual, this ministry is not uni-dimensional. "We have this treasure in clay jars" (2 Corinthians 4:7). Sin and the Fall have implicated and involved the entire created order, and creation too will partake of redemption and restoration (cf. Romans 8:18-25).

Thus we believe in the resurrection of the body. The redemption which is in Christ Jesus has addressed the essential spiritual alienation and estrangement brought by sin and, further, will extend to every trace of sin's influence and effect (with the single exception of the "everlasting punishment" meted out to the Devil, all his minions, and those who remain outside of Christ).

Christian ministry is thus to be coextensive with Christ's ministry in its objectives and comprehensiveness. We are to be concerned with the whole person because of the unity of human personality. What transpires in one aspect of human experience will have impact on every other aspect. Physical problems affect spiritual life, and spiritual struggles have psycho-physical implications. Jesus gave attention to the whole person, and a proper holistic approach to pastoral care will proceed on the basis of His example and teaching. A satisfying definition of the ministry of the cure of souls therefore has the shape of something like: "consisting of helping acts, done by representative Christian persons, directed toward the healing, sustaining, guiding and reconciling of troubled persons whose troubles arise in the context of ultimate meaning and concerns."[1]

This ministry is carried out in the tension between the "now" and the "not yet," the fallenness of this present evil age and the breakthrough into this age by the "powers of the age to come" (Hebrews 6:5). There is an overlap within which we joyously labor. For example, the eschatological verdict of the Judgment is already pronounced in the believer's justification (Romans 8:1). Ultimate and final deliverance awaits our resurrection and seeing Jesus Christ face to face (1 John 3:2). Yet there are anticipations of that ultimate wholeness even now. This is the frame of reference for our delving into the place of healing in ministry today.

THE BREADTH OF OUR FALLENNESS

The undeniable fact of our human fallenness is demonstrated in the multiplication of human misery and the prevalence of sickness, pain and death everywhere on Planet Earth. John Milton in *Paradise Lost* depicts the archangel Michael showing fallen Adam the consequences of primal sin in subsequent human experience:

> *Before his eyes appeared, sad, noysom, dark,*
> *A Lazar-house it seemed, wherein were laid*

Numbers of all diseas'd, all maladies
  Of gastly Spasm, or racking torture, qualmes
Of heart-sick Agonie, all feavarous kinds,
  Convulsions, Epilepsies, fierce Catarrhs,
Intestin Stone and Ulcer, Colic pangs,
  Daemonic Phrenzie, moaping Melancholie
And Moon struck madness, pining Atrophie,
  Marasmus, and wide wasting Pestilence,
Dropsies, and Asthmas, and Joint-racking Rheums
  Dire was the tossing, deep the groans, despair
Tended the sick busiest from Couch to Couch;
  And over them triumphant Death his Dart
Shook, but laid to strike, though oft invok't
  With vows, as their chief good, and final hope.
Sight to deform what heart of Rock could long
  Drie-ey'd behold? Adam could not, but wept.[2]

This continues to be the venue of ministry as modern man, having deposed deity and all finality, finds himself in a universe populated only by whirling stars and circling atoms, with all those around him as totally lost as he is. Thus Richard Rubenstein laments: "We stand in a cold, silent unfeeling cosmos, unaided by any purposive power beyond our own resources." Ortega y Gasset is right that "Twentieth-century man is becoming a technologically competent barbarian." In this unrelieved downdraft of despair, we have the privilege of sharing "the joyful sound" that "Jesus saves."

One very positive emergent out of the malaise of gloom in our time has been an increasing tendency to acknowledge the ontic reality of evil. Myopic notions of the inevitability of progress and the perfectibility of human nature have been dashed on the rocks of empirical reality. Public Television has featured a series on "Facing Evil" which challenged the prevailing modern penchant for overlooking or trivializing the "formidable power of Evil" and asked the question, "Is there any end to Evil?"[3]

The post-secular mind, so vulnerable to New-Age vagaries, is nonetheless far less likely to dismiss out of hand the existence of Satan and the realm of the demonic. What the Bible teaches about the origin of evil in relation to the revolt of Satan and the involvement and fall of one third of the angels of Heaven (Revelation 12:4) is essential background to any understanding of what ministry is today.[4]

The fact is, true Christian ministry of necessity involves spiritual warfare (cf. Ephesians 6:10-18). As ministers of Christ we are contesting the enemy's control of persons and territory. Scripture shares with us the schemes and strategems of the enemy of our souls. In ministry we are challenging that foe's dominion in and through the power of the Lord God who reigns! In his *Screwtape Letters*, C. S. Lewis reflects on the tactics and wiles of Satan, and in *Out of the Silent Planet* he argues that Satan ruled the world before the creation of man. Satan's subsequent revolt against God caused the earth to be abnormal, "the silent planet." Redemption in Christ is God's' reclamation and retrieval project.

It seems that in our times Satan has come out of the closet and has become more bold, perhaps sensing that his time is short. In Christian ministry we always operate as fifth columnists. A recent major study of Martin Luther sees the great Reformer's ministry as a struggle with the Devil "in the shadow of the Last Days and the imminence of eternity."[5] Luther threw an inkwell at his nemesis and contended constantly with the subtle, pervasive onslaughts of the "god of this world" (2 Corinthians 4:4). We are no less in enemy territory.

THE BLESSING OF WHOLENESS

Clearly in Scripture there have been and are certain times and ages when God sovereignly releases healing and miracle power in an extraordinary way. In Old Testament times, the days of the Exodus and the times of Elijah and Elisha were the two chief epochs of signs and wonders. The days of the Savior's ministry on earth, and particularly the early experiences of the infant church, likewise became signal seasons of power and miracle. The miracles of Jesus mirror His great compassion and deep sympathy as "the great Physician," but these miracles have evidential and instructional value as well. The works of Jesus both accredited His claims and were vehicles of His teaching.

No exegetical evidence is convincing that gifts of healings or any spiritual gifts have been withdrawn. Rather, the provision of all of these gifts for the upbuilding of the Body of Christ under God's sovereign allocation seems to be quite clear (cf. 1 Corinthians 12:1-11). I feel that both B. B. Warfield and Sir Robert Anderson overstate the case against any expectation of God's healing today.[6]

On the other hand, the use of a Book of Acts hermeneutic or a Gospel hermeneutic to argue that valid ministry is the precise reduplication of what we see the apostles doing or what we see the Lord Jesus doing, even to the point of expecting resurrections from the dead, is, I feel, going much beyond what the Scriptures would have us expect in terms of what is normative for ministry today.

Some claim healing as a Christian's birthright through the atonement of Christ. These argue, "On Calvary, in His own body, He bare all our bodily liabilities due to sin. Everything that was ever against you, every claim against your body, was met by His body. And there is now no reason why that body of yours should be punished a second time for anything which His body has borne already once for all. The atonement of Christ takes away sin and the consequences of sin for every believer who accepts Him."[7]

While we would recognize that the partial and ultimate deliverance of the body from every mark and consequence of human fallenness is mediated in the final analysis through the merits of Christ's shed blood, it would be a serious mistake to infer that full physical health belongs to every believer through the Cross because it would then inevitably follow that every believer should be delivered from physical death. The mortality rate, even for the most spiritual Christians, is running 100 percent worldwide. No one has more thoughtfully wrestled through the exegesis of the appropriate texts than John Stott, who insightfully shows that the death and resurrection of Jesus Christ do influence our bodies here and now (cf. 2 Corinthians 4:10, 11, 16; Romans 8:11), but that we may not legitimately argue that full physical health belongs to the believer now because of Calvary.[8]

Beyond question God permits sickness, as, for example, with Job and Paul. Sometimes God sends physical malady as a judgment (cf. 2 Samuel 12:15; 2 Kings 15:5; Acts 12:20-25; 1 Corinthians 11:30). Scripture speaks of affliction as being "for the glory of God" (John 9:1-3). Sometimes God is pleased to heal; sometimes He delays healing. J. Sidlow Baxter is correct when he argues that while God has promised to save all who come to him through Christ, He has not promised to heal all.[9]

But God is not indifferent to the plight of His creatures. The Apostle John authentically reflects every spiritual practitioner's concern when he says to Gaius, the elder: "Dear friend, I pray that you may enjoy good health and that all may go well with you, even as your soul is getting along well" (3 John 2). Indeed there are six kinds of divine healing (though in the absolute sense all healing is divine).

1) *Psychosomatic healing.* Some of our problems do not have an organic basis. They result from tensions and stress. The diversification of stress agents, along with better physical and mental health habits, will give relief.

2) *Medical healing.* God uses medical science. Ambrose Pare, the Frenchman who is sometimes called the first modern surgeon, used to say: "I dressed and sutured him, but God healed him." Praise God for good doctors and dentists.

3) *Healing through prayer.* Many have testified to God's healing touch as they came to the Father (cf. John 16:23-28).[10]

4) *Healing from God as James 5:14, 15 is observed.* We shall speak of this more fully subsequently.

5) *The gifts of healings.* Some are specially gifted from the Spirit for special healing ministries.

6) *The ultimate healing.* No one of us will be completely healed until we see Christ and "behold his face in righteousness."

If God delays or denies relief from any affliction we must recognize, as George Müller did, that if there were a better thing for us, He would give it to us because He loves us and cares for us. Pastorally and Biblically none of us could be better off than in the sovereign hands of our gracious God and Father.

THE BREAKTHROUGH OF DELIVERANCE

Too frequently we have left it up to extremists and exhibitionists to offer a significant holistic solution for the human situation. But, thank God, there has arisen within many fellowships a networking of support groups and opportunities to find the healing touch of God. For example, the International Order of Saint Luke the Physician is a Christ-centered, Biblically-based movement in one denomination.[11]

Many congregations provide opportunity for special prayer and anointing for the sick at a special prayer-time set aside for this purpose or after a stated service. On other occasions church elders are called to a home or hospital situation. I always have a cruse of oil (generally olive oil) available. Such an anointing should never be pressed on anyone. Certainly within a context of clear Biblical teaching on this subject, our constituents need to be informed of the meaning of James 5.

Confession and the forgiveness of sin are clearly involved in this type of situation. With the object of concern either seated or kneeling, the anointing with oil in the name of the Lord is accompanied by prayers. Sometimes God will grant a very special touch. One older brother was delivered from fear of the surgery which had been prescribed. Another sister was delivered from bitterness and resentment toward God for a deteriorating disability. Nothing is ever the same after we have prayed in faith.

God can and does heal. I do not believe we have the right to demand anything from God. It is not a cop-out to condition all of our prayers according to the will of God. He knows best. Also, sometimes we pray amiss, and mercifully He does not give us what we seek. Hezekiah sought healing from God and would have been better off had he not received it.

We also need to recognize that signs and wonders are often seen more frequently where gospel showers are falling for the first time. Also, "lying wonders" are wrought by our adversary (cf. 2 Thessalonians 2:9; Revelation 13:3ff.). So we need to be careful and discerning.

THE BOLDNESS OF CHRISTIAN CONFIDENCE

Out on the front-lines we face spiritual antagonists who will yield ground to the forces of righteousness only with the greatest reluctance and the fiercest resistance. Every servant of Christ faces this battle. Every pastor needs the whole armor of God and a continuing spirit of prayer.[12]

We need to be aware of the strategies of our foe.[13] "We are not unaware of his schemes" (2 Corinthians 2:11b). Good solid, basic works on demonology can help us, but there is also the danger of becoming too engrossed in the study of evil. We must not think about the Devil more than we think about Christ. It is advisable to take ten looks at the Cross for each time we look at ourselves or at our enemies.

We used to hear occasionally about overt demonic activity, especially from our missionaries. Pioneer missionaries such as John Nevius gave us some of the first helpful analysis of demonization in a time when modern rationalism was leading many to deny the existence of the demonic.[14] Now the existence of "principalities and powers" and their malignant influence upon human existence is widely recognized. The Cardinal Archbishop of New York has recently identified much heavy metal music as demonic, and two exorcisms in this regard have recently been conducted.

The decisive victory of the Lord Jesus Christ over Satan on the Cross is the basis of the deliverance we offer and experience (Colossians 2:15). The confrontation we may confidently press is in and through Christ (2 Corinthians 10:4, 5). People today can be inhabited by a demon or demons just as described in the New Testament. Such evil spirits can be exorcised. However, exorcism should never be undertaken lightly, hastily or carelessly. Spiritual leaders should spend much time in prayer and waiting on the Spirit before undertaking this challenge. They should then confidently, in the name of Jesus and under the protection of the blood of Jesus, order the unclean spirits to depart. Spiritual leaders can expect to increasingly encounter overt manifestation of the demonic in our culture. We need to be ready.

Christians cannot be inhabited by demons, in my judgment, because that would mean that the indwelling Holy Spirit is put down.[15] I do believe, however, that Christians can be oppressed by demons and seriously harassed, and prayer is the recourse for deliverance.

Praise be to God that believers are on the winning side. There is no question as to the ultimate outcome. To minister for Christ is to do battle with an horrendous enemy of great power and high intelligence. *But he is a defeated foe!* "But thanks be to God, who always leads us in triumphal procession in Christ and through us spreads everywhere the fragrance of the knowledge of him!" (2 Corinthians 2:14).

V
Rethinking

CHAPTER 21

"See to It He Has Nothing to Fear While He Is with You"

The Pastor and the "Fit"

Blessed is that ministry of which Christ is all! (Charles H. Spurgeon)

The one who profits me is the one whose ministry brings most of the awe of a holy and sovereign God on my heart, who discovers to me my sinfulness and my failures, who conveys most light on the path of duty, who makes Christ most precious to me, who encourages me to press forward along the narrow way. (Arthur W. Pink)

The Holy Spirit is indeed no other than God himself approaching us and grasping us; he is our God, the God acting with us and in us through his Word and choosing us to be his children. God is the Creator and Father over us; in his Son he is also with us, and in the Holy Spirit he is in us, in order to open our eyes and ears so that we learn to recognize, love and fear him as our Father in his being with us in the Son. (Eduard Thurneysen in *A Theology of Pastoral Care*)

In this last section, we set ourselves to the task of formulating the outlines of a spiritual strategy for the last decade of the twentieth century and on into the twenty-first century. Nothing can absolve us from the onerous task and the rigors of rethinking and reevaluating the components of Christian ministry. What ministry is and what ministry ought to be and can be impinge heavily on pastoral leadership. The "fit" of pastoral leadership is the particular focus of this chapter.

Times of pastoral change raise all of the issues. The seasoned pastor-teacher with a positive track record agonizes over a new set of expectations and wonders if there really is as much flex and vision as the pastoral search committee assures him there is. The process under any polity is painful and arduous. The theological neophyte finds himself or herself in a swirling vortex of major adjustments far from the familiar setting and frequently in a totally different societal and cultural climate. The professorial models in academia have little relevance in the rough-and-tumble everyday world. Under any circumstances the fledgling must molt for a while before the local rhythms of ministry are established. This is as it always has been, but some things are changing and must be taken into account in the projection of a wise and adequate strategy.

THE MILIEU

Seasons of restlessness are found in any relationship of ministry—in pastor and people alike. The Apostle Paul was concerned about young Timothy's reception at Corinth, given the shyness and reserve of Timothy. This is expressed in Paul's words to the Corinthians: "See to it that he has nothing to fear while he is with you, for he is carrying on the work of the Lord, just as I am. No one, then, should refuse to accept him" (1 Corinthians 16:10, 11a). A congregation should be exercised not only over the ministry which pastors are rendering to the church, but should be equally concerned about what kind of ministry the congregation is rendering to the pastors and their families.

We observe a mounting climate of tension and turbulence on the local church scene in regard to pastoral leadership. A sharp increase in forced terminations, rapid turnover, and difficulties in placement are all symptomatic of the developing situation. The reasons are not difficult to identify. Greater upward mobility and more assertive lay leadership are part of the mix. Nonadaptive church forms lock many a pastor into a vise of frustration. Mega-church models and church growth stereotypes drive many a spiritual leader to an unrealistic and impractical level of expectation. "Success" becomes more important than service.[1] Lack of serious reflection on the transferability of popular models to a local situation is bound to court folly and lead to dead-ends. Apathy, which Harvey Cox calls the sin of our times, hangs like a deadly fog over many a local assembly and is calculated to trigger intermittent episodes of pastoral malaise or some grand blowup in sheer desperation.

No one has been more helpful in analyzing aspects of the current scene than Lyle Schaller. In a recent volume he shares what he sees to be fundamental shifts taking place right now in parish ministry. *It's a Different World*, he argues.[2] And he is altogether correct in his diagnosis. Schaller argues that television has changed the comparison base, and the local pastor is now put up against national figures and personalities rather than over against neighboring functionaries. The erosion of denominational and congregational loyalties, with more people at cabins in the summer and in the sun-belt in the winter, thins out even high holy day support, to the point that traditional Holy Week and Easter musical programs are poorly attended.

Schaller also cites the decline in family stability, feminization of the church, more working wives, less permanent relationships, more competition in a "thirty-one flavors" range of choices as all contributing to the demand for greater emphasis on competence, personality and managerial performance on the part of the pastor. Add to this the "gridlock" which has gripped American's time investments, less homogeneity in the local church, more demands for counseling, shrinking rural and small-town economies in the wake of massive urbanization. The fact is, many local congregations are in the clutches of social and economic upheavals which make their traditional ministries and stabilities up for grabs.

This all boils down to, as one writer put it, "Times of Vast Change Buffet Clergy." This religion editor went on to say: "Also disappearing is religion's tolerance of bumbling, inarticulate and incompetent clergy. Congregations will put increasing pressure on their paid staff members to work efficiently and effectively. Banal sermonizing will not be tolerated."[3]

THE MATCH

As Adam and Eve left the Garden of Eden, G. K. Chesterton imagines, Adam may have said, "Remember, my dear, we live in an age of transition." Making the ministerial match has always represented a major challenge. In whatever polity and in the use of whatever process, seeking the right "fit" is harrowing and awesome in its implications for so many people—not least the pastor and his family. Even denominational fellowships with their computerized profiles face the nightmare of mustard and chocolate cake—each is fine in its own right, but together they make a ghastly combination.

Here our belief in the faithful ministry of the Holy Spirit, while not precluding the possibility of a mismatch, strengthens and assures us that He whose church it is can be counted on in this most crucial enterprise. Frequently the viewing of videotapes, or at least listening to taped sermons, is the first step. Candidature still wisely includes preaching to the congregation, although it is universally recognized that any preacher has at least one good one sermon up his sleeve. The pulpit presence of the prospective pastor is an important step in the "courtship." Even more important is the established track record of the candidate.

Preliminary interviews are now customary, and a visit by the entire family is generally made. A good self-study by the prospective pastor is a necessary prerequisite for significant conversation about the church and its future. On the part of the church, a congregation needs to know itself and where it wants to go, and yet needs to balance that expectation with a respect for gifts and training in a leader whose vision may need to correct and inform stated goals as well as to inspire and fuel their implementation.

The candidate should become acquainted with all the data a local Chamber of Commerce can furnish. Ministry, after all, is not in a barren vacuum, but in a social, economic and political environment. Beyond the statistical data available for the church and the community, what about the school system—public and parochial, morale and tone in education, etc.? It is prudent to talk to denominational officials, neighboring pastors, and others who may possess helpful insights into a given local situation. Discussion with the former pastor may be helpful but must be weighed with other evidence as to the state of the church.

Interviews should be open and candid. The candidate should ask questions as well as answer them. I recall being asked by a search committee what my salary-package expectations were. My reply was, "I would be happy with the average compensation earned by those in this room." As part of the interviewing process the candidate should:

1) *Assess the spiritual climate and mood in the congregation.*

2) *Seek some basic and meaningful understanding of the dynamics of governance.* Is there an unofficial power structure beyond what is represented in the elected leadership of the church? Who are the power brokers, the "tribal chiefs," etc.?

3) *Evaluate the church's past and present philosophy of ministry.*

These are the major considerations in determining "fit" in this "marriage." Obsession with too much fine detail is irrelevant. The basics of the situation are determinative.

Unfortunately some churches are going back to having a series of candidates vie with one another for the call. Perhaps a church has been scalded by a bad experience and so becomes indecisive. But it is unfair to pit candidates against each other. Further, the vote may be divided, so no one is called. This is a sure way to produce fragmentation or strife.

Another lamentable tendency (usually fostered by high-powered entrepreneurs who insist on a managerial model taken from the world of business and industry) is to "buy" a candidate with an astronomical salary package which is way out of balance for ministers in general.

Generally speaking, the pastor search committee should be broadly representative without being too large to be effective.

Congregations are becoming understandably skeptical of ministers who decline a call because "God has told me my work is not done" in their current church and then a month later accept a larger situation without delay. Pastors should never court calls or play games with calls. To accept a call as God's will and then renege only compounds the clergy credibility crisis. Of course, search committees need to scrupulously observe confidentiality in the whole process. Once a pastor engages in serious discussion with another congregation, he makes a statement to his own congregation. Thank God for the ministry of the Spirit of God in all of this or wherever would we be.

THE MARRIAGE

The launch of a ministry is of such importance that it merits careful consideration as to just when and how that important beginning is to take place. As in the candidating sermons, initial discourse should treat the great centralities of the faith and not involve peripheral or bizarre elements. These early occasions should be reassuring to the faithful respecting the foundational commitments of this servant of God to Christ and His Word. These are not the times for radical experimentation. A suitable installation or induction service also helps set the tone for a new ministry.

Helpful materials are available to assist pastors and their families both in concluding a ministry and beginning a new one.[4] A time of pastoral change is a difficult and dangerous time for a congregation. Some members seem to disengage while the church is without a pastor, while others take hold of the burdens and tasks which open up in the absence of a senior shepherd. The day of the three-month notice and a long "lame-duck" period are increasingly less frequent as modern transportation makes supply more accessible. The advantage of an intentional interim pastorate, especially where there has been particular tension and difficulty in the church, seems to be more and more widely used.

As soon as the pastor's resignation is announced, a totally new situation is in place. This is why resignations should not be read after the

Sunday morning sermon (thus totally obliterating any value from the worship service or the preaching), but rather at a business meeting or by letter to the entire congregation. Leaving a congregation involves a joint grief experience, and symptoms similar to bereavement are not uncommon among pastor and family as well as among parishioners. This is a trying time.

Time and space are important in effecting the transition. Roy M. Oswald of the Alban Institute recommends that a departing pastor write a pastoral "obituary" in the interests of healthy closure. He warns against riding Long Ranger-like off into the dust before people have a chance for appropriate expressions of appreciation.[5]

Generally we have counseled caution in making too many drastic changes as the new ministry begins. Some disagree, arguing that the new pastor should strike while the iron is hot and that if he doesn't make changes while the situation is still malleable, those changes will in all likelihood never be made. Such a view is too cynical. A couple of factors argue for gradualism in introducing change.

1) Does the new pastor understand the situation well enough to propose and implement immediate change? This is certainly true of the incumbent ministering staff. While there is some advantage in hiring a whole new staff when the new pastor comes, continuity has advantage because the whole matter of what kind of a staff should be enlisted will hinge on a careful study of the current situation. These need to be unhurried and deliberate decisions. The new pastor's major input is essential, but this input needs to be intelligent and informed. What's the hurry?

2) Precipitous change and radical discontinuity threaten to violate a basic canon of ministerial ethics. Too immediate changes easily become a judgment and criticism of one's predecessor. We have the right to be what God made us to be—unique individuals—but we should not imply in any way that the Lord has not used the former leadership. We have the right to expect no interference from the pastor who has followed God's call to leave, but we only undermine our own effectiveness with those for whom he was a conduit of blessing if we make disparaging comments about this or that which has been the custom.

Pastoral leadership must always be seen as *process*. This process necessarily involves careful and prayerful preparation. Acquaintance with the parish and its situation is prerequisite to genuine progress. Thoughtful and constructive preaching from the Word (for example, taking something very basic and principial such as Philippians for Sunday morning exposition) affords the new shepherd opportunity to touch a wide range of themes which are of abiding relevance for the congregation orienting itself to the new challenge.

THE MATURATION

The whole matter of tenure and length of stay seems to be caught up increasingly in the flux and ferment of our times. Very few pastor-teachers seem to be meant to have a lifelong ministry in a single place. The weaknesses of the pastor generally become the weaknesses of the congregation. Succession is difficult. One brother who had a very distinguished lifelong ministry in a single pastoral charge admitted to me that if he had the chance to do it over again, he would do it differently. Why? "The problem is, the congregation got old along with me."

When is it time to go? How many years should a pastor stay in a given church? When we are younger, we lean toward shorter stays. As we mature, we tend to stay longer. Length of time in number of years is artificial as a criterion. I prefer to think in terms of chapters in a ministry. On what chapter are we working? Is that chapter completed? No one ever truly finishes the work in a given place. There is always so much more to be done. The questions is: have we finished a chapter—what should the next chapter be—are we the persons to embark upon that chapter?

Sometimes a pastor-teacher can stay too long. It is better to leave a little too early than a little too late. But how shall we judge this? The fact that a larger and more attractive opportunity presents itself is not automatic evidence that a move is mandated, for God does not always call us to something larger.

One thing is sure: a move involves cutting the ties where we are and accepting a new opportunity elsewhere. Timing in relation to the life of the church, the experience of one's own family, and the readiness of one's own heart for the new challenge must all be considered. Present difficulties and irritations sometimes make us amenable to a new opportunity, but the crucial consideration in making the decision is: are these difficulties put before me to teach me and mold me, or are they a cue from God that it is time to move along? Perhaps we are meant to overcome the discouragements in our current ministry rather than to opt for greener pastures elsewhere—that is, to face the problems we know rather than the problems of which we know not.[6]

Matthew Henry's plaint at one point in a lifelong ministry in Chester reminds us that ministry inevitably involves times that are "down":

Though the people at Chester are a most loving people, and many of them have had and have an exceeding value for me and my ministry, yet I have not been without my discouragements there, and those such as have tempted me to think my work in that place has been in large done. Many that have been catechized with us and many that have been long communicants with us have left us and very few have been added to us.

We are seeing in our times a crescendo of restlessness in the churches. This makes significant impact upon pastors and their families. Pastoral change is an increasingly costly and traumatic time for goal-oriented congregations. New attention and care must be given to the nurture of our clergy through enhanced support structures and helpful continuing education. This appears not to be a temporary passage but one which will continue to characterize ministry and indeed deepen in complexity as we move into the new century.

CHAPTER 22

"A Great Door for Effective Work Has Opened"

The Pastor and New Forms

Today is not yesterday. We ourselves change. How then, can our works and thoughts, if they are always to be the fittest, continue always the same. Change, indeed, is painful, yet ever needful. (Thomas Carlyle)

Remember the wheel of Providence is always in motion; and the spoke that is uppermost will be under; and therefore mix trembling always with your joy. (Philip Henry)

Preserve sound judgment and discernment,
do not let them out of your sight;
Then you will go on your way in safety,
and your foot will not stumble.
                    (Proverbs 3:21, 23)

And on this rock I will build my church, and the gates of Hades will not overcome it. (Jesus, in Matthew 16:18)

Since the church is always but one generation away from extinction, Christian leaders in the church face the unrelenting responsibility of differentiating between that which is changeless in Christ and the gospel, and that which must be adjusted and adapted in life and practice.

Sitting amid the ideological rubble of state socialism and Marxist determinism as we do in the early nineties, our hearts soar with joy in the assurance that "Jesus Christ is the same, yesterday, today and forever" (Hebrews 13:8). This one of the non-negotiable "givens" of

Biblical faith, changeless verities of Scriptural revelation in which the passing of the centuries fails to find defect or flaw.

Yet there are timebound and culturally conditioned forms which must yield to new situations of opportunity. Tennyson was right that "Our little systems have their day . . . they have their day and cease to be." We cannot recreate past vistas or coast along on the triumphs and strengths of yesteryear. Nor can we afford to chase after the latest fads and fancies in the froth and flurry of modernity.

Cohen and Gooch, in their fascinating analysis of military misfortunes which they subtitle "The Anatomy of Failure in War," suggest that defeat rises out of three basic failures: 1) the failure to learn (as in the early stages of the Battle of the Atlantic); 2) the failure to anticipate (as in Israel's near-debacle in the 1973 Arab-Israeli War); and 3) the failure to adapt to changed conditions (as in the tragic British disaster at Gallipoli).[1]

Continued devotion to forms which need to be changed spells doom. While the church of Jesus Christ has a great future, as promised by its Head, churches and institutions can die. Some die quietly of old age and inanition. Others—for example, the historic seven churches of Asia Minor—see the light go out because of massive spiritual dry-rot. Some churches swoon and seem comatose, but revive. We address here the pressing priority of significant strategizing for appropriate change in our age of breathtaking change.

CHANGE: THE FOES

Change is difficult and threatening. It has been said that there are three kinds of people: the constructive, the obstructive and the destructive. In assessing what the church ought to do and become, we come against the reluctance of human nature generally to anticipate and achieve necessary change. It is estimated that 5 percent are innovators, 15 percent are adaptors, and 80 percent are adopters. There is a passivity in human beings from which believers in Christ are not necessarily immune.

Truly "We've never done it that way before" are the seven last words of a church. This is sclerosis, the hardening of the categories. The favorite Bible verse of such folk is, "I shall not be moved," or perhaps, "My heart is fixed." They love to sing, "Take my life and let it be"; or if they are more high church they prefer, "As it was, in the beginning, is now and ever shall be." This is atrophy and petrification. We can be so set in our ways that life (and opportunity for fruitful ministry) passes us by. We will be for all functional purposes as dead as the extinct bird, the dodo. The indolent repetition of old pious phrases will not do.

Some people seem to have second thoughts before they have first thoughts. There has been a congealing and crusting over of their minds and spirits. In Washington the story is told of a director of the Patent Office who in the early thirties of the last century suggested that the Patent Office be abolished because everything that possibly could be invented had been invented.

We do little to help folk who are seemingly impervious to change by making too broad and too sweeping generalities about the failure of the church. Some paint the situation in such ominous hues of gloom that the hatches are quickly battened down and we face a siege mentality with which it is difficult to cope. It would be well to read and inwardly digest a volume such as William Willimon's *What's Right with the Church*. This is "a spirited statement for those who have not given up on the church and for those who have."[2] Let's not hazard our case by overstating the problems and putting timid souls on the defensive.

We also must not, however, succumb to what C. S. Lewis called "the chronological fallacy"—the idea that the new thing is always the right thing and to be preferred to the old. Likewise, the old is not always good, though the good always stands in significant continuity with values that are old. The tendency of our times to substitute what is modern and up-to-date for what is good can only be lamented. Neologism is idolatry.

Yet, if we intransigently resist change, predictably and inevitably we shall be bypassed in the currents of history. At this stage of the life of the North American church, we need fewer brakemen and more firemen.

CHANGE: FRIENDS

In his epochal little book on "The strategy of innovative leadership," Lyle Schaller identifies those catalyzers we desperately need as "change agents."[3] Schaller analyzes the different kinds of changes and the nature of innovation. He speaks of the "institutional lag" in change and how the "change agent" sorts out a strategy from four contrasting methods of change: 1) coercion; 2) co-optation (bringing the opposition into the supporting group); 3) conflict (drawing up the battle lines); and 4) cooperation.[4] Several of these, or combinations of them, are very time-consuming, but patience in the process is critical. We can ruin it all by pushing too hard too soon. God Himself works with us in process.

Studies are reporting that patience is an important factor in the emotional and intellectual development of the healthy child. Delayed gratification is also linked to higher Scholastic Aptitude Test scores.[5] We have already argued for considerable patience and care in introducing liturgical and worship changes. A brash frontal assault is totally counterproductive. God Himself is a gradualist in working with His children. We Americans like to get things done in a hurry, but the effecting of positive change in the church requires a patient dedication to worthwhile goals.

But thank God for those who want to do something more exciting than watch paint dry. There are brave souls who see that opportunity is purchased with the coin of risk. Thomas Jefferson said, "I am captivated more by dreams of the future than by the history of the past." Babe Ruth hit hundreds of home runs in his career, but he was also the strike-out king, striking out 1,330 times. Without a willingness to risk, nothing can be gained.

The friends of change are those pastors and laypersons who catch the vision, who will not capitulate to a slavish and servile worship of the past. "Forgetting those things which are behind and straining toward what is ahead, I press on toward the goal to win the prize for which God has called me heavenward in Christ Jesus" (Philippians 3:13b, 14).

George Orwell depicts the danger in *1984*. Winston Smith sits at a table in a cell writing, "FREEDOM IS SLAVERY . . . TWO AND TWO MAKE FIVE . . . GOD IS POWER." "He accepted everything," Orwell writes. "The past never had been altered. Oceania was at war with Eastasia. Oceania had always been at work with Eastasia. He remembered remembering contrary things, but those were false memories, products of self-deception. How easy it all was! Only surrender and everything else followed. It was like swimming against a current that swept you backwards however hard you struggled, and then suddenly deciding to turn around and go with the current instead of opposing it." Smith was brought to this point by torture and under duress. We in the church get there so easily on our own. Will we be change agents or will we worship the *status quo*?

CHANGE: FORMATS

We need new forms in the church in order to minister effectively to people in the context of the societal and cultural changes swirling about us. Occasionally these are so drastic as to do us in. A changing rural and small-town population, economic reduction and much else can reduce or destroy the viability of our message. Yet there now seems to be some move back to more rural areas by "gentlemen farmers" who commute long distances to employment centers. While this is no reversal of the demise of the family farm, it does breathe new life and hope into the dwindling prospects of many a rural or small-town parish.

The move to the suburbs and the decimation of urban churches raises important issues. Our large population centers are becoming the home of the very rich and the very poor. But not all are prophets of doom in relation to the city. Some very exciting interracial and ethnic experiments are in evidence. There is even some move back into the city by those who are weary of long commutes from the increasingly distant suburbs. In fact, gentrification is so popular as to seriously compound the problem of finding affordable housing in many cities. William H. Whyte argues that "contrary to previous reports, cities are not dead." He feels that the city is the place of coming together and that the future of the city is guaranteed by this tendency of people to "move toward the center."[6]

Clearly there is a need for intelligent and prayerful study of the data. Our new forms need to be shaped in relation to reality, not fantasy. The use of shopping-mall space for urban and suburban churches presents an alternative to huge capital investment for land, but fails to make a statement to the community about long-range commitment. Yet, this may be a prudent tradeoff.

Sometimes wise strategization would dictate an approach which would not trash what has been, but rather explores meaningful alternatives. Instead of wiping out traditional modes of worship, perhaps an earlier more contemporary service and a second more traditional service would speak to everyone's needs without totally pushing it one way or the other.

Every congregation needs to make regular self-appraisal of its programs and its progress.[7] Leadership retreats, brainstorming sessions, and long-term planning are the matrix out of which significant reforming and restructuring can fruitfully emerge. Several rather obvious areas for evaluation and growth exist commonly in the churches at this time.

1) *Small group experience.* With all of the emphasis on small groups and all of the research and study on the small group process, this continues to be a front-running challenge in many congregations. Smaller congregations are in themselves largely an experience of small group

dynamics The larger the church, the more critical a vital small group experience is.

These groups have included evangelistic Bible studies a la Churches Alive. Others have been care-and-share or support groups, developed and divided geographically or generationally. Leadership has often been a major problem. Leaders tend to be either too dominant and directive or too recessive. It is to be expected that groups generally run their course and need recasting. Small groups seem to follow a cycle.

Wise leadership will seek to sense where on the cycle a given group is. If as some say, "Our church just doesn't go for small groups," something is wrong. The small group affords a dimension which is indispensable. Try some new forms, a new approach. Don't let small groups die. They are a lifeline for many.

2) *The midweek prayer meeting.* Historically this was the hour of power. MacCheyne had thirty-nine prayer meetings weekly in Dundee (of which five were children's prayer meetings). Somewhere along the way our prayer meetings turned into additional preaching services with thin slivers of prayer inserted here and there. Prayer-chains have helped us stand in the gap created by the death of the prayer meeting in North America, but there is still a desperate need in this area. This bodes ill for the church.

A midweek family night in which many activities are held in the interest of clearing the other nights of the week has worked in many places. Sometimes a light supper is made available to relieve the necessity of everyone going home for supper after school or work. This is a superb fellowship time. With a brief Bible study afterwards, and then dividing into small intercessory cells for prayer, several objectives can be attained.

Early-morning men's prayer meetings, women's prayer groups, etc. bespeak the fact that the large, well-attended prayer meetings of yesteryear are probably gone. An occasional concert of prayer or united prayer conference can supplement the proliferation of larger and smaller prayer cells within the life of the congregation. The important thing is that prayer is taking place and that the reality and necessity of prayer are recognized and experienced by leaders and followers alike. Encourage a small cadre of prayer warriors to be on their knees in the pastor's study during the services. Instead of bemoaning the poverty of prayer among us, let us provide vehicles by which prayer can be fostered and nurtured within our common life.

3) *The evening service.* Outside of rural and small-town America and some notable exceptions, the evening service is generally moribund

or nonexistent. The evening service is an opportunity to treat themes and topics of particular interest and to try some innovative experiments not feasible Sunday mornings. I love the evening service—and there are those who need that service. Some of our families need that time at home, to be sure, but people who are employed Sunday mornings, singles, the retired, etc. need such a service.

This service needs to be rethought and reworked in most churches. It may be that in our larger metropolitan centers we will need to move toward a "magnet" evening service in which one church in a given area presents the evening service and other congregations respectively offer other opportunities. Maybe we can't all provide everything, but we can in comity and Christian maturity defer to other congregations to front-window certain other ministries.

Some congregations are offering a Saturday night service. My own view of the Lord's Day in the life of the Christian resists something that seems to be stated in this arrangement. (One such Saturday evening service in the Chicago area is more of an attraction to members of other churches than anything else—and then what is gained?) But we need to remember that the times and formatting of services are not part of "the faith once-for-all delivered to the saints" (Jude 3).

4) *Missionary conferences/special meetings.* Many congregations have tossed in the towel on any kind of special emphasis during the week. But well-planned, prayed-through, purposeful special efforts are necessary for spiritual health in every congregation. Every church needs at least an annual missionary emphasis and a concentrated dose of missionary challenge. The usual missionary slides won't cut it year after year. A missions fair (with displays), panels, home meetings, a supper with ethnic foods, an emphasis on working with international students in this country, and Jewish missions can all enrich and vary the fare.

Special meetings such as a special Bible conference, a week of emphasis on Bible prophecy, a deeper life emphasis or a renewal conference will work anywhere if there is proper preparation and commitment to the the venture.

5) *Evangelism.* The day of mass evangelism is not over.[8] The day of evangelism in the local church is not over either. It can happen right where we are. True Vine Baptist Church in Oakland, California was forced to postpone a series of evangelistic meetings set for the following month "because advance outreach has already brought 1250 new converts in the last five months." This mainly black, Southern Baptist church of 500 members trains its members to go visiting door-to-door Saturday afternoons. They have (as of this writing) handed out twelve

thousand copies of the "New Hope" New Testaments and the SBC is shipping ten thousand more. The church conducts a children's ministry and an outreach to a nearby housing project. This housing complex is now "a different place" as a result, it is reported.[9]

In all of these areas, and many more, every congregation needs some fresh, bold, new strategies and forms with which to share the old gospel. This is not the hour in which we dare sit back in introverted self-adulation, or to sink back into the dregs of despair and depression. This is the time for the people of God to rise up . . .

> *Make us mountaineers;*
>   *We would not linger on the lower slope;*
> *Fill us afresh with hope, O God of Hope,*
>   *That undefeated we may climb the hill*
> *As seeing Him who is invisible.*
>
> *Let us die climbing. When this little while*
>   *Lies far behind us, and the last defile*
> *Is all alight, and in that light we see*
>   *Our Leader and our Lord, what will it be?*
>   (Author unknown)

CHAPTER 23

"The Lord's Message Rings Out"

The Pastor and the Awareness Factor

So the man gave them his attention, expecting . . . (Acts 3:5)

Most experts admit that quality itself is 90% the result of good communication. Communication plays a vital role in achieving quality for any organization. (Wilma Matthews of AT&T Network Systems in *Communication Briefings*)

The extension of the gospel around the world through the media of the electronic church and parachurch groups has given birth to techniques, formats, and methods that on the surface may appear unconventional and unorthodox. But as long as Biblical principles are not violated, let us be grateful for whatever means God may be using and blessing. (Emerson C. Ross, *Alliance Witness*)[1]

Those whom the Lord has destined for this great office he previously provides with the armor which is requisite for the discharge of it, that they may not come empty and unprepared. (John Calvin)

The 330,000 churches in America find themselves awash in a communications revolution. Our business has always been communication and the dissemination of ideas and information, but we now find ourselves in what John Naisbit calls the "Age of Information." Sixty percent of all jobs are in information-related fields, the mass-production of information for public consumption.[2]

Nine out of ten scientists who have ever lived are now living. Each year in our country 800,000 new books are produced; 400,000 periodicals and unnumbered multiple copies of documents are published. This is information overload.[3] To quote Naisbit: "We are drowning in information but starving for knowledge."[4]

The media blitz gives us a constant sense of crisis and a resultant desensitization. The average young person has spent twelve thousand hours in a school classroom by high school graduation, but in that same time 15,000 hours watching the television screen. Computerization and fax machines and all the rest are totally changing the listening and hearing situation. Politics has become the art of "sound bits" rather than substance and ideas. Where are we, and where shall we go in the future?

THE QUESTION OF AUDIENCE

In what kind of soil are we endeavoring to sow the good seed of the Word of God? What are the thought-currents and eddies which bear along both those in the church and those outside the church whom we want to impact with the saving gospel? Thankfully, not all is discouraging to our hopes and aspirations.[5]

Many in the western world have been disappointed and have become disillusioned with the sterilities of secularism and rationalism. Scientism and psychologism in their ruthlessly reductionistic drive have proven to be increasingly unpalatable and unsatisfying. We have moved toward a post-secular mind-set, witnessed by the the fact that one in ten Americans is caught up in the New Age movement. In this whole spectrum of nonsensical horoscopes, channeling, crystals, etc. we see the undeniable fact that many people are reaching out for something beyond themselves. Unfortunately many are becoming caught in a web of evil supernaturalism.

Ecclesiastically the mainline Protestant community is in a serious state of decline. The Presbyterian Church U.S.A. lost more than a million members between 1960 and 1985, with church school membership dropping 53 percent and baptisms 40 percent. The United Methodists in this time period were losing 1,930 members per week. In desperation, as reported by Religious News Service, "a growing movement of United Church of Christ congregations across the United States . . . are adopting mystical practices for spiritual development, including services featuring Tibetan prayer bells, Buddhist chants and various forms of meditation."[6]

The Roman Catholic Church is as theologically confused and mixed up as are some Protestants. Some of the old guard are still very conservative and traditional, some are so liberal as to deny the virgin birth of our Lord, and others are caught up in charismatic renewal. The net effect has become widespread disaffection, dwindling numbers of those entering vocations, and less faithfulness in attending Mass.

Conservative Protestants have enjoyed a growth spurt and high-profile visibility, but a movement tends to founder through its own excesses. The lionization of leaders and personality cults often do us in, and as a result the percentage of Americans who confess to being "born again" has remained at 34 percent for the last seven years. Evidence of theological drift and serious acculturation to the mores of an increasingly narcissistic and sensate culture are in abundant evidence.

"Gridlock grips America" is argued in a *Time* Magazine cover story. Because of a current U.S.A. population of 250,000,000 and because of urbanization, we are becoming more congested and crowded. There have been nine million immigrants in the last decade, the largest foreign influx in our history. Think of the changing demographics. We achieve time-saving breakthroughs but fill up the time we saved with a dozen more things. We wallow in fluff. The toxicity of our culture erodes our moral and relational foundations. None of the old loyalties pull much weight today, including denominational loyalties. Religious consumerism and pluralism are the orders of the day. To this audience we direct the message of Christ.

THE MESSAGE OF APPEAL

There does exist a growing hunger beyond the contemporary fixation on glitz and money. The stock market crash on October 10, 1987, jarred many into realizing that the materialistic fast-track is not altogether dependable.[7] It is at this point that we must realize theological junk food just won't do. There is no special gospel for modern man. We must not give away the store in frantic and futile accommodation. We must not dilute gospel norms or denature the message in a desperate ploy for acceptance. We must not do as was done at the most recent Kirchentag in Germany. There the Communion celebration became a "humanistic travesty" when instead of saying "This is my body" and "This is the new covenant in my blood" the participants inanely said, "We shall pass bread and juice to each other" and "We shall look into one another's eyes" and "We shall say, how lovely that you are here."[8]

There is no use talking about advertising and outreach for the church if there is not a vital message from the Word and substantial content. We can have Visitor's Days and Homecoming Sundays, but if we don't have a top-quality message of hope and grace to share, it is all in vain. Norman Cousins has recently lamented "the decline of neatness"—that is, the trend toward sloppiness, the slipshod, the careless. "Spew and sprawl are taking over," he observes.[9] How tragic when this is true of the church's proclamation of Christ's gospel.

The best P.R. continues to be satisfied customers. The Gallup Poll shows that 91 percent of those attending church regularly began because they were invited by someone they knew. Lyle Schaller has found between two thirds and three quarters of the people he surveyed came to church through friendship or kinship ties. Thus, welcoming visitors and following up on visitors are essential. Newcomer's Classes, Discovery Classes, etc. afford good opportunity early on for getting acquainted and getting over the feeling of strangeness.

Several notable experiments are proving that unconverted people will come into churches which purpose and program to intersect with non-churchgoers where they are. Every church has unconverted people, perhaps even some on the membership roll. The Churches Alive program of Campus Crusade emphasizes outreach activity through small groups in the church. This approach builds soundly on "life-style evangelism." Whatever is used must involve an adequate component of confrontation and actually sharing the gospel. This is especially difficult for some people. Some Christian assertiveness training could be salutary in assisting such persons to be more aggressive in their witness for Christ.[10]

THE QUESTION OF ATTENTION

In such a glut of visual and auditory stimuli, how can we hope to arrest the attention of the people we target for information? The sign-board outside which identifies the church should be sharp and attractive. Our stationery and letterheads convey an image, and a good logo and motto can be useful in projecting identity. If the church is not on a main thoroughfare, some signs to assist people in finding the church are greatly appreciated. Rural and small-town congregations no less than others need to give careful attention to the impression made on those who would like to find and do in fact attend the church.

One of the most significant early impressions made on worshipers is the church bulletin or order of service. Copy machines and relatively inexpensive duplication technology have placed attractive and appealing materials within the expense range of every congregation. A neatly and thoughtfully prepared bulletin makes a good first impression and obviates the necessity of long and often distracting announcement times before or during the service of worship.

To print the full outline of the pastor's sermon in the bulletin is to deprive the preacher of any suspense factor and thus is unwise. Forecasting or preannouncing the main points is considered a negative by almost all homileticians. On the other hand, printing a "skeleton" with blank spaces to fill in invites the hearers to become participants with the preacher in pursuing the journey toward truth.

Every church needs a house organ or parish newsletter of some kind. Some churches mail out the weekly bulletin, and this dated material becomes a weekly medium of communication. People need to receive news about what is happening, to learn about programs and people in the parish, and to see their own names in print from time to time. These can be relatively unsophisticated but immensely useful. Such a piece helps build community. Although the pastor should have a brief meditation or paragraph of contact ("parson to person," we might say), a group of dedicated laypersons with skills and gifts in this area should do most of the work.

We live in an almost embarrassing wealth of helps and resources to assist us in the local church: visuals, contest materials, banquet decorations, etc. Unfortunately, some pastors buy all or nearly all their sermons and/or illustrations from such services, and this is a sure kiss of death.

Each congregation should have some kind of a promo piece, a descriptive and explanatory publication which sets forth the services and opportunities offered in the life of that congregation. The price of creative layout and design is steep. Having a professional in this field in the congregation is an invaluable help. Some publishers make available attractive, multicolor folders which can receive a local imprint. Sometimes an appropriate anniversary publication can double as a promo piece. Congregations should see special occasions as opportunities to interpret and set forth the nature and heart of a local ministry.

Having a float at the local Fourth of July parade or maintaining singly or jointly a booth of witness and testimony at the county fair is an effective way to put forth the claims of Christ and the ministry of the church in a way which boldly says, "We are alive and on the move for God!" We must make continuous forays out of the shelter of our own ingrown community. This is what it means to be "salt" and "light" (Matthew 5:13, 14). Conducting jail services and prison ministries, park and outdoor services in the summer, Lenten noontime services for hospital and business personnel—these and other ministries can find their counterpart in every community of believers.

In some communities we can obtain the names and addresses of people who have just moved into the area from one of the public utilities. Welcome Wagon and other organizations reach out to newcomers at a particularly critical time. One congregation built a powerful cradle-roll ministry by presenting new mothers in the community with gifts for the new babies. There are innumerable angles which creative and resourceful people can pursue to get hold of names for the prospect list.

So often today the church seems to be the bland leading the bland. We need some spiritual spice and spunk, to present to the community appropriately and effectively an image of a caring and alive spiritual people who have surmounted an insipid passivity and an ingrown introversion. What would happen if we prayed as did the early church: "Now, Lord . . . enable your servants to speak your word with great boldness" (Acts 4:20). That prayer might just be answered! "After they prayed, the place where they were meeting was shaken. And they were all filled with the Holy Spirit and spoke the word of God boldly" (Acts 4:31).

THE QUESTION OF ADVERTISING

Some of the most effective advertising a church can do is in the local phone directory. The Yellow Pages present an opportunity to do more than give an address and phone number. Also, hotels and motels in the area usually have a church service display. These boards especially afford a central-city congregation a good opportunity to minister to visitors and guests. Through such advertising we create a reservoir of good will, so when family members move to the area or young people come for college, we have a "foot in the door."

The religion editor or writer of the local newspaper needs to become a friend and an acquaintance of our church. This person is always one of the first calls I would make in a new community. This relationship is one which can be mutually profitable. Most newspapers publish news about church programs *gratis*. Why should we not aggressively take advantage of the opportunities which exist at our doorstep? Materials should be submitted in good form. It would help many pastors to take a course in creative writing. (Good writing form correlates highly with good preaching form.)

Paid advertising presents its own challenges. A weekly contract usually gives a discount. I believe skimping on advertising is a serious blunder. Perhaps the weekend church page is not the best place to use your church's advertising budget. More creative and well-aimed publicity in the press may be possible, but we do need to keep our existence and programs before our own people and before the general public. (One national beverage manufacturer downplayed advertising for several years and almost went out of business entirely.) Again, help with layout and formatting are vital.

THE QUESTION OF THE AVANT GARDE

Radio and television ministry open large vistas for the local church. Rural and small-town congregations may have more opportunity here than many urban or suburban congregations. A fifteen-minute weekly broadcast from "The Little Brown Church in the Vale" may make a significant contribution in a smaller community because it is local and the participants are known.

In some communities, cable TV offers virtually *carte blanche* opportunity for religious organizations without cost, whereas TV time in a metropolitan area is prohibitively expensive for a local congregation. I find I can usually get on local talk-shows in smaller communities without any difficulty and can thus obtain a superb opportunity to publicize the special meetings and get a good word in for the Lord Jesus Christ.

Where we do have a chance in the media, we need to remember that one person shows starring the pastor are the least effective approaches we can take.[11] In some communities various pastors take turns giving a thought for the day on radio or television. These are choice opportunities and should be seized with alacrity. Even a paid thirty-second ad on television has great possibilities.

In every area there needs to be one live or taped service available for shut-ins. I have preached a morning service via a network and two local stations for years. Care should be taken to de-emphasize some aspects of the radio ministry in the worshiping congregation, but that outreach is dynamite. A five-minute daily broadcast in connection with a "read through the Bible" program is a fascinating variant. The use of multimedia for a television special presents an interesting challenge.

The wasteland of the media with its sensationalism, its violence, its addictive character, its total cerebral bypass is here to stay. Couch potatoes and lounge lizards are part of the permanent landscape. The question is whether or not we shall abdicate all effort to counter this phenomenon and to change what exists. The best counsel would seem to be that of Helmut Thielicke: "One must have the courage to make one central point . . . we must let the rabbits go today . . . because today we are hunting stags."[12]

CHAPTER 24

"Perfectly United in Mind and Heart"

The Pastor and Fissures

On February 25 we held our final worship service and now we are in the painful process of closing down the mission. We tried for two and a half years, but it never came together. Why? Perhaps because of its troubled beginnings; perhaps because the core group could not switch their allegiance to me; perhaps because of my inexperience (this is my first pastorate); perhaps because God had another plan . . . but it is closed . . . there is still a keen sense of failure. We did not do what we had set out to do. (Letter from a young, faithful pastor)

Live in harmony with one another . . . if it possible, as far as it depends on you, live at peace with everyone. (Romans 12:16, 18)

Conflict in human experience can be so painful and so destructive, and yet obviously it is endemic to the race. God is not the author of conflict; He is the God of peace, of *shalom*. Strife and struggle are not part of His purpose for His creatures. Conflict has come because of sin and because of humanity's affiliation with Satan in his revolt and rebellion against God.

Immediately after our first parents' sin, mankind clearly became at enmity with God, hiding from God in the Garden. Interpersonal conflict followed between Adam and Eve. Fratricidal conflict between Cain and Abel and further violence was celebrated in Lamech's "Song of the Sword" (Genesis 4:23, 24). The history of war and human strife covers one bloody page after another. The tensions and turbulence between nations and individuals, in homes and marriages, and in all human enterprise comprise one long litany of agony and untold suffering.

God's purpose in redemption is to address the basic cause of this incessant fraying of the human fabric. Christ Jesus is "the Prince of Peace" (Isaiah 9:6), and He came to bring "peace on earth" (Luke 2:14), to "make peace by the blood of his cross" (Ephesians 2:11-22). Jesus pronounces blessing on the "peacemakers" (Matthew 5:9), and Scripture casts believers in the role of "ministers of reconciliation" (2 Corinthians 5:16-21). So believers are to "make every effort to live in peace with all men" (Hebrews 12:14) and to "seek peace and pursue it" (1 Peter 3:11b).

It is no shock or surprise to find hostility and intrigue in the world, but we must confess our disappointment to find them so prevalent in the church. Here our idealism quickly shatters on the hard rocks of realism. Our own hearts know deeply entrenched antagonists (cf. Romans 7:7-25), and this is typical of the church of which we are are part. There is quibbling and carping and controversy within and without, and this has always been so. We even see it in the apostolic band and on the larger canvas in the book of Acts. Our theme seems to be:

> *Roses are red, violets are blue,*
> *You clobber me and I'll clobber you.*

That is so frequently the story as the privatized become the polarized and very soon the pulverized, with much harm to an enlarging circle.

Even Charles Spurgeon observed to his students that "If they resist the Devil, he will flee from them; while if they resist the Deacons, they will fly at you." Here is the hard reality of conflict in the church. Now in a time of rapidly accelerating change in the societal matrix in which the church ministers and therefore a time of mounting pressure on the church as an institution, we are seeing more conflict in the church rather than less. Seminars on conflict in the church are increasing, and consultants in this field are busy. The specter of the Donner party attempting to get over the pass into California on their pioneer trek must haunt us: as community dissolved, they were destroyed.

CONFLICT AS TRAGEDY

It is not difficult to see how conflict in the church rises Hydra-headed out of the carnality and depravity which remain residually even in the most sanctified of the saints. Some see stress as the chief causative agent in creating conflict,[1] and others emphasize the breakdown of communication. Some emphasize Satanic assault (certainly as the "accuser of the brothers," Revelation 12:10, Satan is a continuous advocate of strife and factionalism in the church). But we cannot simply lay the problem at his infernal majesty's door. Growth itself can induce certain tensions and issues.[2] Even spiritual movements tend to die because of their own excesses. As evangelicals still smarting from the scandals of our "holy wars" and "Gospelgate," it is instructive that even the world sees these as reflective of the characteristic excesses of the eighties—the greed, love of glitz, narcissism in which "like vast balloons, these empires had expanded on the breath of faith until they overextended themselves and burst."[3]

The etiology of New Testament conflict in the church is multiform:

1) *Conflict rising out of differences in socioeconomic position* (Acts 6:1-8). Greek-speaking Jews felt they were twisting in the wind as victims of deliberate discrimination by Aramaic-speaking Jews.

2) *Conflict rising out of differences in cultural perspective* (Acts 15:1-35). At the Jerusalem Council an issue was raised concerning Jewish-Gentile differences and the persistence of long-term, deep-dyed cultural disparities.

3) *Conflict rising out of differences in basic personality-types* (Acts 15:36-41). Paul and Barnabas came to a parting of the ways over John Mark, and one cannot escape the conclusion that each saw young Mark through different tinted glasses.

4) *Conflict rising out of differences due to party spirit and intense rivalry*. Personality cults are nothing new, as we see in 1 Corinthians 1—3. Four parties had formed, and the "Christ" party was probably the most trying of all. The fractious spirit here led even to lawsuits and Communion brawls.

5) *Conflict rising out of differences which were picayune*. Paul saw a pulling apart in the Philippian church. That congregation had such a richly variegated charter membership, and yet the sisterhood was having its rifts (Philippians 4:2, 3), and Paul was perturbed. This tension did not stem from any obtuse absolutism, but from insignificant minor issues which grated and galled.

At the least, such conflict distracts and drains a congregation's energies. Friction is lost energy. In some cases we are, pure and simple, dealing with resistance to the plan and purpose of God. A Diotrephes "who loves to be first" (3 John 9) can bring indescribable pain to the Body of Christ. Luecke and Southard see conflict largely on the grid of resistance.[4]

Resistance is sometimes of such a principial kind that it must be confronted and challenged head-on. This is how we must understand our Savior's mysterious words, "Do you think I have come to bring peace on the earth? No, I tell you, but division" (Luke 12:51). Similarly, Paul had to confront and rebuke Peter for the sake of the purity of the gospel (Galatians 2:11-21). Some schisms—for example, the Reformation—are brought about by God. There are divinely ordered divisions which rise out of the fact that truth is not a circle which includes error. Spurgeon's involvement in the "down-grade" controversy and more modern ecclesiastical struggles must be seen as "contending earnestly for the faith once for all delivered to the saints" (Jude 3).[5]

But whether the issue be central or peripheral, we must tell the "truth in love" (Ephesians 4:15). The spectacle of a battling church is a scandal and a disgrace and a grief to the Spirit of God. Why can't we fight like Christians? How can we greet our friends like enemies? Heavy barrages of criticism and complaint with resultant hemorrhage tear the heart out of the servants of Christ. H. Beecher Hicks, a gifted black preacher, has given us a powerful example of preaching in the tempest of church conflict, for he "preached through storm."[6]

Here the pastor-teacher has to wrestle with the issue, shall I pacify or shall I preach? Is the customer going to be the King or the church? Here is where the prophetic and the pastoral roles need to fuse, even in the face of a heavy toll to be exacted by the champions of principle rather than popularity.

CONFLICT AS A TOOL FOR TRANSFORMATION

While we lament the destructive effect of stress and tension, we must also recognize the constructive uses to which stress and tension can be put in an amazing alchemy of spiritual transformation. Psalm 76:10 ("the wrath of men shall praise thee") and Romans 8:28 are still in the Bible. Much personal growth is possible only in the face of difficulty and tension. Conflict is an essential part of growth. Dabrowski's theory of "positive disintegration" is provocative and telling.[7]

Dudley and Hilgert argue that both internal and external conflict have constructive contributions to make to the body politic. Relying heavily on Lewis Coser, they advance the following relevant axioms:[8]

1) *Conflict can contribute to growth.* The hard passages can certainly break down tissue, but they can also build up—in terms of "defining boundaries, disciplining members and fostering higher consciousness of belonging."

2) *Intimacy and ideology (personality and principle) can intensify conflict.* Indeed conflict may be engendered, but mobilization may also be encouraged.

3) *Conflict can unify by defining boundaries and demanding adherence and loyalty.* The potential for destruction is there, but a time of tension can also be a season for the identification and clarification of values.

The word "confront" literally means "with together," and confrontation can awaken and alert a slumbering congregation. I have a problem with euphoric celebration of conflict, as in Tom Peters's recent *Thriving on Conflict.* But I do believe the perspective of faith allows us to see that the grace and power of God can be dramatically catalytic in changing a situation for the good by helping us face the issues.

Luecke and Southard help us grapple with the question, Is this situation redeemable or irremediable? There are limits to constructive conflict. There is a point where too much is torn apart; it's not only "all the king's horses and all the king's men" who cannot "put Humpty Dumpty together again."

Some congregations are like dysfunctional families. They have a reputation and a track record for feistiness and fighting. Moreno's socio-drama oppresses with a monotonous pattern, and some troubled churches are preacher killers. A drastic intervention may be required by denominational leaders in such cases. Kenneth Haugk describes a class of persons who are so bad that there is no hope for resolving disputes with them.[9] Severe neurosis or even psychosis can doom a situation. "With God all things are possible" (Luke 1:37), and yet both Scripture and history testify that God Himself gives up in certain situations (cf. Romans 1:24, 26, 28).

In the church, as in marriage, we recognize that offenses will come. In our finitude and frailty we will have differences. If repressed and submerged for the sake of image or affability, these differences will nevertheless rise to haunt and hurt. But if problems are faced, we have opportunities for growth.

Each difference encountered is an invitation to move on toward greater maturity and understanding. Reconciliation opens new apertures for vision and progress. We must not suppose that by allowing lesions to congeal and simply crust over that we shall experience substantial healing. Let's face our problems and grow! "Like a mighty glacier moves the church of God" may be our experience because we have been unwilling or unable up to this point to face the issues our conflicts contain.

CONFLICT AS TESTING

Sensitive leadership should seek to anticipate conflict and to address it wisely before it flares up into a full-blown conflagration with possible catastrophic consequences. Some persons are so afraid of conflict they will bury their heads in the sand like the proverbial ostrich in hopes that it will go away. Is someone miffed? Has there been a misunderstanding? Does the unofficial church communications network yield a disaffected member? What is gained by letting the wound or offense or perceived slight exacerbate? Wouldn't it be advisable to make a call by phone or in person *now*?

Charles A. Daily identifies danger signals, moving from the least serious to the most serious:

1) voting patterns indicating the rise of opposition to the leadership
2) direct protest of a policy or decision
3) change in attendance at meetings
4) change in revenue
5) a persisting issue of abrasive quality
6) withdrawal of support by the power structure
7) increase of polarization
8) withdrawal of key persons or groups from communication.[10]

These are significant alarm bells and should be taken seriously. Sometimes we get uptight and unnatural around perennial critics. Shawchuck speaks of five different styles in handling conflict or crisis: avoiding (the turtle), accommodating (the teddy-bear), collaborating (the owl), compromising (the fox), and competing (the shark).[11]

The best way in which to prudently avoid destructive conflict is to walk in the wisdom of the book of Proverbs. What if we learned to take reproof, advice and criticism as we are admonished to do in that holy document? "Listen to advice and accept instruction, and in the end you will be wise" (Proverbs 19:20) is good for all of us. What if we learned to weigh our responses more carefully before answering? What if we avoided needless arguing? "It is to a man's honor to avoid strife, but every fool is quick to quarrel" (Proverbs 20:3). What if we avoided gossip and were not so dedicated to proving we are right? This approach to life and interpersonal relations would deliver us all from much fruitless and unproductive strife.[12]

CONFLICT AND THE TURN-ABOUT

But what if the situation deteriorates into a vicious knockdown/drag-out all-out war? There is a point at which an additional flow of information is counterproductive because communication has broken down so completely that even well-intentioned overtures and gestures are misconstrued. G. Douglas Lewis is right in describing creative management of conflict as analogous to the artist's ability to bring something into existence which does not now exist. It "means forging new relational possibilities, new alternatives for action that can be satisfying to both parties."[13] Coercion through dominance and demolition is never the solution.

In his approach Lewis suggests the following principles:
1) *Help others feel better about themselves.* This is an important place to begin. This was certainly where the Apostle Paul began with problem churches.
2) *Strive for effective communication.*
3) *Examine and filter assumptions.*
4) *Identify goals*, what is wanted and sought—ask "what," not "why," questions.
5) *Identify the primary issue.*
6) *Develop alternatives for goal achievement.*
7) *Institutionalize conflict management processes*; i.e., build these processes into the very structures and procedures.[14]

In some situations, the collapse of confidence and communication is so painful and so drastic that a referee, mediator or ombudsman needs to be sought. Speed Leas likes the word "referee" in this context "because it does not have the connotation of declaring a winner and keeps before us the notion of neutrality, which is so crucial to the third-party role in conflict management."[15] The careful choice of such a referee is critical. Denominational leaders are often seen as having too much vested stake in an outcome favoring existing pastoral leadership. The use of outside resources is often the wisest in these circumstances.

The ideal process for resolution, as described helpfully by McSwain and Treadwell, involves: step 1—diffusion through greater awareness of facts and history, enlargement of group, and delay; step 2—problem-solving by the collecting of data and listing of options, developing a consensus; step 3—decision-making by stating the purpose, outlining the rules, observing and engaging emotions, rejecting games, deciding and celebrating.[16]

Before us in all of the process must be the objective of restoring the body and all of its parts to normal and healthy function. The enemy of our souls would divide Christians and debilitate the church. What if an award-winning band began its performance with the trumpet players trying to trip each other? What if the percussionists played so loudly you couldn't hear anyone else play? What if the clarinetists felt over-looked and sat in a circle playing only for themselves? And in all of this the drum major is attempting to restore order. This may be how the church often appears, but this is not what the Lord of the church desires. He says to us today: "And over all these virtues put on love, which binds them all together in perfect unity" (Colossians 3:14).

CHAPTER 25

"He Who Has Begun a Good Work Will Carry It On"

The Church of the Future

The future is not what it used to be. (A current adage)

'Tis all in peeces, all cohaerance gone;
  All just supply, and all Relation:
Prince, Subject, Father, Sonne, are things forgot,
  For every man alone thinkes he hath got
To be a Phoenix, and that then can bee
  None of that kinde, of which he is, but hee.
                    (John Donne)

I beg of you to think. (Demosthenes to Athens)

Christians with their linear view of history are properly entitled to a realistic optimism with regard to the future. We must honestly face the disintegration and decomposition of modern western culture and its increasing estrangement from the norms of historic Christian orthodoxy. Yet there is no question as to the ultimate outcome: *Christ is the victor!* The church of Jesus Christ, whatever may be her debilitations, is on the winning side.

Christians are the people of the future, the children of the resurrection. We are already participating in the age to come because we have eternal life (John 3:36; 5:24). But we also eagerly anticipate the consummation in the coming again of our Lord Jesus Christ. Then the church will be completed and conformed to Christ's image (Romans

8:29ff.). We await the coming of Christ for His own, but also take seriously the Savior's admonition to "Put this money to work until I come back" (Luke 19:13b).

Thus ministry is conducted in the dynamic tension between Christ's imminent return and the necessity to wisely plan for the future. Luther advised believers to live as if Christ died this morning, rose again this afternoon, and is coming back this evening. Here is motivation for service and holiness in a context of urgency and passion. But Luther also said that even if he knew Christ were coming back tomorrow, he would plant his apple tree today. We are not to be idle in our confidence of our future with Christ.

A vibrant hope should be a distinctive mark of the Christian. To refuse to hope is an act of spiritual treason because of who Christ is and what he has done. As futurologists plot what is ahead, and as much thought and discussion are being given to what the shape of things will be by 2000 A.D., Christians rejoice in that "We have the word of the prophets made more certain, and thou will do well to pay attention to it, as to a light shining in a dark place, until the day dawns and the morning star rises in your hearts" (2 Peter 1:19).

SOCIETY

Secular think-tanks are overwhelmed with gloom. The population explosion (we are now 5.2 billion and increasing by 93,000,000 annually), the AIDS epidemic, ecological crises, terrorism, the continued proliferation of nuclear capability—all taken together lead some to say, "We don't know enough about the future to be absolutely pessimistic."[1]

And the information explosion doesn't help much. As Coleridge said of the Enlightenment: it is full of enlighteners but lacking in light. There is today much knowledge but much ignorance and little wisdom. Analysis of the problems may be perceptive, but no substantive solutions are proposed.[2]

The trends which portend the church of the future are as follows:

1) The mainline Protestant denominations continue to experience massive losses.

2) The Roman Catholic Church, now suffering from the same theological confusion as Protestants, has seen significant shrinkage in church attendance and faces huge problems in vocations and red-button issues (for example, birth control) which exacerbate the divisions and sense of alienation in the church.

3) Conservative Protestants have plateaued in growth—at about 34 percent of the population for the last seven years—and have been scarred by scandals and vitiated by acculturation. With few exceptions, evangelicals have the "blahs" in North America—maintaining a cerebral commitment to Christianity but lacking in significant dedication.

4) New-convert growth is continuing in the Two-Thirds World on an unprecedented scale and is replacing North America and Europe as the "senders" in Christian world missions. Persecution and martyrdom are part of this story (with an estimated 330,000 martyrdoms for Christ every year).[3]

5) There is undiminished urbanization throughout the world. This has immense implications for ministry. We see the continued decay of the infrastructures in American population centers, with cities increasingly the home of the very rich and the very poor. The gap between the "haves" and the "have nots" continues to widen in this country and abroad. The question of the distribution of wealth will continue to fester and will become increasingly volatile.

6) With globalization "in" and one-world consciousness increasingly prevalent, the viability of spiritual and moral absolutes will become more and more tenuous. What has been described as *The Divine Super-market: Shopping for God in America* will be more, not less, the case.[4] The spread of the cults and eastern religions as well as the New Age movement with all its spurious progeny caters to the very notions which will give rise to the Antichrist at the end of the age.

7) There will be increasing generational tension. Those who are older than the baby-boomer generation don't seem to be in touch with their thinking at all. As the percentage of senior adults balloons, the likelihood of "control" conflict grows. Old loyalties don't cut it anymore. The multi-option society—thirty-nine flavors—will not hold these restless persons in the old molds.

8) The consistent decline in rural and small-town population is posing challenges of gargantuan proportions. Formerly rural areas within driving distance of metropolitan centers will boom unless there is another fuel crunch.

9) There will be a continuing erosion of the family unit as we move rapidly toward 50 percent of American homes operating on a single-parent basis. Two thirds of the jobs held in this country will be held by women. Day-care will become a chief employee benefit.

10) We will still be in the "mega-church" age. The large church can do so many things, and small dynamic churches have their place. The pressure will be on the medium-sized church.

11) Biotechnology will be big in such areas as animal rights, children's rights, ecological concerns.

12) The emergence of large new trade-blocs—Europe (1992), Japan and the East (will China come in?), and the USA—will have unbelievable economic and sociological implications. Are we too stuck in the old forms? Peter Drucker says that our institutions as a whole are still stuck in the world of 1960, and "What we face now is totally new and dynamic."[5] "Yankee impatience" has proven to be one of our primary weaknesses in international competition.

The pundits and prophets of secularity speak of the next one hundred years as "one of the most dangerous periods since the origin of life" (Jonathan Weiner). Are we so sedated by the *status quo* that we are paralyzed by the changes taking place around us? Will our congregations become isolated islands of archaic irrelevance? The changeless Christ is our fixed center of stability in the swirling sea all about us.

There can be no progress without change. We're in a seething caldron of revolutionary upheaval. One in two churches in the U.S. uses a personal computer. This is a minuscule adaptation. We need to aim and adapt on a much larger scale.

STRATEGY

The need for serious strategizing is clear. Innovation has been defined as "the process of bringing new problem-solving ideas into use." Here is where we can learn from business and education. "The children of this world are wiser in their generation than the children of light" (Luke 16:8). Effective organizations utilize long-range planning—where we believe we are going, where we want to be way down the road. "Visioning" is common in the corporate world—what do we want to become in seven to ten years? When this vision is agreed upon, the next step becomes identifying the changes which must take place if that vision is to be realized.

Our spiritual strategy for the end of the century needs to be based on the final words of the risen Christ to His disciples, as found variously in the four Gospels and the book of Acts. The essential foundations of this charge are:

l) *We are to be a commissioned people.* Christians are under divine orders. We cannot be autonomous. "Then Jesus came to them and said, 'All authority in heaven and on earth has been given to me . . . therefore go . . .'" (Matthew 28:18, 19a). The risen Lord is the Lord of history. In all the flex and ferment of the Revelation of Jesus Christ given to John, the throne is mentioned twelve times. This is our foundation— the sovereign, supreme Lordship of Jesus Christ.

It is Christ who would enlarge our vision and draw us to a Great Commission life-style. "All the world" is our field (Mark 16:15)—"To all nations" (Luke 24:47)—progressive penetration geographically, sociologically, psychologically (Acts 1:8). John Wesley exclaimed, "The world is my parish!"

This means we cannot abandon the cities of our country or the world. The demographic shifts are staggering. Besides the problems of homelessness and hunger among the underclass, we have the acutely painful problem of shrinking economic opportunity in the cities as factories and businesses are lured to the suburbs. People in the cities will not commute to the suburbs as suburbanites have commuted to the cities. The cities and their financial woes, ineffective school systems, overloaded social services agendas, problems of law and order and drugs—all this and more is part of our world that must be reached for Christ.

The small churches cannot be abandoned. Smaller churches have strengths: there is more intimate fellowship—everyone is needed—they are more intergenerational, more lay-centered. Half of the congregations in America could be called "small." There are special perils there as well: introversion, hypochondria, institutional neurasthenia, feelings of inferiority, constant wrestling with morale and money problems. Turnover of clergy and difficulty in maintaining youth and music programs are endemic. But what a marvelous place for a young pastor to begin ministry, and there are those who feel called to rural and small-town ministry for a lifetime.

Trouble on the farm has made a difficult situation worse. With soaring productivity, fewer farmers are needed. The bigger, low-cost operators remain. A string of bad crop years and heavy debts have put many farmers out of business. This has exacted a tragic toll in rural America. But this is part of our world, and we are commissioned to be involved for Christ in "all the world."

2) *We are to be a committed people.* The main verb in the Matthean text is "to make disciples" (Matthew 28:19)—i.e., to seek followers and learners for Jesus Christ. Conversions are the immediate goal, but initiation into lifelong learning in the school of Jesus Christ is our paramount purpose. The other coordinated participles in the passage support and enhance this chief goal. Baptism is the outward sign of this identification with Christ, but we are nurturing a growth process. "Take my yoke upon you and learn of me," the Savior said (Matthew

11:28-30). Our strategizing for the church of the future needs not only to deal with church planting and goals for numerical growth, but with in-depth discipling of men and women and young people in lives of significant commitment.

Baby-boomers (those born from 1946-1964) have been making some movement back toward the church, but it is largely in the interests of getting certain services and support. This group is very fluid and is highly allergic to commitment. Their "return" is on "distinctly different terms than in past generations."[6] The "calculated choices" of this largest generation in American history are generally made "not on the basis of doctrine or denominational loyalty but because of a first-rate day-care program, congenial music, or preaching lively enough to compete with television." This is a consumer attitude toward spiritual things.

Strategizing for the future must make serious provision to address this population which will quickly take their business elsewhere. No congregation can be without significant small group experience. We need a variety of support groups. Strong clergy dominance and passive laity simply play into the hands of those who resist the Biblical mandate that Christians are to be the "company of the committed."

Little Mother Theresa won't partake of refreshments in the homes of the rich and famous, though they be presidents or prime ministers. Her rationale is, if the word gets out to the masses of the poor that I accept refreshments, they will spend money they don't have to offer me refreshments in their deprivation. How strange and curious such discipleship seems to us!

3) *We are to be a conspicuous people.* We are to teach believers "to obey everything I have commanded you" (Matthew 28:20). Recent studies emphasize the importance of Christian education. The recently reported three-and-half-year study of the Search Institute in Minneapolis, although dealing chiefly with the mainline and Southern Baptist denominations, shows current deficiencies in our programs. Only a minority of adults evidenced "integrated, vibrant, life-encompassing faith."[7] Shockingly the study showed that only three in ten Protestant high school students and adults are presently involved in Christian education.

Here is where a flexible style of leadership needs to make serious adaptation to the need as it exists. Do we have the desire and drive to strategize for what we believe the will of God is for the next ten years should our Lord tarry? Tom Peters in his arresting study of American business abroad contrasts American and Japanese interests in capturing the Chinese market.[8] The Japanese mean business—they have three hundred firms there, while we have 170. They build a strong infrastructure and learn Chinese. (In their Sanwa Bank, nine of twelve Japanese working there know Chinese. In Citicorp, only one American knows Chinese.) In 1973, eight thousand Americans were studying Japanese; in 1989, the figure has risen only to ten thousand. Ninety percent of American business people living in Japan never attempt to learn the language. Are there are not similarities in church situations? Do we really mean business for Christ or do we not?

SPIRITUALITY

The bottom line for the church of the future must be, of course, the leading of God. That very special visit of God among His people which is described in the Old and New Testaments and which we call revival is desperately needed. Our God is faithful to His promises, but think what could take place for His glory and praise were there to be a deep spiritual quickening and renewal of North American and European churches.

The great awakenings in our country in the eighteenth and nineteenth centuries (with their counterparts overseas) have not been matched in this century, and we are coming down the stretch. The Welsh revival in the first decade of this century and some episodic movements of the Spirit in the New Hebrides, in certain American colleges at mid-century, and on the Canadian prairie provinces a while back never became the type of sweeping spiritual conflagration which shakes society and changes cultural structures.

Have gospel rains moved off our shores permanently? Is it our task today to minister, as it were, "out of season" (2 Timothy 4:2) and to hear only of divine visitations from newer churches abroad? It was said of one older pastor in my own communion that he never achieved noteworthy status and never served more than smaller or medium-sized congregations, but in each charge there was a special visit of God while he and his wife served there. Would this could be said of each of us, and that God might once more visit us in revival before Christ returns.

The Great Commission closes with that promise which enables us to be a confident people—"And surely, I will be with you always, to the very end of the age" (Matthew 28:20). We see here the attitude and posture which so delights our God as to invite the mighty manifestation of His glorious presence among His people. This must be at the heart of all of our strategizing and dreaming for the future. David Brainerd captures it in these words:

> I prayed privately with a dear Christian friend or two; and I think I scarce ever launched so far out on the broad ocean that my soul with joy triumphed over all the evils on the shores of mortality. I think that time and all its gay amusements and cruel disappointments never appeared so inconsiderable to me before.

The Seasons
of Ministry

There is a time for everything, and a season for every activity under heaven. (Ecclesiastes 3:1)

Be prepared in season and out of season. (2 Timothy 4:2b)

In due season we shall reap if we faint not. (Galatians 6:9b)

The ministry of the pastor-teacher as all of life is caught up in a series of cycles and undulations. Physically, emotionally, intellectually and spiritually we are caught up in process and passage. Many have aptly and appropriately addressed these issues, and it is our purpose here to address nuances and aspects of ministry in relation to these factors in human experience.[1]

Four seasons fill the measure of the year.
There are four seasons in the mind of man.
(John Keats)

STABILITIES

In contemplating ministry in our time with its unrelenting demands and increasing complexity, all of us closely identify with the Apostle Paul's cry, "And who is equal to such a task?" (2 Corinthians 2:16b).[2] We know our own frailty and fragility and naturally shrink back from such an onerous calling. The fact that we have been "sent from God" (2 Corinthians 1 :17b) and sense His hand upon us stabilizes and strengthens us. We are all inadequate for the ministry, but the work is His, the church is His, the battle is His, and He has guaranteed the resources required. "Not that we are competent to claim anything for ourselves, but our competence comes from God. He has made us competent ministers of a new covenant—not of the letter but of the Spirit; for the letter kills, but the Spirit gives life" (2 Corinthians 3:5, 6).

The continuity and stability of the work of the Lord reside in the character and unchanging fidelity of our sovereign God, His ever-present Son (Hebrews 13:8), and His gentle but indefatigable Holy Spirit. Christians are the people of the future. We are the sons and daughters of the resurrection. We come to the flux and ferment of time-space history with a basic bias toward optimism and hopefulness because we know who is in charge (cf. Romans 8:18-25). We do not deny or trivialize the tragic dimensions of human existence, nor would we minimize the implications of the cosmic struggle for truth and right. But we are confident as to the outcome for us personally, for the people of God corporately, and for our planet ultimately.

In the book of Revelation, where we are often appalled by the seeming chaos and confusion into which humanity descends in the climactic scenarios of history, we read twelve times of "the throne," and we see "the Lamb" who is on that throne. He is the "King of Kings and the Lord of Lords" (Revelation 19:16). We can rest on these foundational certainties and revel in the eternal victory the Lord Jesus Christ has achieved over all the minions of darkness. This is the context for Christian ministry.

OPPORTUNITIES

Matthew Henry's dying words (after being thrown from a horse) were: "A life spent in the service of God is the most pleasant life that anyone can live in this world." And this life has its shifting phases.

1) *Springtime: looking forward.* At last the years of preparation conclude and one is launched into ministry. This is a time of resilient optimism, unflagging idealism, and considerable trepidation and apprehension. Little wonder that after the first five years of ministry there is need for expectation revision. Highly favored is that young servant of Christ who is blessed with some good mentoring relationships in this period. To spend the first years in a small-town or rural setting affords the young minister the very choice opportunity needed to study, study, study without constant interruption, to integrate the insights of seminary with the realities of life "out there." As I look back I can see that I drove too hard in those early years—I was so eager and so excited about ministry and desperately longed to see growth. My blunders

were understandable but nonetheless lamentable. There was spring in the air!

2) *Summertime: serving in strength.* This is the time when growing experience and confidence allow for aggressive reach. The days are long, and the demands are great. Cecil Paul characterizes aptly the danger of a "chronic overextension pattern" and "personal neglect of needs, tasks and crises." This is a very rigorous time in family life—the time of "generativity . . . the task of helping one's children to become whole and fulfilled" (Erik Erikson). This is a prime time for burnout, and wise is that Christian worker who carefully learns to handle the stress-agents of life in the interests of the long-distance race at hand. To the praise of God, as John Henry Newman observed, "Faith has large reserves."

3) *Falltime: coping with our finitude.* Here Christ's servants come to terms with the fact that many of our fondest dreams and hopes and aspirations are not to be realized—vocationally, relationally, personally, spiritually. Cecil Paul itemizes the ingredients in this crunch:

a) family problems—empty-nest syndrome
b) feelings of loneliness and isolation
c) economic pressures
d) the tyranny of evaluation
e) absence of recreational values
f) motivational problems
g) spiritual crises.[3]

The frost is on the pumpkin in what can be such a beautiful season, but the days are growing shorter and there is a chill in the air. This is a time for renegotiation and renewal in ministry. Some are swallowed up in depression and despair (like J. B. Phillips and Dean Inge), while others are like Jonathan Edwards who had to move on after twenty-four years at Northampton but showed no bitterness or rancor at his farewell. Why take swipes and digs in the letter of resignation? Who is served by such petulance and peevishness?

4) *Wintertime: finishing our course.* Here we face the challenge of stepping aside gracefully. Here is retirement and the nexus of challenges faced in the aging process. Cecil Paul identifies the chief adjustments in this season as physical changes, environmental changes, social and cultural changes.[4] F. B. Meyer used to pray: "Lord, help me not to become a mean old man." What we now lack in physical energy we compensate for, hopefully, with wisdom. We can be an encouragement to younger ministers and to the church, perhaps share an interim pastorate or pul-

pit supply, do some writing, visiting and travel. I do not intend to resign in a final sense, but to re-sign to appropriate ministries within the limitations at hand.

Surely there is no higher calling than that of the pastor-teacher in this country or abroad. To preach and love for Jesus' sake until I have no more breath is my passion and longing.

RESPONSIBILITIES

At whatever stage or juncture we find ourselves now, the injunction of the Apostle Paul needs to be foremost: "Discharge all the duties of your ministry" (2 Timothy 4:5d). These duties could be summed up in the following terms:

1) *We have an eternal responsibility.* We will give an account at the Judgment-seat of Christ, as will all believers (1 Corinthians 3; 2 Corinthians 5). We have great responsibility because we have had great privilege. We have had the indescribable joy of companying much with the Word of God and with the people of God.

2) *We have an intellectual responsibility.* We need to live on the growing edge and keep learning. Our library needs to reflect the reaching out and up and on of our thought processes. We need grown-up growth. New vistas should be conquered, new trails should be blazed, new continents of awareness should enthrall us.

3) *We have an ethical responsibility.* How concerned we need to be "that the ministry be not discredited" (2 Corinthians 6:3). How sensitively we need to relate to our predecessor, our successor, our brothers and sisters in neighboring congregations. How deeply we must be concerned with the handling of finances and all of our interpersonal relationships, so Christ will be honored and no shadow will fall over the cause of Christ or His church.

4) *We have a spiritual responsibility.* We have a solemn duty to live close to God and to walk with His Son in the fullness of the Spirit. We shortchange the people of God when we are prayerless or spiritually careless. "In season and out of season" (2 Timothy 4:2), whether we feel like it or not, when we are up and when we are down, when we are encouraged and when we are discouraged—at all times we need to take that extra step of seeking the renewing and refreshing touch of God.

And when we come to the end of our life's journey and give account of our stewardship of the mysteries of God, may we not have to be ashamed, but rather hear Him say, "Well done, good and faithful servant, enter into the joy of your Lord" (Matthew 25:23).

Your Church and My Church

Your church and my church, and may it ever be
  A place of refuge from the turmoil on life's stormy sea,
A holy place for worship, where our souls may be blessed,
  A place of consecration, for the weary a place to rest.

Your church and my church, in which to work and pray,
  And bring to the Saviour those who have gone astray;
To send to every nation the gospel full and free
  And thus fulfill Christ's own command to you and to me.

Your church and my church, where fellowship we may,
  As "saints of the Lord" awaiting the coming day;
When with "bright and shining raiment" we meet him
    in the sky
  Or rise to life immortal if meanwhile we should die.

Oh glorious institution, by Jesus Christ ordained,
  And hallowed through the ages by love and sacrifice
    sustained;
Grant, blessed Lord and Master, that we may always be
  Faithful and loyal to your church, its mission, and to thee.

E. S. Larsen

Sample Description of the Annual Program Theme of Elim Church

A YEAR OF EVANGELISM AT ELIM CHURCH

As is true of evangelicalism generally, our weakest area is our evangelistic pulse. It is in vital outreach and soul-winning that we seem to make the least effective impact. It is proposed that we designate 19__ as a year of emphasis on evangelism throughout our church—reaching out into the homes and lives of our neighbors with the gospel of Christ. It is proposed that we:

1. During prayer week, January 3-10, undergo "An Evangelistic Measurement" in which each organization in the church seeks to discover its unused evangelistic potential. The leaders' prayer breakfast is keyed to this emphasis.

2. Increase our emphasis on our monthly visitation night and broaden our participation by further training sessions. Perhaps a light supper for fellowship and inspiration prior to the visiting could be employed.

3. Observe February 28—March 1 which is followed throughout our denomination as Visitation Evangelism Week. The apartments south and east of us will be our special goal.

4. Develop further and systematize our friendship evangelism program in which our homes are opened to newcomers and outsiders.

5. Intensify our program for literature and tract distribution.

6. Crusade for Christ: eight great days of evangelism with Dr.—— —, with outstanding musical team to lead the music. Prepare by small group prayer meetings during the four months prior to the campaign. April 25—May 2.

7. Deacons to set membership recruitment and other goals for the year.

8. Each organization to set goals and implement them through outreach.

9. Sunday morning services devoted to an exposition of the book of Romans—tremendous evangelistic material.

10. A week of Children's Evangelistic Meetings in the Fall with evangelists. A great time of ingathering of our boys and girls.

11. Develop through the Board of Deacons and Board of Deaconesses a definite method whereby inquirers can seek counsel and prayer following each service. Each decision to be reported to the pastors.

12. Develop a strong follow-up program for those who profess Christ.

13. Encourage personal work by the members in every possible way—training sessions, seminars, prayer groups, etc.

It is now our fervent desire to implement this program and carry it into fruitful realization by God's Spirit.

A Theology of Christian Stewardship

Aim: to explore and understand better the Biblical and theological bases of Christian stewardship.

"Stewardship is not simply giving. It is the wise handling of that which God has entrusted to his children, to take care of our needs and to support his work. Giving according to a well thought out plan is stewardship at its best. Stewardship is what we do after we have said: 'I believe.'"

Scripture Lesson: Matthew 25:14-30.

I. God is the owner to whom all things belong—Ezekiel 18:4; Psalm 50:10; 1 Timothy 6:7.

II. God is the giver who has entrusted possessions to his servants. "Property is not an earthly treasure but a heavenly trust."

    A. The right of possession is established by God's gifts (cf. with Plato, Marx. Possessions can be a great evil—cf. 1 Timothy 6:10; Mark 10:23). This right is recognized throughout Scripture: 1 Timothy 6:17; Genesis 27:28; Deuteronomy 8:17ff.; Matthew 20:15; Acts 5:4; Psalm 112; Job 1:8 (cf. James 5:11).

    B. There is proper and lawful acquisition of possessions.

        1. Lawful ways of acquiring possessions:

            a. Gifts and inheritance—1 Kings 21; Numbers 27:8-11.

            b. Wise investment—Matthew 25:27; Luke 19:23.

            c. Work—Luke 10:7; 1 Timothy 5:18; Colossians 3:22ff.

        2. Unlawful ways of acquiring possessions:

            a. Stealing—Psalm 37:21; Amos 8:5; Hosea 12:7.

            b. Exploitation of the less-privileged—James 5:4; Exodus 22:25; Deuteronomy 23:19.

      c.   Gambling—Isaiah 65:11.

III. We are caretakers of what has been entrusted to us.

    A.   A good caretaker is clear as to his relationship to his master—2 Corinthians 8:5. "Man's presumption of autonomy is an expression of his sin, of the egocentricity which separates him from God and flaws his life."

    B.   Stewardship embraces 10/10 of our possessions.

        1.   We are on an expense account.

        2.   Misuse of money is to be guilty of misappropriation of funds. Study 1 Timothy 6:17—for enjoyment and employment.

    C.   Our attitude toward giving is so crucial. The New Testament picture—Mark 12:41.

        1.   Joyfully and eagerly—Exodus 25:2; 2 Corinthians 9:7; 8:4.

        2.   Purposefully and systematically—2 Corinthians 9:7; 1 Corinthians 16:2.

        3.   Worthily and sacrificially—Mark 12:41; 2 Corinthians 8:3; 2 Samuel 24:24.

        4.   Secretly and with humility—Matthew 6:1ff.

    D.   We shall give an account of what has been entrusted to us.

    E.   Parable of the Good Samaritan—three attitudes toward life and possessions:

        1.   The robber: "What's yours is mine, I'll take it."

        2.   Priest and Levite: "What's mine is mine, I'll keep it."

        3.   Good Samaritan: "What's mine is yours, I'll share it."

The above are drawn from K. F. W. Prior, *God and Mammon: The Christian Mastery of Money* (Philadelphia: Westminster, 1965); Stephen Olford, *The Grace of Giving: Thoughts on Financial Stewardship* (Grand Rapids, MI: Zondervan, 1972).

NOTES

INTRODUCTION

1. The Granville-Sharpe Rule provides that in the case of two coordinate nouns, repetition of the article distinguishes the nouns from each other while the use of a single article associates them, as is the case in Ephesians 4:11.
2. For further probing of this issue, cf. Erik H. Erikson, "The Problem of Ego Identity," in *Journal of the American Psychoanalytic Association*, 4, 1956, pp. 56-121. An illuminating case study is to be found in E. N. Hirsch, *The Enigma of Felix Frankfurter* (New York: Basic Books, 1981).
3. Anwar el-Sadat, *In Search of Identity* (New York: Harper and Row, 1977).
4. Miguel de Cervantes, *The History of Don Quixote de la Mancha*, Volume 29 (Chicago: Great Books of the Western World, 1952), p. 112.

CHAPTER 1: "The Church Which Is Christ's Body":
The Nature of the Church

1. Thomas C. Oden, *Pastoral Theology: Essentials of Ministry* (San Francisco: Harper and Row, 1983), p. 55.
2. Robert Bellah *et al*, *Habits of the Heart* (New York: Harper and Row, 1986).
3. K. L. Schmidt, in *Bible Key Words*, Volume I (London: A. and C. Black, 1956).
4. T. W. Manson, *Ministry and Priesthood: Christ and Ours* (London: Hodder and Stoughton, 1948), p. 14.
5. Ray S. Anderson, ed., *Theological Foundations for Ministry* (Grand Rapids, MI: Eerdmans, 1979).
6. G. W. Bromiley, *Christian Ministry* (Grand Rapids, MI: Eerdmans, 1959), p. 11.
7. *Ibid.*, p. 17.
8. A. T. Hanson, *Pioneer Ministry* (London: SPCK, 1975).
9. Oden, *Pastoral Theology*, pp. 64, 65.
10. Bromiley, *Christian Ministry*, p. 79.
11. J. N. D. Kelly, *A Commentary on the Pastoral Epistles* (Grand Rapids, MI: Baker, 1963).
12. Thomas M. Lindsay, *The Church and Its Ministry in the Early Centuries* (London: Hodder and Stoughton, 1902), p. 173.
13. Thomas Oden, *Becoming a Minister* (New York: Crossroad, 1987), p. 102.
14. John Henry Jowett, *The Preacher: His Life and Work* (Grand Rapids, MI: Baker, 1912).
15. Kelly, *A Commentary on the Pastoral Epistles*, pp. 111-121. An additional recent volume of great interest on this point is Bonnie Bowman, *The Widows: A Women's*

Ministry in the Early Church (Minneapolis: Augsburg, 1989).

CHAPTER 2: *"Christ's Ambassadors" and "Witnesses of the Resurrection"*: The
Mission of the Church

1. *Religion Report*, Volume 3, Number 12, June 5, 1989, p. 2.
2. Charles Jefferson, *The Minister as Shepherd* (New York: Thomas Y. Crowell, 1912), p. 19.
3. *Ibid.*, p. 35.
4. *Ibid.*, p. 37.
5. Other choice materials on the shepherd include: Thomas C. Oden, *Becoming a Minister* (New York: Crossroad, 1987), pp. 41-53; John Killenger, *The Tender Shepherd* (Nashville: Abingdon, 1985); Derek J. Tidball, *Skillful Shepherding* (Grand Rapids: Zondervan, 1986).
6. Charles Haddon Spurgeon, *Lectures to My Students* (Grand Rapids: Zondervan, 1954).
7. See Appendix A for more detailed description.

CHAPTER 3: *"God's Household . . . The Pillar and Foundation of the Truth"*: The
Governance of the Church

1. Nicholas Ridley, *Works* (London: Parker Society, 1843), pp. 122, 123.
2. Richard Hooker, *Ecclesiastical Polity*, 3.1.19.
3. Bengt Holmberg, *Paul and Power* (Philadelphia: Fortress Press, 1978), p. 193.
4. F. W. Dillistone, *The Structures of the Divine Society* (Philadelphia: Westminster, 1955), p. 132.
5. Daniel Jenkins,*Traditions, Freedom and the Spirit* (Philadelphia: Westminster, 1956), pp. 115-123.
6. Lloyd M. Perry and Gilbert A. Peterson, *Churches in Crisis* (Chicago: Moody Press, 1981), pp. 11, 12.
7. Avery Dulles, *Models of the Church* (New York: Doubleday, 1974).
8. John MacArthur, *Answering the Key Questions About Elders* (Panorama City, CA: Word of Grace Communications, 1984); Alexander Strauch, *Biblical Eldership* (Littleton, CO: Lewis & Roth, 1986).
9. W. D. Davies, *A Normative Pattern of Church Life in the New Testament: Fact or Fancy?* (London: Clark, n.d.).
10. C. Peter Wagner, *Leading Your Church to Growth* (Ventura, CA: Regal Books, 1984).
11. Howard A. Snyder, *The Community of the King* (Downers Grove, IL: InterVarsity Press, 1978); Strauch, *Biblical Eldership*.
12. Ezra Earl Jones and Robert L. Wilson, *What's Ahead for Old First Church?* (New York: Harper and Row, 1974), pp. 68-73.
13 Lyle E. Schaller, *The Small Church Is Different* (Nashville: Abingdon, 1982).
14. Findley B. Edge, *The Greening of the Church* (Waco, TX: Word, 1971), p.161ff.
15. Stephen Kliewer, *How to Live with Diversity in the Local Church* (Washington, D.C.: Alban Institute, 1988).

CHAPTER 4: *"A Holy Nation . . . Chosen in Him to Be Holy"*:
The Integrity of the Church

1. W. Graham Scroggie, *The Psalter* I (New York: Harper, n.d.), pp. 87, 88.
2. Paul Johnson, *Intellectuals* (New York: Harper, 1988).

3. Harold Hazelip and Ken Durham, *Becoming Persons of Integrity* (Grand Rapids, MI: Baker Book House, 1988).
4. Homer A. Kent, Jr.,*The Pastoral Epistles* (Chicago: Moody, 1958); J. N. D. Kelly, *A Commentary on the Pastoral Epistles* (Grand Rapids, MI: Baker Book House, 1963); Gordon H. Clark, *The Pastoral Epistles* (Jefferson, MD: Trinity Foundation, 1983); A. T. Hanson, *New Century: The Pastoral Epistles* (Grand Rapids, MI: Eerdmans, 1982).
5. Kent, *The Pastoral Epistles*, p. 125ff.
6. Kelly, *A Commentary on the Pastoral Epistles*, p. 75.
7. See Ed Glasscock, "'The Husband of One Wife' Requirement in I Timothy 3:2," in *Bibliotheca Sacra*, July-September 1983, pp. 244-258.
8. Richard Baxter, *The Reformed Pastor* (London: Epworth Press, reprint, 1939), p. 24.

CHAPTER 5: *"The Followers of This Way": The Servanthood of the Church*

1. Robert C. Worley, *A Gathering of Strangers* (Philadelphia: Westminster, 1976), p. 121.
2. R. M. Stogdill, *Handbook of Leadership* (New York: Free Press, 1974), vii
3. W. J. Phillips,"Styles of Leadership," in *Church Development*, November 1987, pp. 4-6.
4. Derek J. Tidball, *Skillful Shepherds* (Grand Rapids, MI: Zondervan, 1986), pp. 322-327.
5. Howard Butt, Jr., *Velvet Covered Brick* (New York: Harper and Row, 1973), p. 73.
6. Stephen E. Clapp, *Ministerial Competency Report* (Sidell, IL: C4 Resources, 1982), p. 26.
7. "Where Did the Gung-ho Go?" in *Time* Magazine, September 11, 1989, pp. 52-56. Cf. also Max DePree, *Leadership Is an Art* (New York: Doubleday, 1989).
8. J. Oswald Sanders, *Spiritual Leadership* (Chicago: Moody Press, 1978); Eugene H. Peterson, *Working the Aisles: The Shape of Pastoral Integrity* (Grand Rapids, MI: Eerdmans, 1987); Eugene H. Peterson, *The Contemplative Pastor* (Carol Stream, IL: Christianity Today Inc., 1989).

Chapter 6: *"Preach the Word": The Pastor as Communicator of the Truth*

1. Sidney Greidanus, *The Modern Preacher and the Ancient Text* (Grand Rapids, MI: Eerdmans, 1988), p. 183.
2 David L. Larsen, *The Anatomy of Preaching: Identifying the Issues in Preaching Today* (Grand Rapids, MI: Baker, 1989).

CHAPTER 7: *"Come, Let Us Bow Down in Worship":*
The Pastor as Leader of Worship

1. Robert Webber, *Worship Old and New* (Grand Rapids, MI: Zondervan, 1982), p. 11.
2. Paul Hoon, *The Integrity of Worship* (Nashville: Abingdon, 1971). This is a remarkably rich and provocative treatment.
3. Browne Barr, *High-Flying Geese* (New York: Seabury, 1983), pp. 40, 41.
4. In William Willimon, *Worship and Pastoral Care* (Nashville: Abingdon, 1979).
5. Geoffrey Wainwright, *Eucharist and Eschatology* (New York: Oxford, 1981).
6. C. S. Lewis, *Letters to Malcolm* (New York: Macmillan, 1972), p. 4.
7. David Rambo, *Alliance Witness*, September 13, 1989, pp. 30, 31.

CHAPTER 8: *"Whatever You Do . . . Do It All in the Name of the Lord Jesus":* The
Pastor as Administrator

1. Lloyd M. Perry, *Getting the Church on Target* (Chicago: Moody Press, 1970), p. 42.
2. David S. Luecke and Samuel Southard, *Pastoral Administration* (Waco, TX: Word, 1986), p. 11.
3. See Appendix B.
4. For materials on the types of budgets I am indebted to President Kenneth M. Meyer of Trinity Evangelical Divinity School, whose most helpful volume *Minister's Guide to Financial Planning* (Grand Rapids, MI: Zondervan, 1987) is a practical resource for the pastor in this and many areas.
5. *Church Leadership Resource Catalog*, Church Growth, Inc., 2670 South Myrtle Avenue, Suite 201, Monrovia, CA 91016. The title of their volume is *The Church Building Sourcebook*.
6. *Church Information and Development Services*, 3001 Redhill Avenue,Suite 2-220, Costa Mesa, CA, 92626.

CHAPTER 9: *"Comfort Ye, Comfort Ye My People":*
The Pastor as Counselor

1. Paul Johnson, *Intellectuals* (San Francisco: Harper and Row, 1988).
2. Derek J. Tidball, *Skillful Shepherds* (Grand Rapids, MI: Zondervan, 1986), pp. 218-221.
3. Lars I. Granberg, "Counseling," in *Baker's Dictionary of Practical Theology* (Grand Rapids, MI: Baker, 1967), p. 193.
4. Frank Wright, *The Pastoral Nature of the Ministry* (London: SCM Press, 1980), pp. 58-60.
5. Lesley Hazleton, *The Right to Feel Bad* (New York: Dial, 1984).
6. Michael R. Saia, *Counseling the Homosexual* (Minneapolis: Bethany House, 1988).

CHAPTER 10: *"Visit the Orphans and Widows in Their Affliction":*
The Pastor as Minister to People

1. For a superb discussion of this see Ray S. Anderson, *Theological Foundations for Ministry* (Grand Rapids, MI: Eerdmans, 1979).
2. E. Brooks Holifield, *A History of Pastoral Care in America* (Nashville: Abingdon, 1983), p. 12.
3. Richard John Neuhaus, *Freedom for Ministry* (San Francisco: Harper & Row, 1984).
4. Thomas C. Oden, *Crisis Ministries* (New York: Crossroad, 1986).
5. Ralph L. Underwood, *Empathy and Confrontation in Pastoral Care* (Philadelphia: Fortress Press, 1985), pp. 89-119.
6. Eldon Weisheit, *God's Word in a Child's World* (Minneapolis: Augsburg, 1986); Andrew D. Lester, *Pastoral Care with Children in Crisis* (Philadelphia: Westminster Press, 1985).
7. Horace L. Kerr, *How to Minister to Senior Adults in Your Church* (Nashville: Broadman Press, 1980).

CHAPTER 11: *"As for Me and My House . . .":* The Pastor and the Family

1. Edith Schaeffer, *What Is a Family?* (Old Tappan, NJ: Revell, 1975), pp. 30, 31.
2. *International Standard Bible Encyclopedia*, Volume II, "Family" (Grand Rapids, MI: Eerdmans, 1939), pp. 1094-1097.

3. *Homebuilders Couple Series* (Waco, TX: Word, 1989).
4. *The John Ankerberg Show Letter*, May 1989.
5. Marilyn Brown Oden, "Stress and Purpose: Clergy Spouses Today," *Christian Century*, April 20, 1988, pp. 402-404.
6. Cameron Lee and Jack Balswick, *Life in a Glass House: The Minister's Family in Its Unique Social Context* (Grand Rapids, MI: Zondervan, 1989).

CHAPTER 12: *"Hold out the Word of Life": The Pastor and the Community*

1. "The Preacher of a Militant Creed," *Insight Magazine*, February 1, 1988, p. 60.
2. William J. Wilson, *The Truly Disadvantaged* (Chicago: University of Chicago Press, 1987).
3. Richard John Neuhaus, "Those Turbulent Bishops," in *National Review*, December 31, 1989, pp. 32, 33.
4. Michael Medved, "Hollywood vs. Religion," in *Imprimis*, Hillsdale College, Volume 18, Number 12 (December 1989).

CHAPTER 13: *"Servants of the Church" and "Fellow Workers":*
The Pastor and Team Ministry

1. J. N. D. Kelly, *A Commentary on the Pastoral Epistles* (Grand Rapids, MI: Baker, 1963), pp. 158, 159.
2. A. B. Bruce, *The Training of the Twelve* (New York: Harper, 1956); David L. Larsen, *In the Savior's School* (Chicago: Covenant Press, 1961).
3. D. A. Carson, *Showing the Spirit* (Grand Rapids, MI: Baker, 1987); Ralph P. Martin, *The Spirit and the Congregation* (Grand Rapids, MI: Eerdmans, 1984). These are both choice and careful expositions of 1 Corinthians 12—14.
4. Quoted in Dallas Willard, *The Spirit of the Disciplines* (New York: Harper, 1988), p. 50.
5. David S. Belasic and Paul M. Schmidt, *The Penguin Principles* (Lima, OH: C. S. S. Publishing Co., 1986).
6. Jerry W. Brown, *Church Staffs That Win* (Nashville: Convention Press, 1979, p. 35.
7. Kenneth Blanchard and Spencer Johnson, *One Minute Management* (New York: Berkeley Books, 1983).
8. W. J. Phillips, "Styles of Leadership," from *In Search of a Leader* (Vancouver, BC: Center for Study of Church and Ministry, n.d.).
9. Herman Sweet, *The Multiple Staff in the Local Church* (Philadelphia: Westminster ,1963); Marvin Judy, *The Multiple Staff Ministry* (Nashville: Abingdon, 1969); Lyle Schaller, *The Multiple Staff and the Larger Church* (Nashville: Abingdon, 1980); Harold J. Westling, *Multiple Staff Handbook* (Grand Rapids: Baker, 1985).

CHAPTER 14: *"Are You Not to Judge Those Inside?":*
The Pastor and the Unruly

1. Dietrich Bonhoeffer, *The Cost of Discipleship* (New York: Macmillan, 1949).
2. Jay E. Adams, *Handbook of Church Discipline* (Grand Rapids, MI: Zondervan, 1986).
3. *Ibid.*, p. 39ff.
4. J. Carl Laney, *A Guide to Church Discipline* (Minneapolis: Bethany House, 1985), p. 48ff.
5. J. Carl Laney, "The Biblical Practice of Church Discipline," in *Bibliotheca Sacra*, October-December 1986, p. 358.
6. Mark R. Littleton, "Church Discipline: A Remedy for What Ails the Body," in

Christianity Today, May, 8, 1981, p. 33.

7. Laney, "The Biblical Practice of Church Discipline," p. 357.
8. Gordon Addington, *Discipline: The Proof of Love and Caring in the Family of God* (Minneapolis: Evangelical Free Church of America, n.d.).
9. Adams, *Handbook of Church Discipline*, p. 81ff.
10. John White and Ken Blue, *Healing the Wounded* (Downers Grove, IL: InterVarsity Press, 1985).
11. Don Baker, *Beyond Forgiveness* (Portland: Multnomah, 1984).
12. Ralph D. Mawdsley, "The Modus Operandi of Church Discipline," *Fundamentalist Journal*, November 1984, p. 23.
13. William H. Tiemann and John C. Bush, *The Right to Silence* (Nashville: Abingdon, 1983).
14. R. C. Sproul, *In Search of Dignity* (Ventura, CA: GL Publications, Regal Books, 1983), quoted in J. Carl Laney, "The Biblical Practice of Church Discipline," p. 353.

CHAPTER 15: *"There Are Many Parts, but One Body":*
The Pastor and the Vitality of the Body

1. For examples of the encouraging resurgence of contemporary emphasis on discipleship, see Bill Hull, *Jesus Christ: Disciple-maker* (Colorado Springs, CO: NavPress, 1984); Francis M. Cosgrove, Jr., *Essentials of Discipleship* (Colorado Springs, CO: NavPress, 1980); Keith Phillips, *The Making of a Disciple* (Old Tappan, NJ: Revell, 1981); David Watson, *Called and Committed* (Wheaton,IL: Harold Shaw Publishers, 1982).
2. Gene A. Getz, *Building Up One Another* (Wheaton, IL: Victor Books, 1976).

CHAPTER 16: *"The Household of Faith":*
Baptism and the Presentation of Children

1. James M. Stifler, *The Epistle to the Romans* (New York: Revell, 1897), p. 109.
2. David W. Wright, "Baptismal Trends," in *Scottish Bulletin of Evangelical Theology*, Spring 1989, p. 1.
3. Ronald S. Wallace, "Sacrament," *Baker's Dictionary of Theology* (Grand Rapids, MI: Baker, 1976), p. 465.
4. *Ibid.*, p. 466.
5. Donald Bridge and David Phypers, *The Water That Divides* (Downers Grove, IL: InterVarsity, 1977). In this book a Baptist and Anglican explore the issues.
6. Augustine, *Epist.* 54, quoted in P. W. Evans, *Sacraments in the New Testament* (London: Tyndale Press, 1946), p. 5.
7. G. W. Bromiley, *Sacramental Teaching and Practice in the New Testament* (Grand Rapids, MI: Eerdmans, 1957), p. 20.
8. R. E. O. White, *The Biblical Doctrine of Initiation* (Grand Rapids, MI: Eerdmans, n.d.), p. 87.
9. *Christian Century*, January 24, 1990, p. 73.
10. Evans, *Sacraments in the New Testament*, p. 23.
11. Dwight Hervey Small, *The Biblical Basis of Infant Baptism* (New York: Revell, 1958).
12. Joachim Jeremias, *Infant Baptism in the First Four Centuries* (London: SCM Press, 1960).
13. Kurt Aland, *Did the Early Church Baptize Infants?* (Philadelphia: Westminster, 1963).
14. Johannes Warns, *Baptism* (Grand Rapids, MI: Kregel, 1957), p .60.
15. John Baillie, *Baptism and Conversion* (New York: Charles Scribner's, 1963), pp.

13-15. Cf. O. Hallesby, *Infant Baptism and Adult Conversion* (Minneapolis: Augsburg, 1924).
16. Bromiley, *Sacramental Teaching and Practice in the New Testament*, p. 35.
17. *ibid.*, p. 38.
18. John A. Simpson, "The Sacraments and Ordinances," in *Baker's Dictionary of Practical Theology* (Grand Rapids, MI: Baker, 1967), p. 390.
19. Aland, *Did the Early Church Baptize Infants?*, p. 95.
20. Bridge and Phypers, *The Water That Divides*, p. 93.

CHAPTER 17: *"Proclaiming the Lord's Death Until He Comes":*
The Lord's Supper

1. Max Thurian, *The Mystery and the Eucharist* (Grand Rapids, MI: Eerdmans, 1984), p. 13.
2. G. W. Bromiley, *Sacramental Teaching and Practice in the Reformation Churches* (Grand Rapids, MI: Eerdmans, 1975), p. 59.
3. O. Cullmann, *Early Christian Worship* (Bristol, IN: Wyndham Hall, 1987).
4. Ronald S. Wallace, "Lord's Supper," in *Baker's Dictionary of Theology* (Grand Rapids, MI: Baker, 1976), p. 331.
5. G. W. Bromiley, *Thomas Cranmer Theologian* (New York: Oxford, 1957), p. 53.
6. Eugene M. Skibbe, *Protestant Agreement on the Lord's Supper* (Minneapolis: Augsburg, 1968).
7. Bromiley, *Sacramental Teaching*, p. 75.
8. Andrew Murray, *The Lord's Table* (Chicago: Moody Press, n.d.).
9. *The Covenant Book of Worship* (Chicago: Covenant Press, 1981).
10. Bromiley, *Sacramental Teaching*, p. 72.
11. William H. Willimon, *Preaching and Leading Worship* (Philadelphia: Westminster Press, 1984), p. 58.
12. Bromiley, *Sacramental Teaching*, p. 60.
13. *The Covenant Book of Worship*, p. 105.
14. Martin E. Marty, *The Lord's Supper* (Philadelphia: Fortress Press, 1980); Geoffrey Wainwright, *Eucharist and Eschatology* (New York: Oxford University Press, 1981).
15. Wainwright, *Eucharist and Eschatology*, p. 116.

CHAPTER 18: *"The Two Will Become One Flesh":* The Wedding

1. For example, Ruth Muzzy and R. Kent Hughes, *The Christian Wedding Planner* (Wheaton, IL: Tyndale, 1984).
2. For example, Charles M. Sell, *Achieving the Impossible: Intimate Marriage* (Portland: Multnomah, 1983); H. Norman Wright, *Seasons of a Marriage* (Ventura, CA: Regal, 1983).
3. Paul E. Steele and Charles C. Ryrie, *Meant to Last* (Wheaton, IL: Victor, 1983).
4. Jay E. Adams, *Marriage, Divorce and Remarriage* (Grand Rapids, MI: Baker, 1986).
5. George W. Peters, "What the Bible Says About Divorce," in *Moody Monthly*, May 1970, p. 35ff.; June 1970, p. 36ff.
6. Guy Duty, *Divorce and Remarriage* (Minneapolis: Bethany Fellowship, 1967). Another excellent discussion is: Stanley A. Ellisen, *Divorce and Remarriage in the Church* (Grand Rapids, MI: Zondervan, 1977, 1980).
7. John Murray, *Divorce* (Philadelphia: Westminster, 1953), pp. 91, 92.
8. Robert L. Saucy, "The Husband of One Wife," in *Bibliotheca Sacra*, July 1974.
9. "Divorce and Remarriage—A Policy Statement," The Evangelical Covenant Church, 1976.

10. Arthur M. Vincent, ed. *Join Your Right Hands* (St. Louis: Concordia, 1965).

CHAPTER 19: *"Man Is Destined to Die Once": The Funeral*

1. Malcolm Forbes with Jeff Bloch, *They Went That Way* (New York: Simon and Schuster, 1988). This book deals with the deaths of seventeen people of interest.
2. Jessica Mitford, *The American Way of Death* (New York: Simon and Schuster, 1963). A rather bitter, scathing exposé. There is a modicum of important truth here.
3. William E. Phipps, *Death: Confronting the Reality* (Atlanta: John Knox, 1967), pp. 10-26.
4. Edgar N. Jackson, *For the Living* (Des Moines: Channel Press, 1963), p. 21.
5. Paul E. Irion, *The Funeral and the Mourners* (Nashville: Abingdon, 1954).
6. Morton T. Kelsey, *Afterlife: The Other Side of Dying* (New York: Crossroad, 1979).
7. Herbert M. Luckock, *After Death* (an examination of the testimony of primitive times respecting the state of the faithful dead and their relationship to the living) (London: Riverton's, 1886); S. D. F. Salmond, *The Christian Doctrine of Immorality* (Edinburgh; T. and T. Clark, 1895); T. A. Kantonen, *Life After Death* (Philadelphia: Muhlenberg, 1962); Rene Pache, *The Future Life* (Chicago: Moody Press, 1962) (this is exceedingly rich); Loraine Boettner, *Immortality* (Philadelphia: Presbyterian and Reformed, 1956); W. Graham Scroggie, *What About Heaven?* (London: Pickering and Inglis, 1940); Billy Graham, *Facing Death* (Waco, TX: Word, 1987).
8. Herbert Lockyer, *The Funeral Sourcebook* (Grand Rapids, MI: Zondervan, 1967); John R. Chiles, *A Treasury of Funeral Messages* (Grand Rapids, MI: Baker, 1966).
9. James L. Christensen, *Difficult Funeral Services* (Old Tappan, NJ: Revell, 1985). A rather fascinating treatment of hospice care and its unique aspects is found in Beverly Hall, *Caring for the Dying* (Toronto: Anglican Book Centre, 1988).

CHAPTER 20: *"The Prayer Offered in Faith Will Make the Sick Person Well": Anointing for Healing and Exorcism*

1. William A. Clebsch and Charles J. Jaekle, *Pastoral Care in Historical Perspective* (Englewood Heights, NJ: Prentice Hall, 1964), pp. 4-10.
2. John Milton, *Paradise Lost*, Book XI, 478-492.
3. Paul Woodruff and Harry A. Wilmer, eds. *Facing Evil* (LaSalle, IL: Open Court, 1988).
4. Edward M. Bounds, *Satan: His Personality, Power and Overthrow* (Grand Rapids, MI: Baker, 1963); Lewis Sperry Chafer, *Satan* (Findlay, OH: Dunham, 1919); Hal Lindsey, *Satan Is Alive and Well on Planet Earth* (Grand Rapids, MI: Zondervan, 1972); Herbert Lockyer, *Satan: His Person and Power* (Waco, TX: Word, 1980); Frederick Tatford, *Satan: The Prince of Darkness* (Grand Rapids, MI: Kregel, n.d.); Warren W. Wiersbe, *The Strategy of Satan* (Wheaton, IL: Tyndale, 1979).
5. Heiko A. Oberman, *Luther: Man Between God and the Devil* (New Haven, CT: Yale University Press, 1989).
6. B. B.Warfield, *Counterfeit Miracles* (Edinburgh: Banner of Truth Trust, repr. 1976); Sir Robert Anderson, *The Silence of God* (Grand Rapids, MI: Kregel, repr. 1975).
7. A. B. Simpson, *How to Receive Divine Healing* (Minneapolis: Bethany, n.d.), pp. 2, 3.
8. John R. W. Stott, *The Cross of Christ* (Downers Grove, IL: InterVarsity, 1986), p. 244ff.
9. J. Sidlow Baxter, *Divine Healing of the Body* (Grand Rapids, MI: Zondervan,

1979).
10. John G. Mitchell, "Does God Heal Today?," *Bibliotheca Sacra*, January 1965, p. 51ff.
11. *Christian Healing* (Richmond, VA: International Order of St. Luke, 1981).
12. See Frank E. Peretti, *This Present Darkness* (Westchester, IL: Crossway Books, 1986); *Piercing the Darkness* (Westchester, IL: Crossway Books, 1989).
13. Merrill F. Unger, *Biblical Demonology* (Wheaton, IL: Van Kampen, 1952); *Demons in the World Today* (Wheaton, IL: Tyndale, 1971); Mrs. George C. Needham, *Angels and Demons* (Chicago: Moody, n.d.); Jessie Penn-Lewis, *War on the Saints* (Ft. Washington, PA: Christian Literature Crusade, n.d.).
14. John Nevius, *Demon Possession and Allied Themes* (Old Tappan, NJ: Revell, n.d.).
15. A different view is argued in C. Fred Dickason, *Demon Possession and the Christian* (Westchester, IL: Crossway Books, 1989). Dickason takes the position that while Scripture does not say Christians can be inhabited by demons, clinical experience would indicate they can. Unger, in *What Demons Can Do to the Saints* (Chicago: Moody, 1977), veers in the same direction.

CHAPTER 21: *"See to It That He Has Nothing to Fear While He Is with You": The Pastor and the "Fit"*

1. Kent and Barbara Hughes, *Liberating Ministry from the Success Syndrome* (Wheaton, IL: Tyndale House, 1987). A very helpful address to this topic.
2. Lyle Schaller, *It's a Different World* (Nashville: Abingdon, 1987). Also by Schaller, *Reflections of a Contrarian: Second Thoughts on Parish Ministry* (Nashville: Abingdon, 1989).
3. Clark Morphew, "Times of Vast Change Buffet Clergy," in *St. Paul Pioneer Press Dispatch*, May 21, 1988, p. 3B.
4. J. Keith Cook, *The First Parish: A Pastor's Survival Manual* (Philadelphia: Westminster, 1983). Also William Bud Phillips, *Pastoral Transition: From Endings to New Beginnings* (Washington, D. C.: Alban Institute, 1989).
5. Roy M. Oswald, *New Beginnings: A Pastorate Start-up Book* (Washington, D. C.: Alban Institute, 1989).
6. Kevin A. Miller, *Secrets of Staying Power* (Carol Stream, IL: Leadership/Word Books, 1988).

CHAPTER 22: *"A Great Door for Effective Work Has Opened": The Pastor and New Forms*

1. Eliot A. Cohen and John Gooch, *Military Misfortunes: The Anatomy of Failure in War* (New York: Free Press, 1989).
2. William H. Willimon, *What's Right with the Church?* (San Francisco: Harper and Row, 1985).
3. Lyle E. Schaller, *The Change Agent* (Nashville: Abingdon, 1972).
4. *Ibid.*, p. 129.
5. *Insight Magazine*, August 21, 1989.
6. *Time* Magazine, August 7, 1989, pp. 9, 10.
7. Lyle E. Schaller, *Looking in the Mirror: Self-Appraisal in the Local Church* (Nashville: Abingdon, 1984).
8. Cf. an interesting update, Luis Palau, "Evangelism Is Social Action," in *World Vision Magazine*, April-May 1990, pp. 4-8.
9. *National and International Religion Report*, Volume 4, Number 7, March 26, 1990.

CHAPTER 23: *"The Lord's Message Rings Out":*

The Pastor and the Awareness Factor

1. Emerson C. Ross, "Are You Flexible?," *The Alliance Witness*, September 2, 1981, p. 3.
2. John Naisbit, *Megatrends* (New York: Warner Books, 1982), p. 141.
3. David McKenna, *Megatruth* (San Bernardino, CA: Here's Life, 1986), p. 51ff.
4. Naisbit, *Megatrends*, p. 52.
5. David Larsen, "What Is the Climate for Today's Sermonic Communication?," in *The Anatomy of Preaching* (Grand Rapids, MI: Baker, 1989), pp. 35-46.
6. Religious News Service, April 11, 1989.
7. Laurence Shames, *The Hunger for More: Searching for Values in an Age of Greed* (New York: Times Books, 1988).
8. Harold O. J. Brown, *The Religion and Society Report*, August 1989, p. 1.
9. Norman Cousins, "The Decline of Neatness," *Time* Magazine, April 2, 1990, p. 78.
10. Randolph K. Sanders and H. Newton Maloney, *Speak Up! Christian Assertiveness* (Philadelphia: Westminster, 1985).
11. Charles Somervil, Chapter 7 ("The Uses of Media for Church Leaders"), *Leadership Strategies for Ministries* (Philadelphia: Westminster, 1987).
12. Quoted in John W. Bachman, *Media: Wasteland or Wonderland* (Minneapolis: Augsburg, 1984). This is one of the best books in print on the media, treating both its opportunities and its dangers.

CHAPTER 24: *"Perfectly United in Mind and Heart": The Pastor and Fissures*

1. Larry L. McSwain and William C. Treadwell, Jr., *Conflict Ministry in the Church* (Nashville: Broadman, 1981), p. 51ff.
2. Horace L. Fenton, *When Christians Clash* (Downers Grove, IL: InterVarsity, 1987), p. 49.
3. A most remarkably perceptive article on this subject is Frances Fitzgerald, "Reflections: Jim and Tammy," *The New Yorker*, April 23, 1990, pp. 45-87.
4. David S. Luecke and Samuel Southard, *Pastoral Administration* (Waco, TX: Word, 1986), p. 136ff.
5. Chester A. Tulga, *The Foreign Missions Controversy in the Northern Baptist Convention* (Chicago: Conservative Baptist Fellowship, 1950).
6. H. Beecher Hicks, Jr., *Preaching Through a Storm* (Grand Rapids, MI: Zondervan, 1987).
7. Kazimierz Dabrowski, *Positive Disintegration* (Boston: Little, Brown and Co., 1964).
8. Carl S. Dudley and Earle Hilgert, *New Testament Patterns and the Contemporary Church* (Philadelphia: Fortress, 1987), p. 105ff.
9. Kenneth C. Haugk, *Antagonists in the Church: How to Identify and Deal with Destructive Conflict* (Minneapolis: Augsburg, 1989).
10. Luecke and Southard, *Pastoral Administration*, p. 146.
11. Norman Shawchuck, *How to Manage Conflict in the Church* (Irvine, CA: Spiritual Growth Resources, 1983).
12. For a rich, nourishing study, see Charles Bridges, *Proverbs* (Edinburgh: Banner of Truth, 1846, 1968).
13. G. Douglas Lewis, *Resolving Church Conflicts* (San Francisco: Harper and Row, 1981), p. 49.
14. *Ibid.*, p. 49ff.
15. Speed Leas and Pasul Kittlaus, *Church Fights: Managing Conflict in the Local Church* (Philadelphia: Westminster, 1973), p. 62.
16 McSwain and Treadwell, Jr., *Conflict Ministry in the Church*, pp. 30, 31.

CHAPTER 25: *"He Who Has Begun a Good Work Will Carry It On"*:
The Church of the Future

1. For a fascinating and most instructive approach to many of these issues, cf. E. Calvin Beisner, *Prospects for Growth: A Biblical View of Population, Resources, and the Future* (Westchester, IL: Crossway Books, 1990).
2. Paul R. Ehrlich and Anne H. Ehrlich, *The Population Explosion* (New York: Simon and Schuster, 1990).
3. Kevin Perrotta, "Church Growth Picks Up," in *Pastoral Renewal*, September 1987, p. 9.
4. Malise Ruthhven, *The Divine Super-market: Shopping for God in America* (New York: William Morrow, 1989)—this book is rough and critical; see also Randall Balmer, *Mine Eyes Have Seen the Glory: A Journey into the Evangelical Subculture in America* (New York: Oxford, 1989)—this is somewhat less critical and more understanding.
5. Peter Drucker, "Facing the 'Totally New and Dynamic,'" in *Time* Magazine, January 22, 1990, pp 6, 7.
6. Peter Steinfels, "Beliefs," in *The New York Times*, January 6, 1990.
7. "Study Highlights Importance of Christian Education," in *Christianity Today*, April 23, 1990, pp. 48, 49.
8. Tom Peters, *Thriving on Chaos: Handbook for a Management Revolution* (New York: Knopf, 1987).

EPILOGUE

1. Cecil R. Paul, *Passages of a Pastor* (Grand Rapids, MI: Zondervan, 1981); John Killenger, *Christ in the Seasons of Ministry* (Waco, TX: Word, 1981). For a secular but very thoughtful volume on winter blues and seasonal affective disorders, see Norman E. Rosenthal, *Seasons of the Mind* (New York: Bantam, 1989).
2. One of the choicest treatments of this classic section is in G. Campbell Morgan, *The Corinthian Letters of Paul* (Old Tappan, NJ: Revell, 1946), pp. 229-249.
3. Paul, *Passages of a Pastor*, p. 50ff.
4. *Ibid.*, p. 81.

SCRIPTURE INDEX

GENERAL INDEX

Abel, 209
Abortion, pro-life concerns, 109, 110, 113
Abraham, 24
Achan, 124
Activism, 16, 111
Acton, Lord, 33, 108
Adam, 24, 99, 147, 176, 187
Adams, Jay, 52, 83, 124, 125, 127, 160
Adler, 82
Administration, 73 (Chapter 8 *passim*)
Aland, Kurt, 144
Alexander, Archibald, 62
Amos, 20
Anderson, Sir Robert, 178
Ankerberg, John, 104
Apollos, 20
Aquinas, 16
Arnold, Matthew, 81
Art of Ministering to the Sick, The (Cabot and Dicks), 92
Atlee, Clement, 51
Augustine, 142, 150

Bach, J. S., 51
Baillie, John, 144
Baptism, spiritual and water, 16, 25, 70, 141 (Chapter 16 *passim*), 149, 150
of infants, 144, 145, 158, 221
Barnabas, 27, 106, 116, 211
Barr, Browne, 68
Barth, Karl, 65, 144

Barth, Markus, 144
Baruch, 50
Baxter, J. Sidlow, 179
Baxter, Richard, 46, 82
Bede, Venerable, 52
Berger, Peter, 155
Blanchard, Kenneth, 120
Blue, Ken, 127
Bonhoeffer, Dietrich, 123
Book of Common Prayer, The, 58, 175
Borgias, the, 39
Brainerd, David, 224
Brandon, Thomas S., Jr., 129
Bromiley, 17, 142, 145, 150, 152, 154
Brown, 120
Brunner, Emil, 24
Building Up One Another (Gene Getz), 132
Bunyan, John, 146, 167
Burnout, 45, 227
Burns, Bobby, 103
Bushnell, Horace, 114
Butt, Howard, 50
Buzzard, Lynn R., 129

Cabot and Dicks, 92
Cain, 209
Calvin, John, 20, 33, 67, 147, 150, 151, 152, 155, 201
Campus Crusade, 103, 204
Candidating, 59, 187, 188, 189
Carlyle, Thomas, 193
Celebration of Discipline (Richard